TRADITION:
The Quest for a Championship

How Ed Pepple Led the Mercer Island High School
Boys' Basketball Team to its First State Title

SCOTT A. WEISS

HEADLINER BOOKS
Seattle, Washington

The book is dedicated to the memory of Ed Pepple, a coach I never had the chance to play for but whose tireless work ethic, integrity and commitment to excellence made an impact on countless lives both on and off the court.

AUTHOR'S NOTE

This story is told in chronological order using the words and images of the Mercer Island Reporter during the years 1980-1985. In each case where a writer's name was present alongside a story when it first appeared in print, that name appears below the headline and date of the original article.

TRADITION:

The Quest for a Championship

PROLOGUE

Ed Pepple was a man of his times, but even as the times changed around him, his ideas, attitude and spirit never went out of style. Growing up in Seattle, Pepple played basketball for Lincoln High School and graduated as a member of the class of 1950. He took his basketball talents to nearby Everett Community College, where he met his future wife, and spent two years there before transferring to the University of Utah.

Upon graduating from Utah in 1955 he enlisted as a member of the Marine Corps. Those close to him would often say that it was his time in the military, more than anything else, that influenced the unique brand of coaching he would later bring to the game of basketball.

Pepple never gave up his love for the game. With his playing days behind him and his stint in the military complete, he launched his high school coaching career in 1958 in Fife, a blue-collar community situated along Interstate 5 just north of Tacoma, where he stayed for six years. He took an assistant coaching position at Meadowdale High School and stayed only a short time before landing the head coaching job at Mark Morris High School in Longview, another blue-collar town nestled in the shadow of Mount St. Helens, on the banks of the mighty Columbia River.

After one season at Mark Morris, Pepple was hired as the head basketball coach at Mercer Island High School in Mercer Island, a bedroom community accessible only by bridge or boat in the middle of Lake Washington, just east of Seattle and directly west of Bellevue. There, he would go on to coach for 42 years, becoming something of an icon in the community and Washington state's all-time winningest basketball coach with 952 wins (882 at Mercer Island, along with 15 league titles and four state championships.)

Mercer Island was a different place when Pepple arrived there, and he had been warned by several people not to take the job. "There was a thing called, 'Mercer Island-itis.' It was like a label," he told the Seattle Times in 2004. "It was, 'If we're ahead, we can't protect a lead. And if we're behind, we quit.' "

He quickly made an impression. In the first "Islander" football game of the fall season in 1967, the team gave up a lead in the final minutes and ultimately lost the game. The athletic director of the school hosted a post-game party to welcome new staff members, where Pepple overheard one of the assistant coaches complaining about how the kids had "choked" again.

"I got into it with this football coach a little bit," Pepple told the Times. "I told him, 'You know, we need to stop that nonsense. All we're doing is reinforcing that concept.' I said, 'These kids, from what I've seen so far, seem like every other kid.' "

Players on Pepple's team during his inaugural season said they noticed something different about their new coach. Steve Hawes, a 6'9 forward who starred for Mercer Island and would go on to play college basketball at the University of Washington and spend 10 seasons in the NBA, told the Seattle Times that "our first impression was that here was a guy from another planet. He's a disciplinarian and real feisty and energetic. He had a real strong sense of how he wanted things to be run and we hadn't seen that before."

The first step? Haircuts. Pepple instituted a policy that players had to cut their hair above the ears, like the crew cuts he'd grown familiar with in the Marines. It was a policy he would loosen up on in later years, but at least initially, his players did what was asked of him. Hawes had his head practically shaved, and Pepple told him he thought by doing so, Hawes was demonstrating leadership qualities. "The reality was I didn't want to pay another $1.75 to have to go back and get it cut shorter," he joked to the Times.

That year, Pepple also introduced the maroon blazers that came to be synonymous with Mercer Island High School basketball. He felt that if his players wanted to be champions, they had to first look like champions. In keeping with the school colors (maroon and white), he created a signature look for his team, one that every successive team after that first one would emulate: cropped hair, maroon blazer, maroon and white practice ball.

Early in his career at MI, Pepple developed a concept that, while groundbreaking at the time, has become ubiquitous in today's youth sports world. Pepple, with the help of his high school players, rounded up the local kids in grades 5-8 with an interest in basketball and put together teams who would learn his offensive and defensive schemes from an early age. He called it "feeder" ball and named the program "Little Dribblers". Many of his future championship players would get their first taste of Pepple as a 10-year-old: high school kids drilling them on weekends during the season, so that by the time they got to high school, their coach's playbook would be as familiar to them as anything else. Little Dribblers also gave Pepple a chance to scout for future talent.

"It was not a thing that other communities were doing at that time," says Brian Schwabe, Class of 1985 who played under Pepple. "I think since then, a lot of schools have kind of picked up on that because it totally makes sense to develop the players at a young age and get them involved. But back then, at least in the state of Washington, there was nothing going on."

Pepple, led by Hawes' 30 points a game, took the Islanders to their first state tournament appearance in his first season, 1967-68. They didn't place, but were back in 1970, this time led by Steve's younger brother, Jeff. Unfortunately, they again came up short during that campaign. Two seasons later, in 1972, the Islanders took third at state with a roster of only 7 players. They finished 7th at state in 1974, and that team featured Terry Pepple, Ed's older son who went on to play college ball at Cheney in eastern Washington. In 1976, led by 7'2 Peter Gudmundsson, Pepple's Islanders traveled again to the state tournament but didn't place, and the following year, they finished third.

In 1978, the squad finished 8th. 7 attempts in 11 years, nothing better than a third-place finish for Pepple and the hardscrabble Islanders.

Their luck would appear to change in the 1980-1981 season.

KingCo AAA Athletic Conference

Crown Division
Juanita

Lake Washington

Inglemoor

Sammamish

Newport

Crest Division
Bellevue

Mercer Island

Interlake

Bothell

Redmond

PART ONE

1980-1981

"The 1981 team had to win 9 loser-out games to get to the championship game. It was an inspirational, never give up group that knows how good they were and knows what they accomplished."

- Ed Pepple

November 19, 1980

Basketball team faces 'exciting' season

By Bob Ogle

When other boys' basketball teams in the KingCo League think of the Mercer Island squad, it's probably viewed as a "good news – bad news" story.

For those teams, the good news is that the Islanders have seven lettermen returning from a squad which finished with the poorest record in Coach Ed Pepple's 13-year reign.

But the bad news is that the "poor record" was really anything but poor, 13 wins and 8 losses, which was good enough for second place in the Crest Division. Such a record would leave many high school teams in ecstasy.

So it's understandable why nobody is smiling -- except maybe Pepple. At 7:30 p.m. Tuesday, November 25, he will unveil his 1980 squad for the public at "Parent's Night" in the Mercer Island High School gym. Introductions and practice games involving sophomore, junior varsity and varsity teams are slated. The following Saturday, a scrimmage game is scheduled, also open to the public.

"The problem we had last year," Pepple said, "was that we had seniors on the varsity with a group of good sophomores. There wasn't any team cohesiveness. They just weren't close enough."

No such problem is expected this year. The seniors of last year are gone and the sophomores of 1979 are now a more mature crop of juniors.

"Most of these kids have been playing together since they were fifth-graders," Pepple said. "They've got a good feel for each other. They're unbelievably close as close a team as I've ever had. It's going to be an exciting team."

Pepple probably will include six seniors in his varsity group. Chris Kampe, a 6-1 guard, will be one key player, as will 6-5 center

Scott Driggers. Erik Nordstrom, 6-4 and Mark Aldape, 6-2, will see some action as forwards, while Doug Gregory, 6-2 and Tom Uczekaj, 5-10, will handle guard chores.

But the juniors will be the key. Forward Al Moscatel (6-1) returns to fill a starting role with his 13.5 points-per-game average of last year. He was tabbed second-team all-KingCo, a notable achievement for a sophomore.

Also present will be juniors Kyle Pepple, 5-11, at point guard; Joe Thompson, 6-4, a starter last year, at forward; Eric Schwabe, 6-4 at forward and backup center; Paul Jerue and Rich Dewey, 6-2 at forward.

All are more mature and more experienced. Pepple, son of the coach, played last summer for the state AAU squad. Several other players were included on a team which toured Australia.

"Balance and depth are going to be our strong points," Ed Pepple predicted. "There aren't any kids who really stand out above the rest. There are a lot of things each one can do well."

However bright the outlook though, there are going to be one or two problems. Lack of size is the main nemesis for the Islanders.

"We're not real big inside." Pepple conceded. "The kids can shoot, pass and play defense, but handling the other teams inside could be a problem."

The Islanders' biggest competition in the Crest Division will come from division champ Bothell and from Interlake and Bellevue.

Pepple knows his team will be a strong contender, but nothing is being taken for granted.

"We've got a long way to go before the playoffs or anything like that," he said, using a line coaches have used since time began. "We're just not going to worry about that. We're an intelligent team. If all the kids have a good start, then we can have a good season."

That season will officially open Dec. 2 in a jamboree against Lake Washington, Kent-Meridian and Shorewood at Mercer Island High School.

December 3, 1980

Island cagers face tough rival Tuesday

By Bob Ogle

It's unusual to face a crucial game early in the high school basketball season, but that's the situation facing coach Ed Pepple's Mercer Island High School team next week.

After a non-league game at Eisenhower of Yakima on Saturday the Islanders will prepare to face tough division rival Bothell next Tuesday at 8 p.m. in the high school gym.

"And the team that wins is going to be in the driver's seat," Pepple predicted.

Last year, Mercer Island took both league games from Bothell 50-49 and 77-63.

"They're a very experienced team," Pepple said. "They've played together for a long time. They're probably a little more physical than we are but they still like to run and go with the ball."

For the two games, Pepple said, he will probably start Scott Driggers (6-5) at center, Joe Thompson (6-4) and Al Moscatel (6-1) at forwards, and Chris Kampe (6-1) and Kyle Pepple (5-11) at guards.

Bothell will likely start Tom Parrish (5-11) and Kevin Morris (6-1) at guards, Joe Shaffet (6-4) and John Hanrahan (6-3) at forwards and will alternate Paul Cronkite (6-5) and big John Jensen (6-9, 260 lbs.) at center.

"We match up all right with them, except for Jensen," Pepple said. "When he comes in, we might have a problem. If we control him, we'll be alright."

That job will be made more difficult with the loss of 6-5 Eric Schwabe, one of the Islanders' tallest players. Schwabe is out indefinitely with a bout of mononucleosis.

It really doesn't bother Pepple that his team has only one non-league contest before Bothell.

"We'd rather have a couple of non-league games first," he admitted. "But you've got to play them (Bothell) sometime. It's a good way to start the season. It adds a little excitement to the season, since it could be a game that makes the difference in our division."

Eisenhower, he said, will have to serve as a tune-up for his club.

"We're going to try to win, but we want to get a chance to look at everybody we have," he said, "We're not going to sacrifice the game for substitutions, but it isn't as crucial as our league games."

Eisenhower is coached by former Mercer Island assistant coach Ed Aho. Last year, when the two teams met, Mercer Island nipped Eisenhower 56-55.

December 10, 1980

Hoopsters win 'confidence builder' against Yakima team
By Bob Ogle

It was supposed to be a tune-up game, but last Saturday's 78-41 romp with Eisenhower of Yakima showed Mercer Island High School boys' basketball coach Ed Pepple that his "machine" is in fine working order.

It has to stay that way. The Islanders have two tough games coming this week, Friday at home against Interlake and Saturday in Tacoma against Wilson High School. The following Tuesday, the Islanders return home to face Redmond.

Four players scored in double figures for Mercer Island against Eisenhower. Al Moscatel led the charge with 14 points, followed by Joe Thompson with 11, Paul Jerue with 11 and Kyle Pepple with 10. Pepple added six assists and contributed on the defensive side with eight steals.

Overall, defense was probably the Islanders' strongest point. They held Eisenhower to only four field goals in the first half and outrebounded them 44-16 at the final buzzer. Center Scott Driggers hauled down 11 of those rebounds in his first major test of the season, and he got help from both Moscatel and Thompson, who contributed nine apiece.

"I was very pleased,' Pepple said. "Defense is what we key on in practice and we were very aggressive defensively. We did have a few silly fouls (a total 23), but nobody fouled out. We showed that we have enough depth in our line up to protect anybody who gets into foul trouble."

Although his team shot 48 percent from the field, Pepple said, he was less than pleased with that figure.

"We didn't shoot the ball as well as we normally can," he said. "We didn't shoot badly but we've got the capability to be a 50-percent shooting team."

All things considered the game turned out to be more of a confidence builder than a true test.

"This wasn't the strongest team they've ever had," Pepple said. "They weren't a strong team physically. But when we do come up against a physical team, I think our kids will still be able to go inside. Moscatel, for example, isn't extremely big but he is very aggressive."

Pepple said he expects the Islanders' next three games to be more challenging. Interlake is a team much like Mercer Island, not overly big but very aggressive and tough defensively. Wilson has earned a reputation in the past for being one of the tougher teams from the Tacoma City League.

December 17, 1980

Islander cagemen 4 and 0

By Bob Ogle

Mercer Island High School's boys' basketball team had three games last week against some of the toughest competition around. When the smoke cleared, the Islanders had come away with three wins, pushing their season record to a perfect 4-0.

Tuesday night, in the toughest test, the Islanders used last-second free throws to beat KingCo League rival Bothell 52-50. Friday night, the going got a little easier as they survived a first half scare to handily outdistance Interlake, 64-48. The following night, the Islanders traveled to Tacoma to take on Wilson High School, and they smashed the Abes 82-67 in a non-league contest.

But it isn't going to get any easier. Friday night, Mercer Island will take on last year's division champ Bellevue in an 8 p.m. away contest. Like all other contests against KingCo League teams, it will be crucial.

Mercer Island center Scott Driggers hit three of four fourth-quarter free throws, including a game-icer with seven seconds left, to help beat Bothell. Guard Kyle Pepple also added two key baskets during that period.

"Neither team played exceptionally well," said Mercer Island coach Ed Pepple. "We figured it would be a close game, but we also thought there would be more points scored."

Indeed, Mercer Island had only one player in double figures, Kyle Pepple with 13. And, regardless of the number of points scored, it still puts another mark in Mercer Island's win column.

"It puts us one game ahead of Bothell in the league," Ed Pepple agreed.

The two teams will meet again January 27, in a game which could decide the divisional championship.

Against Interlake, it looked like the Islanders had left some of their intensity on the court against Bothell. During the entire first half, they shot only 33 percent from the field, falling behind 28-21 at intermission.

Somebody must have found the intensity, or at least conjured up some more. Mercer Island ripped off a 21-point scoring spree in the third quarter, while holding Interlake to only three. Driggers led the charge with seven points that quarter and 15 for the entire game. Joe Thompson chipped in 10 before fouling out, and Paul Jerue added nine.

Pepple gave much of the credit for the second half to assistant coach Bill Woolley, who delivered an inspirational talk at half-time.

"We talked about distractions," Pepple said. "Bill talked to them about how they had approached the first half and how they had to approach the second half."

The rest of the credit had to go to the field goal percentage, which improved drastically to 55 percent.

Complacency was the Islander's worst enemy.

"We try to fight complacency," Pepple said. "We let down a little bit and they came out smoking against us in the first half. You have to give them credit for playing well."

Things were a little less complicated against Wilson. Or as Pepple phrased it, "We basically ran them into the ground. They were quick, but we were able to outrun them."

It was Mercer Island's best effort to date, Pepple said, with each player performing to the best of his potential.

"As a team we played our best because we had more guys playing their best," Pepple explained.

December 17, 1980

Islanders long shots in Vegas

By Bob Ogle

Jimmy the Greek would have to agree – Mercer Island High School's chances of leaving the Las Vegas High School Holiday Basketball Tournament with a championship would best be described as "long-shot" or at least "dark-horse."

Among the 16 teams entered in the tournament, scheduled for Dec 26-30, are teams best described as national powerhouses. Witness: Daniel Murphy High School of Los Angeles, ranked 18th in the nation. Valley High School of Las Vegas, defending Nevada state champs. Inglewood High School of Los Angeles, ranked second in the nation last year and East High School of Salt Lake City, defending Utah state champions.

Other cities represented include Providence, R.I.; Beaverton, OR; Boise, Idaho; Beaver Falls, PA; Carson City, Nev; Staten Island, N.Y.; Uniontown, PA; and Las Vegas locals Gorman, Rancho, Clark and Western high schools.

Despite the odds, Mercer Island High School coach Ed Pepple said he believes his team can stay with any of the competition. He'll find out early – the Islanders' first contest is against Valley of Las Vegas. If they defeat Valley, Mercer Island will likely play Murphy of L.A.

"We definitely have our work cut out for us," Pepple agreed. "There are a lot of different playing styles there. A lot of those teams have a strong black player influence, while the Las Vegas teams tend to have been influenced by the running-gunning style of the University of Nevada Las Vegas."

If anything, Pepple has an ace-in-the-hole of sorts. The last time he brought a team to the tournament (1978), it finished third. Defense was the key then, he said, and it will likely be the key now.

The Islanders won't be lonely for support. Pepple said he expects more than 75 Mercer Island fans to be in Las Vegas for the games. Many are traveling with the team on a charter flight, while others will meet the team at its destination.

Not every basketball team is fortunate enough to compete in a tournament of such magnitude, Pepple said, and that's precisely why Mercer Island is participating.

"It's something which sets our program apart from all the others," he explained. "We try to do something like this every year. It gives the kids something to look back on and remember. Also, there are some good teams down in this tournament, so it'll bring out the best in our players."

December 25, 1980

Islanders sink Redmond and Bellevue, head for Las Vegas

By Donna Cool

Defense was the key factor when Mercer Island's boys' basketball team defeated Bellevue, 58-43, in the crucial game of the season.

Bellevue, last year's division champions, tried to slow the pace against the Islanders in a Friday game which saw the majority of points scored in the last quarter.

Al Moscatel fired 14 of his 20 points at that time, making up for a five-minute period in the third quarter when neither team scored.

Just the opposite happened in the Islanders game against Redmond, 70-55, which marked the return of Coach Gene Yerabeck, Ed Pepple's former assistant coach to the Island.

"He had the team performing pretty well," said Pepple of Yerabeck. The Mustangs met the Islanders with a 5-1 season record.

"The game was closer than what the score indicates," Pepple added.

The game was close with a 31-27 margin at halftime. Redmond cut its deficit to two points early in the third quarter, but Mercer Island eventually pulled away to a 55-35 lead in that period.

The Islanders hit 55 percent of their shots in this contest against a familiar face, while Redmond hit 46 percent.

Chris Kampe led the island team in scoring with 15 points. The performance of the 6-foot-3-inch senior guard marked the fourth time this season Mercer Island has had a different scoring leader.

"But" said Pepple, "the nature of the game is not built around the points."

Moscatel put 13 on the board and Kyle Pepple aided in 11 assists.

The Islanders will travel next to Las Vegas on Dec. 26 for the Nike Holiday Classic tournament. Mercer Island's first match-up is against Valley High School, the defending champions from Nevada.

"We're looking forward to beating them," said Pepple.

The Las Vegas team has a 6-foot-4-inch forward and all-state player and a 6-foot-6-inch center, Walter Jones, who is the top-rated player in the country, Pepple said.

Although the Las Vegas players are taller, Pepple feels the teams are fairly well-matched.

January 7, 1981

Islanders take seventh in Vegas; face Sammamish Totems Friday

Mercer Island High School's boys' basketball squad returned from Las Vegas with a seventh-place finish in last week's Nike Holiday Classic tournament, as the Islanders lost their final game, 80-

73, against Clark, Nevada. The Islanders won two and lost two during the Las Vegas tourney, bringing their overall season record to 8-2.

Al Moscatel, a 6-foot-2-inch junior forward, was named to the all-tourney team. Moscatel had a game high 20 points and 12 rebounds against the Clark squad. The winner of the tournament was Daniel Murphy High School of Los Angeles which edged Mercer Island, 57-54, earlier in the tourney.

The Islanders were overwhelmed by Clark's 6-foot-10-inch center Duane Kendall, an all-stater who plans to play at South Carolina next year. The Clark center scored a game-high 28 points against the Islanders.

"We played super defense most of the game, but we just couldn't handle the big dude," said Mercer Island coach Ed Pepple.

Scott Driggers, 6-foot-6-inches, and Joe Thompson, 6-foot-5-inches, Mercer Island's tallest players, both fouled out trying to stop Kendall.

Chris Kampe contributed 18 points and Paul Jerue 15 for the Islanders.

Coach Pepple complimented both the offensive and defensive work of Kampe, Jerue, Uczekaj and Pepple during last week's competition. "I was impressed with our guard play in Las Vegas," Pepple said. "All four played very well, both offensively and defensively. We need a little more consistency from our front liners offensively to be an outstanding team."

Pepple added he is looking to the Islanders' next contest, Friday night against Sammamish, as "an excellent time for everyone to play well."

The contest between the Islanders, who lead the Crest Division, and the Totems, who are number 7 in the Seattle Times rating of the top 20 high school teams since upsetting Juanita, should be one of the season's biggest games, Pepple said. The Totems also have an 8-2 season record.

Sammamish is led by third year letterman guard Ron Simone, who is averaging 17 points a game.

"Sammamish is definitely one of the KingCo's top teams, and ranks with the best in the state," Pepple said. "We're looking forward to this game because it matches the two divisional leaders. It should be an outstanding contest."

Tip-off time for the Friday night game is at 8 p.m. in the Islander gym.

January 14, 1981

Islander offense comes home

By Bob Ogle

Yawn.

Once you go to Las Vegas for the holidays, beat two of the nation's best high school basketball teams and darn near beat two more, thrashing teams in your own backyard just doesn't seem quite as exciting as it used to.

That's what the Mercer Island High School boys' basketball team has been facing. After leaving the Las Vegas Holiday High School Tournament with two big wins and a seventh-place finish, life in the good ol' KingCo League proved fairly easy.

Refusing to be complacent about returning, the Islanders belted Lake Washington last Tuesday 84-57. On Friday, they used a tremendous first-half effort to whip Sammamish, 62-47, to retain a hold on first place in their division with a 6-0 record.

But during the next two weeks the Islanders will face Issaquah (Friday) and state power Juanita (next Tuesday) both in 8 p.m. away contests, and then meet Inglemoor at home (Jan. 23) and divisional rival Bothell at Bothell (Jan. 27) in what could be the most crucial matchup of the year.

The Islanders will lean heavily on the Las Vegas experiences for all four contests.

"There's nobody around here any tougher than the teams we played in Las Vegas," Mercer Island coach Ed Pepple said.

Certainly, neither Lake Washington or Sammamish would be placed in the "awesome" category. As it has been all season, defense was the key to both wins.

"It's a key for us because it triggers us offensively," People said. "Defensively, I don't think we've had our best game yet. Against Sammamish, the first half was probably the best half we've had all year."

That fact was reflected in a 42-18 halftime lead. Problems in the second half kept it from being the Islanders best game all year. Guard Chris Kampe had 15 points to lead the way.

"We got so far ahead that it was tough for us in the second half," Pepple said. "We stopped doing anything defensively, so we didn't do anything offensively. Only 20 points in a half is just ridiculous. We came out flat."

Kampe finished the game with 15, being shut out in the second half. Al Moscatel, a member of the Las Vegas all-star team, chipped in 13, Kyle Pepple added 13 and Joe Thompson contributed 10. Kampe also led the way defensively, holding Sammamish hot shooting guard Ron Simone to only two points in the first half.

Against Lake Washington, Pepple and Moscatel both led with 15 apiece, followed by Rich Dewey with 12 and Scott Driggers with 10.

The Islanders next two opponents both feature strong front lines. Juanita, in particular, will be troublesome. The Rebels are led by

6-8 all-state candidate Rodnie Taylor and burly 6-5 forward Don Sparling.

Pepple is a little concerned about Juanita, but he's not losing any sleep. A loss or a win against the Rebels will have little effect on his team's playoff chances since both teams are in different divisions.

"So far, we've done what we have had to win," he said.

"The kids have a lot of confidence in themselves."

January 21, 1981

Hoop road to get tough for Islanders in Bothell

By Bob Ogle

Sooner or later, it's going to get tougher for Mercer Island High School's boys basketball team. The chances are more than likely it will be sooner.

Not only did the Islanders play KingCo powerhouse Juanita last night, but they will face divisional rival Bothell next Tuesday in what is likely to be the second biggest game of the season.

As a point of information, the biggest game of the season was the first matchup against Bothell, which the Islanders won 52-50 on Dec. 9.

But a lot of water has gone under the proverbial bridge since then. Mercer Island is undefeated in league play, with Newport (70-31) last Tuesday and Issaquah (81-41) last Friday being the latest casualties. Bothell has also gone unbeaten since playing Mercer Island, running over Juanita (60-48) along the way.

Against both Newport and Issaquah, MIHS coach Ed Pepple said, the key was typical Islander basketball – tough defense.

"We played a good, full-game of defense against both of them," he said. "We also had well-balanced scoring. There's nobody that the other team can key on. We can spread the scoring around."

Indeed, in the 81-point effort against Issaquah, only one Mercer Islander was in double figures, Joe Thompson with 14. Against Newport, the story was a little different, as team scoring-leader Al Moscatel hit for 17, guard Chris Kampe added 10 and reserve guard Tom Uczekaj hit for 10 more.

Pepple is hoping for more of the same against Bothell.

"We think that if we play our best, we can beat them," he said.

"We've already beaten them once. I hope it will come down to our bench against their bench."

Bothell, he said, is a team much like his own. "They have good balance, a lot of flexibility," he offered.

"They're a lot like us in that way. They're a good shooting team, they run well and they're big inside.

"I think it'll come down to defense. They play a tight zone, and we play man-to-man. But I also think it'll come down to who can shoot the ball against the other's defense."

Prior to Bothell, the Islanders will face Inglemoor. That contest is slated for Friday night at home at 8 p.m.

January 28, 1981

Islanders overwhelmed by Rodnie Taylor Show

By Bob Ogle

It was supposedly a game between two of the state's finest AAA boys' basketball teams. But sometimes, it looked more like the Rodnie Taylor show.

Mercer Island High School lost a 74-64 contest to the Juanita Rebels last Tuesday night, and Taylor, the Rebels' 6-8 center, was the man chiefly responsible.

Witness: 31 points, 6 rebounds, 6 blocked shots. And, oh yeah. Two slam dunks.

The Islanders were able to get back on the winning track with an 82-54 win over Inglemoor last Friday night, pulling their season record up to 14-3, in preparation for a showdown tilt last night at Bothell.

The Inglemoor win made the Juanita bitter pill a little easier to swallow.

"He's a very good player," said Mercer Island coach Ed Pepple, pointing out the obvious. "We want to put pressure on their other players so they couldn't just come down the floor and dump the ball off to him easily. But we were slow putting pressure on their forwards downcourt and they got the ball inside to him early in the game.

"He was just a better player than any of our players."

It was largely through Taylor that the Rebels opened up a 16-6 lead at the end of the first quarter, as he grabbed eight points during that period, then six straight to open the second period, making for a 23-12 wound.

To their credit, the Islanders stayed even and made a rush late in the first half on foul shots by Joe Thompson, Kyle Pepple and Scott Driggers, and on a three-point play by Rich Dewey. That closed the Islanders to within four at the half, 31-27.

It should be noted that Taylor sat out the final few minutes of that half. When he decided to come back and play some more, it was the early stages of the third quarter. He got the first two baskets. Erv Kuebler added another and Don Sparling nailed a three-point play. Presto - a 40-27 lead.

Mercer Island made another run, fighting back to 48-41 at the end of the third period. But one more time, they allowed Juanita three straight baskets at the beginning of the final period for a 54-41 lead. From then on, the Islanders would come no closer than six points.

"We might have been too intense," Pepple said after the game. "We might have been trying a little too hard. We had two bad streaks that made the difference for the whole ball game. Those few minutes really told the story.

"But I was really impressed with the way our kids kept coming back."

Against Inglemoor, the intensity was there, but in smaller quantities.

"We played fairly aggressively in the first half, but not with a lot of intensity," Pepple pointed out. "We played very well in the third quarter."

In fact, in the entire second half, the Islanders found enough intensity for 47 points, while holding the Vikings to only 29.

Against Juanita, Paul Jerue led all Islanders with 14 points, coming off the bench. Kyle Pepple added 11, with Thompson scoring 10 and Chris Kampe with 9. Kampe also grabbed high scoring honors against Inglemoor with 12 points, followed by Tom Uczekaj with 11 and Pepple with 10.

Next on tap for Mercer Island is Interlake in a Friday night away contest and Redmond in another away game next Tuesday night.

February 4, 1981

Cold shooting gives Bothell a 66-51 edge over Islanders

By Bob Ogle

Mercer Island High School's boys' basketball coach Ed Pepple has a problem. During most of his team's games this season, the Islanders field goal percentage has hovered at 50 percent or above.

But for four games, two against competition in Las Vegas and one each against Juanita and Bothell at home, the team's field goal percentage has decided to go AWOL, as in "on vacation." Or more appropriately, "poof!"

During those four losses, the only blemishes on an otherwise clean state, Mercer Island has shot poorly as a team. Last Tuesday's 66-51 loss in an important game against Bothell was no exception, as the Islanders shot a dreary 30 percent from the floor. That figure improved slightly as they came back last Friday to whip Interlake 61-49.

"We missed our first nine shots against Bothell and that was the key," offered Pepple. "We had to play catch-up ball all night long. By not doing well on offense, we never had a chance to set up our defense.

"Field goal shooting is the key to our success. The four games we've lost this year, we haven't shot well at all."

It was particularly annoying against Bothell. Both teams were tied for first place in the Crest Division of the KingCo League, with 9-1 records. Barring any unforeseen complications, that game was for the division championship and the right to play Juanita for the league championship. Juanita is title-winner from the Crown Division.

"Now, we're behind the eight ball as far as the league championship goes," Pepple said. "In order to finish first in our division, Bothell has to lose one of its remaining games (against Interlake, Bellevue and Redmond) and we have to win the rest of ours. I don't see them losing if they play like they did against us, but it could happen.

"We're more disappointed with the way we lost against both Juanita and Bothell than just the fact that we lost. When you don't play your best game, it's disappointing."

Cougar guards Tom Parrish and Kevin Morris hammered the Islanders from the outside, combining for 39 points which stung the nets to the tune of 17 field goals. Bothell's two big men, John Jensen and John Hanrahan, each copped 10 points.

Mercer Island could offset that production only with Kyle Pepple's 12 points and 10 apiece from Chris Kampe and Al Moscatel.

In a strong effort against the Saints last Friday, MIHS center Scott Driggers took his team's scoring honors with 14, and Kampe provided 13 more.

The situation isn't all gloom and doom for the Islanders, not by a long shot. They have already clinched a berth in the KingCo League playoffs, regardless of whether Bothell loses again. If the Islanders win one of their next two or if Bellevue loses one of its next two then Mercer Island would be in as No. 2 team. As such, they would likely play either Inglemoor or Newport, whichever team finishes third in the Crown. That playoff game would be at Mercer Island probably on Feb. 13. If the Islanders do finish third, they would likely travel to Sammamish for a qualifying game on Feb. 13.

In any case, in either game, the loser would be out of postseason competition and the winner would advance to the West Central District playoffs.

Supposing Bothell was to lose one of its remaining games, both Mercer Island and the Cougars would be tied for the Crest title with two losses apiece. Both teams would face off one more time for the division championship. It would also be a series-deciding game, since each team has beaten the other once this season. Mercer Island won the first meeting 52-50 in December.

And Pepple's team would like nothing better. "We look forward to playing them again for the rubber game in the series," he said.

The only question is, would a decent Islander field goal percentage be on hand to watch such a game?

February 11, 1981

Island hoop squad takes aim at playoff

The regular season for Mercer Island High School's boys' basketball team is over. Granted, it hasn't been an easy season, but what's in store for the Islanders is a different story.

For as anybody will tell you, the playoffs are a whole new ball game (pardon the pun).

As a result of wins last week against Redmond (72-55) and Bellevue (65-64) the Islanders enter into the KingCo playoffs as the No. 2 entry from the Crest Division, unless first-place Bothell was to lose last night against Redmond, an unlikely development.

Should the Islanders finish in the No. 2 spot, they will play at 7:30 p.m. this Friday at home in the first round of the league playoffs against either Inglemoor or Newport, whichever finishes third in the Crown Division. A loss by Bothell last night would mean a playoff game against the Cougars for sole possession of first place in the division. Mercer Island is 1-1 this season against Bothell.

If Mercer Island loses this Friday night against Newport or Inglemoor the Islanders can put away their basketball shoes because the season will be over. The winner Friday advances to the game for third and fourth places next Tuesday at Hec Edmundson Pavilion at the University of Washington. That game will take place at 5:30 p.m. with the championship game (probably Bothell versus Juanita) at 8:30 p.m.

Assuming the Islanders win on Friday night, they will automatically be assured a berth in the West Central District tournament Feb. 20 and 21. A third-place finish in the KingCo tourney would mean the Islanders would play at Auburn, a fourth would put them into competition at Renton. To make things even worse, the West Central District tourney will likely be the toughest in the state, containing as many as five of the top 10 teams in the state.

While Redmond was little problem for the Islanders, Bellevue was another matter.

"They're a good ball club," coach Ed Pepple said, "and they've made a lot of changes since we played them earlier this season. It was a tough ball game."

With three minutes left in the third quarter, the Islanders were down 41-32. Then, tough defense took hold and guards Tom Uczekaj and Kyle Pepple started hitting with field goals. At the end of the quarter, it was 46-46.

Mercer Island pulled away to a 65-61 lead with 1:26 left. Controlling the ball, they played keep-away for about a minute, then played throw-away with 36 seconds left, giving the ball back. Bellevue hit a three-point play, but Mercer Island regained possession and didn't give it up until the buzzer sounded.

Chris Kampe led the Islanders against Bellevue with 14 points. Pepple ended up with 13 and Uczekaj finished with 11.

Against Redmond, forward Al Moscatel had one of his best offensive nights of the season with a 17-point effort, followed by Kampe with 12, Eric Schwabe with 12 and Paul Jerue with 11.

February 18, 1981

Islanders cross one hurdle; face several more this weekend

By Bob Ogle

For Mercer Island High School, last Friday night's 79-41 smashing of Newport in the first game of the KingCo League playoffs was just the first of several hurdles.

The win catapulted the Islanders into the West Central District basketball playoffs this weekend. The only question remaining - where the Islanders will be playing – was resolved last night, in a game against Sammamish for third and fourth place in the KingCo.

Mercer Island already has beaten Sammamish once this season, a 62-47 decision at home. The winner of last night's game at Hec Edmundson Pavilion at the University of Washington will play Friday night in a 7 p.m. game at Auburn High School, against the No. 2 team from the South Puget Sound League. Such a game would prove to be a big hurdle – the opponent would be Federal Way (14-3), a team with a 6-8 center, David Syring.

The KingCo's fourth-place team, last night's loser, will participate in the WCD tourney at Renton High School. That game, at 7 p.m. Friday, will be against the Tacoma-Narrows League's No. 2 team, either Lincoln, Stadium or Foss high schools. That league, always a tough one, will provide no patsies to the tournament.

Regardless of which game they play Friday night, the Islanders will have a rough time on Saturday night, should they pass the first hurdle. If they defeat Federal Way, they will face Auburn in a 7 p.m. Saturday night tilt at (gulp) Auburn High School. Auburn is led by 7-0 center Blair Rasmussen and has lost two games all season.

Beating Narrows No. 2 on Friday night would be even worse. The following night at 7 p.m. at Renton High School, the Islanders would face top-ranked and undefeated Lakes of Tacoma.

Against Newport, the Islander's future was unclear for the first four minutes, as they fell behind 8-6.

Then, Mercer Island's defense took hold. Guard Kyle Pepple grabbed a steal, one of six for the evening, and drove it in for a bucket. That triggered a scoring spree which saw Mercer Island outscore Newport 33-7 over the next 16 minutes.

Pepple not only keyed the Islanders offense, but their defense as well, with 11 assists. That gives him a season total of 138, tying the school record.

"Both he and several other kids were trying to take charge out there," said Kyle's coach (and father) Ed Pepple. "Kyle was keying the defense. When our defense is playing like it was, the offense also does well."

Kyle finished with only five points, but his assists were responsible for 22 more. Not bad for only playing half the ball game.

Al Moscatel also stepped forward to take charge of the Islanders, hitting for 15 points while playing less than three quarters of the game. In fact, when Newport finally did recover their offense, almost all the MIHS starters were on the bench and the Islander reserves were getting exercise on the court.

Mercer Island shot a better-than-average 55.3 percent from the field, hitting 31 of 56 shots. Newport also shot extremely well, 54 percent. But when you only take (or are allowed, as it were) 26 shots, it makes a big difference.

Friday night, regardless of where they play, the Islanders will be faced with a loser-out situation. With a win Friday, they would be forced to win one of their next two games to qualify for state AAA regionals.

There are quite a few good teams – or hurdles – in the West Central District for the Islanders and all will have to be jumped in order for the team's goal to be realized – a chance for a berth in the state finals.

"Federal Way or Lincoln would be good opponents," Pepple said of the outlook for Friday night, "But we'll have to play good teams throughout the tournament."

February 25, 1981

Heartbreaking loss in Auburn: Islanders overcome 14-point deficit; but lose to Trojans in final seconds

By Bob Ogle

Mercer Island High School's 56-55 loss to Auburn High School in the second round of the boy's AAA West Central District basketball tournament last Saturday was a real disappointment.

Sort of like having your paycheck chewed up by your dog. Or, if you prefer, like running a world-record time in the mile only to find out that the stopwatch broke midway through the race.

You know. A REAL disappointment.

In what would prove to be a modern-day version of "Casey at the Bat," the Islanders battled back from a 14-point deficit midway through the final period to take the lead with 1:33 remaining, only to blow the game at the end.

If "blow" seems like a harsh word, just ask coach Ed Pepple.

"We won it," he flatly announced after the game. "We had the ball game until 36 seconds left and then we lost it."

The Islanders, fresh from a win the night before against Federal Way (59-47), had played the Auburn Trojans evenly for three quarters, behind by six at the end of the third, 40-34.

Then, all sorts of havoc broke loose. Auburn started going inside to 6-10 center Blair Rasmussen, as had been the case all evening. Rasmussen hit four free throws and two buckets as part of a 10-2 Auburn scoring surge.

With slightly more than five minutes left, Mercer Island called time, regrouped and started to rise from the ashes.

"There wasn't anybody in that whole place," Pepple noted afterward, "who didn't think we had lost the game right then." Guilty as charged.

The Islanders sent a harassing, tight-pressing defense into the game and it paid off. Kyle Pepple hit a free throw and Eric Schwabe followed with a basket of his own. The Islanders stole the ball and Al Moscatel hit another basket. They stole the ball again and this time Paul Jerue hit the hoop. Taking matters into his own hands, Jerue stole the ball and popped in another. After another Auburn turnover, he threw in one more just for good measure and the Trojans were suddenly on a wild ride. Mercer Island had pulled within three with 3:20 left, 50-47.

Auburn stopped momentum briefly, until it took over again with 1:52 left, as Eric Schwabe hit an 18-footer to give Mercer Island a 53-52 lead. Rasmussen threw in his final basket with 1:41 left, giving him a total of 34 for the night, putting the Trojans back up. With 1:33 left, he fouled Moscatel, who sank both free throws to put Mercer Island back up, 55-54.

Moscatel rebounded an Auburn miss at the other end with 1:10 to go and Mercer Island went into a stall.

And if you like happy endings, this is your stop.

Because, with 36 seconds left, Mercer Island was called for charging near the top of the key. Auburn's Mark Kovacevich got a one-and-one situation at the foul line, since the Islanders' fouls had put Auburn in the bonus situation. He sank both to give the Trojans a one-point lead.

Mercer Island then proceeded to: (1) Throw the ball away with 15 seconds to go, as an errant pass drifted into backcourt for an over-and-back call; (2) Foul Auburn's Steve Kearney, who missed the first part of his one-and-one; (3) Send two more Trojans to the line after failing to rebound each missed free throw. Finally, on the third try, Rich Dewey hauled in the rebound and Mercer Island called timeout with three seconds left. (4) The Islanders threw the ball away on the inbounds pass.

The only thing that hurts more than losing is winning and then losing. Mighty Casey had struck out.

"It's a heartbreaker," Pepple confirmed. 'The kids battled their hearts out to get back ahead. All we had to do was run out the clock. Who'd foresee that we'd run over somebody?"

While he gave Jerue a lot of credit for the comeback - "He's a hard-nosed, aggressive kid" - it was a team effort, according to Pepple.

"Jerue sparked us, but it wasn't a one-man deal," he said. "It was just too bad we had to play our worst ball of the season during the last 36 seconds."

For sure, it ended a great week on a sour note. To finish third in the KingCo League, Mercer Island beat Sammamish the previous Tuesday night, 58-55, then dominated Federal Way to open the WCD tourney.

Against Federal Way, there was very little doubt of the outcome. Mercer Island grabbed an 18-6 lead at the end of the first period, and that held up quite nicely throughout the remainder of the evening.

Moscatel led all Islanders against Federal Way with 19 points. He also led in the Auburn effort, with 14 points. Eric Schwabe added 12, including a couple of shots over the towering Rasmussen, and Kyle Pepple collected 11.

Of course, the Islanders are anything but dead in the West Central District. They play Friday night, at Auburn High School, in a 7 p.m. tilt against Kentridge, the No. 2 team from the North Puget Sound League. Kentridge lost in Saturday's nightcap to Juanita, 87-58. Juanita will play Auburn at 8:30 p.m. Friday.

As it was against Federal Way, Kentridge will be a loser-out situation for Mercer Island. If the Islanders win, they will play the winner of Sammamish and Rogers the following night at 6 p.m.

A win against Kentridge would also secure a spot for Mercer Island in the next round of the journey to a state championship, the regionals. Regional competition is scheduled for March 6 and 7 at various sites throughout the Puget Sound area.

March 4, 1981

Two wins propel Islanders into play-offs against Everett

By Bob Ogle

Last weekend's West Central District basketball tournament went just the way Ed Pepple wanted.

His Mercer Island High School club whipped Kentridge, 79-53, last Friday night and Rogers of Puyallup, 75-44, the following evening. That was Pepple's main desire.

The win over Kentridge propelled the Islanders into the next phase of the basketball playoffs: the regionals. That was wish No. 2 on Pepple's list.

Beating Rogers made Mercer Island the fourth-place team in the West Central District and secured a spot in the Region 1 Playoffs this weekend at Seattle Center Arena. While fourth place wasn't exactly what he had in mind, Pepple doesn't deny that it will be nice to play close to home again. The WCD tournament was held at Auburn High School.

Two wins this weekend would go a long way toward fulfilling Pepple's final wish, since they would put the Islanders in the following weekend at Seattle Center Coliseum.

And as anyone could tell you, a shot at the state title is just what Ed Pepple wants. In fact, it's probably No. 1 on the wish list of his 12 basketball players.

There was never any doubt about the outcome last Friday or Saturday night. Against Kentridge, the Islanders ran up a 10-2 lead in the first quarter, let the Chargers come back to 14-12 at the end of the period, then stretched the lead out again to 27-15 midway through the second period. This time, Mercer Island made the lead stick and then some, stretching it out to as much as 27 points.

Four Islanders hit double figures, with Al Moscatel firing for 17 points to lead the way. Guard Chris Kampe ticked off 14 and Scott Driggers and Paul Jerue added 10 each.

Rogers, the No. 3 school from the South Puget Sound League, looked a bit on the hapless side the following night, as the Islanders ran off a 16-0 lead in the first period. Rogers didn't get its first basket until five minutes had gone by and only had two baskets the entire quarter. Moscatel did most of the damage, with eight of his game high 15 points in that quarter, but Kyle Pepple, Eric Schwabe and Chris Kampe also did some damage before the smoke had cleared from a 20-4 first quarter lead.

Things got no better for Rogers as the night wore on. Mercer Island built leads as large as 34 points on route to the final verdict.

Moscatel again led Mercer Island, this time with 15 points. Kyle Pepple and Eric Schwabe each contributed 12 to the cause.

Moscatel has made a full recovery from a mild slump which caught him near the end of the regular season. In the four WCD games, he has contributed 60 points and an immense amount of determination.

"Al's a great competitor," his coach praised. "It seems like the tougher the competition, the tougher he plays. I think near the end of the season, he just got burned out for a while."

Everything seemed right on both nights, but one problem did appear. Upon building a large lead, the Islanders tended to become complacent and allow the other teams to get rolling. This is a trait Mercer Island shares in common with almost every other basketball team – a 30-point lead tends to make you complacent.

"Yeah," Pepple quipped, "when they get that far ahead, I have to beat 'em with a switch just to keep them going."

The Islanders had a lot of time last week to think about a one-point loss to Auburn in the second game of the tourney. A few days of easy practice and clear thinking set the stage for two nights of success.

"I haven't been working them that hard lately." Pepple said. "We've had a lot of energy for what we've had to do the last two nights. I think we were mentally ready to play. We thought we could win both games. We came in confident because we have been playing well lately."

The regional tournament will require a similar degree of readiness. Mercer Island's first opponent will be Everett in a loser-out contest. The winner will play the winner of a game between Shorecrest and Auburn in the finals on Saturday at 7:30 p.m. The ultimate victor will continue to state; losers will go home to lick the wounds.

Everett, Pepple said, "Doesn't seem to have a whole lot of depth. But they're a scrappy team, and they have good quickness with their guards."

Everett's main source of points comes from a 6-3 sophomore forward, Chris Chandler.

It is entirely possible that Region 1 may be the easiest region of all during the tournament, but that's not the main reason Pepple wanted to enter that particular region.

"We wanted to be in the Arena to be close to home," he said, "It's been a tough drain for everybody from Mercer Island to have to come all the way down to Auburn to play."

The fact that both games will be loser-out situations may help, too. With three wins in postseason, loser-out games, the

Islanders are developing a response to pressure. They have won all loser out games by handy margins.

March 11, 1981

State-bound!

Islanders break 100; gain tourney berth

By Bob Ogle

After they had barely squeaked by Everett, 51-49, in the first round of the Region 1 high school basketball playoffs at the Seattle Center Arena, coach Ed Pepple decided it was time to have a chat with his Mercer Island High School players.

They talked about the usual things - about playing to win, about team goals, and other such stuff which teams usually discuss following a mediocre effort.

Needing another win to advance in the playoffs, they annihilated the Shorecrest Scots the following night to the tune of 101-60, and that isn't a misprint.

Now, the Islanders will embark on the biggest journey of all, the dream of any kid who has ever played in a high school basketball game. They are going to get a shot at a state championship.

Mercer Island will play tomorrow (March 12) at 8:30 pm against Richland in an opening round game of the State AAA Basketball Tournament finals at the Seattle Center Coliseum. That is the goal which has been in mind since the season started last December.

"It's the draw we were hopin' for," People said of his team's first content. "We're excited about the prospect of playing Richland. They're a prestige team, and a first-class program. It'll be an exciting game."

Tickets for the contest are on sale at the high school, $3 for students and $4 for adults. Mercer Island High School will receive a percentage of the profits from all tickets sold at the school.

Should the Islanders defeat Richland, they will play the winner of the 10pm contest tomorrow night between Lakes and KingCo nemesis Juanita Friday at 8:30 pm.

If they lose, they would face the loser of that game at 10pm Friday.

And should they win both nights, they would play for the championship Saturday at 8:30pm.

As far as last weekend is concerned, it wasn't that the Scots were such a lousy team. They had finished first in their Western Conference division with an 11-1 record and had whipped Everett 73-50 in a district playoff game the previous weekend.

The Islanders played their best ballgame of the year. Period. Just ask Pepple.

"We know we didn't play our best the night before, against Everett," he admitted. "We had to play like we were enthusiastic about it. That's what we talked about after the game."

"It worked out better than my fondest dreams. We blew Shorecrest out of the gym."

Indeed, they did. After building a 24-17 lead at the end of the first period, the Islanders stepped into the proverbial phone booth and changed into supermen, running off a 17-2 scoring spree against the Scots during the next six minutes.

The result was a 45-23 lead, which grew to 54-29 by the time the quarter ended. The only question left was whether the Islanders would break 100 points.

It was reserve Doug Gregory who hit a 15-foot jump shot with 16 seconds left to break the barrier. The game eclipsed the previous record for most points scored in a tournament game, 94 by Mount Rainier in 1971.

Hard to believe but breaking 100 points was not that big a deal with Pepple.

"We don't like to rub it in," he said. "Only two things were important to us. One, we won the game, and two, it was a team effort. As far as breaking 100 points goes, nobody deserved to score that basket more than Doug Gregory."

All 12 Islanders got into the scoring column against the Scots. Forward Eric Schwabe had his best game of the year, leading all scorers with 21 points and some tough inside play. Al Moscatel and Chris Kampe added 12 apiece, Tom Uczekaj hit 11 and Kyle Pepple added 10.

While that game was a total team effort, Everett was a different case. Two players, Moscatel and Kampe, carried the load for Mercer Island, as they hit 19 points each.

With the game tied at 49-all and three minutes left on the clock, Mercer Island got possession of the ball and began a stall, working for the last shot. They never got to take it.

Everett was called for a technical foul with 18 seconds left for refusing to come out to the halfcourt line and challenge the stalling Islanders. The rulebook says the defense must initiate action, and if they don't, a technical foul is in order.

Moscatel went to the line and canned the free throw for a 50-49 edge. Kampe was fouled with four seconds left, after the Islanders retained possession following the technical, and hit one of two free throws to ice the win.

Part of the problem against the Seagulls was an injury to point guard Kyle Pepple, a thigh bruise which left him hesitant on defense.

Now, at the major risk of oversimplification, all that stands between Mercer Island and a state championship is three wins. It is, as Ed Pepple says, one of the most evenly matched state finals in recent history.

"Any of the eight teams could go all the way," Pepple said. "We're not afraid to play any of them. Our team has a good chemistry, and tremendous versatility. Anybody who sells these guys short of going all the way doesn't know what makes them tick.

"The most important thing now is for the community to get behind these guys. There's nothing more exciting than the state high school basketball finals. It's going to be a real showcase for our school and for the community."

State AAA Tournament: on eighth trip, Pepple's still excited

By Peggy Reynolds

The state AAA basketball tournament should be old stuff by now to Mercer Island coach Ed Pepple, but this year on his eighth try at the state title, Pepple seems more excited than ever.

What's new this time is the company he keeps: three teams from the KingCo Conference, the others being Juanita and Bothell. On occasions in the past, two conference teams might get into the final eight, and in 1976 Mercer Island and Juanita played each other in the final round. But three? Incredible. It attests the quality of basketball on the east side of Lake Washington.

Like in 1978, the last state try by the Islanders, this is a team without a star. Rather, according to Ed, it's "a team with 12 stars." Everybody scored Saturday night against Shorecrest, when the Islanders piled up their all-time high of 101 points, and that's how Pepple likes to see his guys play.

In a trip along Memory Lane, Pepple recalls his first season here, 1967-68, with a team led into state by Steve Hawes, then 6-foot-

8, a 4.0 standout, and a scorer who consistently broke 30. Hawes later starred for the Huskies, and has since been in pro ball, playing presently with Atlanta. The Islanders failed to place in the tournament, however.

By 1979 Steve's "little" brother Jeff, only 6-4, led the Islanders to state for some excitement but again, no place.

In 1972 the Islanders placed third in state, with the miracle combination of Greg Jack, Steve Biehn, Mickey Smith, Doug Gribble, Gary Weddell, Mark Morgan and Jim Johnson. They played the state tourney with a squad of only seven, but it was a lucky number.

Again in 1974 with Gribble then a senior, the Islanders played in state and finished seventh. That team featured Terry Pepple, Ed's oldest son, who went on to play college ball at Cheney and a core of Mike Ginn, Kevin Haynes, Randy Mitchell, and Matt Yeagar.

By 1976 the locals had acquired "Mercer Icelander" Peter Gudmundsson, 7-foot-2, and teammate Marty Mattila, 6-8. They made it into state that year but didn't place, the following year they again went to state and finished third.

In 1979 a squad led by Mark Jerue and Paul Bain finished eighth.

Like the last several squads of Islanders, the current group has been playing together since fifth grade. Among his first activities upon arriving on Mercer Island that 1967-68 season, Ed Pepple founded the Little Dribblers for fifth and sixth graders, a pilot group for the area. Among this year's eight long-time teammates is Kyle, Ed's younger son. When Kyle was little Ed said he would "go after anything that rolls, bounces or flies" and Kyle's still doing it.

Last year someone started a rumor that Ed Pepple would move up to college ball once Kyle was through school. Ed says the rumor's entirely untrue. "I have no intention of leaving. I enjoy what

I'm doing. I love the community and the kids in it, and they'll probably have to bury me here."

And as for the community, "I hope I see all of 'em out tomorrow night. Richland knocked us out of the championship in 1977 and now we want to return the favor. We're very excited about playing them."

Little Dribblers shoot toward Texas tourney

Teamwork. Fundamentals. With Mercer Island High School's varsity boys' basketball team going on to the state playoffs, these aspects of basketball are being stressed.

But how did those varsity players learn their skills? Through participation in Mercer Island's Little Dribblers program, which concluded its regular season March 7 with the championship playoffs.

High school basketball coach Ed Pepple has headed the program during its 13-year existence and feels Little Dribblers "helps in a lot of ways," by giving kids the opportunity to play competitive basketball.

Little Dribblers concentrates on fundamentals and teamwork and gives the players experience. The all-star team is also able to travel, which Pepple calls "a broadening experience."

All 12 of the high school's varsity players were Little Dribblers competitors, and two-thirds of them were members of at least one all-star team. Incidentally, that team won the National Championship as sixth graders, and placed second as eighth graders.

"The fact that the high school is competitive has some reflection on Little Dribblers," Pepple said.

A number of high school basketball players, as well as a few junior high competitors, coach the Little Dribblers teams.

The 1981 All-star Little Dribblers team will host a game against Issaquah Thursday, March 19 in the Mercer Island High School gym.

The Issaquah game will be the first of a three-game contest to determine who will represent Washington state at the national championships in Texas April 15 to 19.

The Mercer Island team has a long history of success in the Texas tournament and has usually placed well. However, to get to Texas, Mercer Island must win two of its three games against Issaquah.

Team members will be selling game tickets door-to-door in the business district.

Ticket proceeds will go toward the hoped-for Texas trip.

March 18, 1981

On the road to the finals: Islanders upset Lakes, Richland

By Bob Ogle

Richland. It's a name synonymous with basketball excellence. A record 27 years of post-season high school tournament appearances and 11 times placing in the top three at the state AAA basketball tournament is indicative of the quality of Bomber basketball. Heck, they even sell a 52-page booklet detailing the history of Richland High School basketball.

It's too bad that, in 1981, they came all the way from Richland to the state AAA finals for nothing. This tournament probably will not go too well in the history books. It was not to be a good year for Richland at the state finals.

Instead, the glory belonged to the Islanders, who pulled off what many considered the upset of the tournament by knocking off the second-ranked Bombers 58-56 in a first-round game last Thursday night. It was only Richland's second loss of the season.

The margin of victory came courtesy of point guard Kyle Pepple. After being fouled with seven seconds left in the game, he stepped to the free throw line and calmly canned the two biggest free throws of his life for the win.

Following the game, he passed the two shots off as part of the job. "I just figured that if I hit them," he said, "we'd win." His reasoning was perfect and so was his aim.

It was the kind of arrangement upsets are made of. Richland came into the game with a 34-1 record and a lineup that included four starters who averaged double-digit totals and a fifth who averaged just under 10 points a game.

Mercer Island? Well, all they had was one double-figure scorer - Al Moscatel with a 12.2 average. They did have one other thing called desire.

The desire paid off, showing itself quickly. Mercer Island fell behind 2-1 at the outset after a dunk by 6-5 Richland center Dennis Soldat. After regaining a 5-4 lead, Mercer Island ran off with seven straight points and the Bombers were down 12-4, with slightly more than half the period gone. At the end of the period, the Islanders held a 19-11 lead.

Richland came back hard in the second period, pulling within two at the half, 32-30. The Bombers would spend the rest of the night clawing their way back from such deficits.

Just when it looked like Mercer Island might get some breathing room, after running off eight consecutive points in the third period, which meant a 40-32 lead with 5:40 left, Richland ran off a string of its own, tying the game at 42-all with 1:49 left in the third.

It was toe to toe from there. Richland took a 48-47 lead with 5:52 left in the fourth period, and the two teams proceeded to trade the honor of leading back and forth.

Chris Kampe hit two free throws with 2:07 to go, giving the Islanders a 56-54 lead. Richland's Dave Keller tied the game at 56 with a bucket at the 1:50 mark. With the ball again, Mercer Island went into a slowdown offense, working and waiting for the final shot. With 13 seconds left, they began to work the ball inside for the game winner when Pepple was fouled.

The rest, as they say, is history.

"This was something we had been looking forward to for a long time," coach Ed Pepple said. "We had to play a smart ballgame to win."

Part of the game plan was to play tough defense and shut down the inside game of Soldat. They ran right at him all night offensively.

"We initiated our offense to do that," Pepple said. "We made Soldat play defense all night long. He didn't contest us too much inside."

Down the home stretch, the Islanders got a big break when Soldat picked up his fifth foul. He was benched for good with 4:34 left to go.

"Having him out of there at the end made a lot of difference," Pepple said. "He's an outstanding player. But we felt we could go inside on him all night long. That's how he got into foul trouble."

Soldat ended the night with 11 points, far behind the 23 points of teammate Matt Haskins. No other Richland player scored in double figures.

Conversely, Kyle Pepple led Mercer Island with 18 points, a rash of assists and some key defensive plays. Moscatel contributed 16, while center Scott Driggers hit for 10, most of those over Soldat in the middle.

Richland, Ed Pepple said, played a magnificent game.

"Every time we were up, they just kept coming back," he praised. "It's easy to fold up and roll over when somebody keeps coming at you like that, but our kids showed a lot of poise and did all the things they needed to do."

It's not often that you get to play in the second round of the state AAA high school basketball finals.

It's also not often that you get a chance to show your stuff against the No. 1 team in the state, a team with a 22-0 record.

Mercer Island High School got its chance Friday night, playing the undefeated Lakes Lancers of Tacoma at Seattle Center Coliseum.

The Islanders exited the game with their second upset in as many nights, making the Lancers look like so much junk, handing them a 64-48 shellacking to advance into the Saturday night championship game against Shadle Park.

It didn't start out looking like an upset, though. Mercer Island had a little trouble getting untracked. A bad pass here, a missed shot there, and Lakes was able to run up an 18-10 lead by the end of the first period.

From then on, the game would be controlled by the Islanders, thanks to one of the toughest defenses ever seen at the state finals. Mercer Island virtually shut the Lakes scoring threat down, allowing the Lancers only one field goal and four free throws enroute to a 29-23 halftime edge.

Things didn't get much better by the end of the third, as the Islander defenses again held Lakes down, this time to only nine points. The Mercer Island lead would get no smaller than eight the rest of the night.

The main reason for the second quarter surge was largely guard Kyle Pepple, who coordinated defensive sets during the game. The Islanders used seven different defenses in all, from a full-court press to a couple of different types of zone defenses. The ploy worked, as Pepple kept switching the Islanders from defense to defense, and Lakes never knew what to look for.

The second half belonged almost totally to forward Al Moscatel, who hit 15 of his game-high 21 points in the final two periods, while shooting 9 of 14 from the field the entire night. Many of the points came from muscling inside Lakes' defense for easy lay-ins.

After the game, he spread the praise to his teammates.

"When you have people who can get the ball inside to you," he said, "you have to start going inside. Everybody on the floor was throwing great passes tonight."

Mercer Island coach Ed Pepple chose to leave the praise with Moscatel.

"He's got to be the biggest 6-2 player in the world," Pepple said. "He plays with a lot of emotion. He's a supreme competitor and he does not like to lose. He provides us with an anchor."

Crafty as ever, coach Pepple had decided that using a number of different defenses might shale Lakes up a bit. The way son Kyle called the sets, it looked like a family stroke of genius.

"They had a hard time adjusting to what we threw at them," Ed Pepple said. "I didn't think they were a good shooting team. We thought they might have trouble when we changed up our defenses. And Kyle did a great job of calling the defenses."

The first quarter slump, Pepple said, was just a matter of not knowing what to expect.

"I think we underestimated Lakes' actual raw talent," he explained. "We may have come out a little tired, too. We gave them some easy points in that first quarter."

One player did all the damage for Lakes, Calvin Harris with 19 points. On the Islanders side, Eric Schwabe turned in some outstanding play on his way to a 15-point performance.

The state championship game against Shadle Park was played the following night, Saturday, March 14.

March 18, 1981
Cheap shot? Islanders protest "winning" basket
By Teresa Wippel

"When we started the year, we had three goals: to win KingCo, to win district and to win state. Two games took KingCo away from us. Two calls took district away from us. And I don't think two acts of God are going to take state away from us." - Chris Kampe, captain, MIHS basketball team

The Mercer Island community isn't likely to forget Saturday, March 14, 1981. It will be remembered as a day that began with happiness and excitement and ended in anger. It will be written in Island history books as the day the high school basketball team won, but didn't receive, the State AAA championship trophy.

And although most of the memories are unforgettable, few of them are pleasant.

"Would someone please let me know," asked head coach Ed Pepple as he paced outside the Seattle Coliseum locker room last Saturday night, "how I can go in and explain that to those kids?"

Muffled sobs and cries or frustration found their way outside the locker room door, echoing in the hallway. For a team that had played together since grade school and for a man who was in the state finals for the first time in his 14-year coaching career, the dream of a state championship had turned into a nightmare.

THE CAUSE OF the heart wrenching frustration came just 45 minutes earlier, at the end of the Islanders' championship game against Shadle Park High School of Spokane.

Behind by five points, 19-14, at the end of the first quarter and by one, 36-35, at the half, Mercer Island took the lead in the third quarter and never again trailed.

With six seconds left and the score tied, 64-64, Pepple son and star guard, Kyle, made one of two foul shots, giving Mercer Island a 65-64 edge. After regaining possession, Shadle Park's Dave Ray dribbled the ball, then made a long pass to teammate Greg Schmidt, who was waiting near the Highlanders basket. Schmidt put up a 9-foot baseline shot that swished through the hoop, but the clock had run out, the Islanders thought. One referee standing under the basket, Chris Manolopoulos, signaled the shot as good. The other, Dave George, standing at mid-court near the scorer's table, indicated the shot was too late. The scoreboard registered a 65-64 win lor Mercer Island.

Meanwhile, Mercer Island fans had rushed on to the court to celebrate. Players Kyle Pepple and Doug Gregory climbed on top of the basket and began cutting down the net (a tradition for the winning team).

Then, 30 seconds after the game's end, the scoreboard changed to read 66-65, in favor of Shadle Park. Highlander fans began celebrating, while Mercer Islanders stood frozen, disbelieving and stunned.

The referees had already left the floor. Pepple, his coaching assistants and players went to the scorer's table to argue with officials. Don Davis, the official timer, told assistant coach Bill Woolley and player Al Moscatel that Schmidt's shot was late and shouldn't have counted. But, Davis added, he could only give his opinion if asked by the referees. And they didn't ask.

And Davis wasn't the only non-Islander who disagreed with the call. Prep and collegiate coaches, off-duty officials and members of the media watching the game agreed that the shot was no good.

However, the Shadle Park coach, Dave Robertson, commented he thought the shot was made in time.

To add to the confusion, the automatic buzzer which signaled the end of the game wasn't working that evening and had to be operated manually.

TENSION MOUNTED as the angry crowd gathered on the Coliseum floor. Some Island basketball players dropped to the ground, sobbing and beating their fists on the floor, while others wandered from one side of the court to the other, tears streaming down their laces. Assistant coach Woolley sat on a chair, a towel covering his bent head.

Islander fans stood on the Coliseum floor for 45 minutes, preventing an awards ceremony from taking place. Finally, Pepple took the microphone and told the Island fans to leave the Coliseum and meet back at the high school gym.

The coach and his team went to the locker room, where they stayed for another 45 minutes.

"We had it won," sobbed Al Moscatel as he walked to the locker room. "They took it away from us."

"We've worked six years for this," added Kyle Pepple. "It's ours."

Painfully reflected in the tear-stained faces was the frustration of being declared a loser on what was considered an unfair judgement, after beating the state's top teams and fighting as underdog status from the beginning of the tourney.

What Coach Pepple said when he went into the locker room was simple and firm. "We're still state champs, no matter what the score is."

He relayed those same sentiments to an estimated 3000 Mercer Island fans who gathered in the high school gym after the game.

"I don't know if we can get our own gold ball. I don't know if we can have patches on our jackets or not. I don't know what can be done. But I do know this. As long as I live, the student body, the administration, the animal band and especially the basketball team are the state triple-A champs of 1981," Pepple declared.

BUT HIGH SCHOOL officials are trying to rewrite this chapter in history. On Monday morning, District Superintendent Craig Currie delivered an official protest of the game to Hank Rybus, executive secretary of the Washington Interscholastic Athletic Association (WIAA).

Currie would not release the details of the protest, but he did say it is based on a WIAA rule that allows a school to protest "a misapplication or misinterpretation of the rules or game conditions that have an unfair effect on the outcome of the game."

When contacted Monday, Rybus said the WIAA could not hear protests of a referee's judgement call, but only those objections based on improper game "mechanics" - how an official handles a particular situation, for example.

A decision is expected sometime today (Wednesday) or early Thursday from the WIAA office, on whether the WIAA's executive board will agree to hear the protest.

If the board IS willing, Rybus said he doesn't know when the case will be heard. The board's next regular meeting is in April, although members may decide to call an earlier meeting.

Rybus said that if the protest is heard, the board would use any evidence available to make its decision, including video tapes and statements by referees and other officials.

Mercer Island High School video tapes all of its basketball games and has two tapes of the final shot. The tapes have been viewed by school administrators and were shared on KING-TV's Sunday evening newscast.

Since the publicity has hit the local media, both referees have been interviewed on the final call. Manolopoulos, who lives in Richland, said he believes he made the right call. But the most interesting testimony has come from Dave George, the other referee, from Yakima.

ALTHOUGH MANY PEOPLE, including an off-duty referee, said they definitely saw George signal that the shot was no good, George has denied he ever made such a call. In fact, George said, he and Manolopoulos agreed that the shot counted.

Pepple stated that the Islanders would not be content with a second-place trophy. "Second place doesn't mean anything to us.

"We won on the court and we'll win off the court," Pepple said. "We're going to fight this thing as far as we can."

Oddsmakers made a mistake in overlooking Island team

By Bob Ogle

It was a meeting of the high school basketball elite. Richland, Lakes, Shadle, Auburn, Juanita, Bothell, Foss...

...and Mercer Island. Somehow, with all the big to-do surrounding the state AAA high school basketball tournament finals, the kids from the rock got overlooked.

That was a mistake.

Item: The final results of the state Associated Press sportswriter basketball poll showed all eight finalist teams placed in the top eight positions. Lakes was first. Richland was second. Shadle Park was third and so on down the list. Mercer Island? Look down that list, next to the number eight.

Eighth-ranked in state, and therefore considered least likely to win the state title.

That was a mistake.

Item: A Seattle daily newspaper picked Lakes at 3 to 1 and Richland at 5 to 1 as odds-on favorites to win the championship. Mercer Island? Uh, sorry guys, how 'bout 25 to 1, the worst odds of any team participating?

That was a big mistake.

Item: Mercer Island's first game was against Richland, a team rich in basketball tradition. With slightly more than a minute gone, Richland runs a fast break, gets the ball to big Dennis Soldat who slams it through with a dunk for two points. A broad, confident grin spreads across his face as he runs back down court. The grin seems to say, "Mercer Who?"

Soldat couldn't find much to smile about after the game was over and his team had been upset 58-56. When confronted with the lack of confidence in his troops by those not connected with the program, Mercer Island coach Ed Pepple shook his head and sadly smiled.

"I just can't believe that anybody would not take us seriously," he said. "I sent $10 to the guy who gave the 25 to 1 odds and told him I wanted a piece of the action."

After the win over Richland, the daily newspapers blared the news on the front page of the sports section. Still, a few believers had yet to be won over. A 64-48 annihilation of top-ranked Lakes took care of that. More headlines, more believers.

Said Pepple· "Those were upsets only for those people who didn't know this team." But realistically, why would anyone think Mercer Island would have a shot at the state title? No superstar-type players. No real big scorers. Nobody in the lineup taller than 6-6. To top it off, the Islanders had the worst record of any team in the field of eight, with five losses.

All the doubters overlooked one thing - desire. They forgot that it's not the size of the dog in the fight, but the size of the fight in the dog.

It was this desire which earned Mercer Island High School its second-place finish.

Al Moscatel knew why he and his teammates fell behind Lakes 18-10 in the first quarter of that ballgame.

"We needed to be more patient," he said. "In the first quarter, we played like individuals. We're not good enough to win just as individuals. In the second, third and fourth quarter, we were a team. If we play like a team, like we know how, we can beat anybody."

Moscatel, who led Mercer Island in scoring during the tournament, knew he was a good bet for tournament MVP kudos.

"Forget it," he said after the Lakes game. "It means nothing. If we win, who cares?"

So, what can be learned by looking at the final results of this year's tournament?

There's no limit to what a group of individuals can do when they pull together as a team. All the other teams and sportswriters forgot that. All they needed was a reminder, and sure enough, they got it. Mercer Island's success in the tournament proved that the only limitation to achievement is a lack of imagination and determination.

And what of the guy who brought all this together in one place, coach Ed Pepple, now in his 14th year at Mercer Island? Saturday night was his first trip to the state championship game as a coach.

Never before had any of his teams finished higher than third place. That was 1977.

Pepple was more than a little miffed at the lack of attention given his team.

"The only thing that counts in something like this is what happens at the end of it all," he said.

"What do sportswriters know about it? They saw that we had lost five games, but they forgot who we lost those games to. We lost two in a national tournament in Las Vegas and three to teams which were in the final eight. We didn't lose to anybody who was a patsy. What the sportswriters think isn't important. What is important is the way the kids look at it."

Pepple knows what it's like to be in a championship situation as a player. He played in the 1950 AAA title game as part of a Lincoln

High School (Seattle) team which lost to South Kitsap in overtime, 40-37. He remembers.

"These kids are only going to get one time around," he said last Friday. "All of my emotion is for them. It's a once-in-a-lifetime opportunity. It's something they'll always remember."

But don't think that the coach doesn't feel any of the sense of pride, the sense of achievement against the odds, that his players feel. That isn't the case at all.

"Let's put it this way," Pepple said after pausing for a moment to reflect. "If you were sitting on the bench during these games in my place, watching this team play and knowing that you may have had something to do with it, how would you feel?"

Nobody's perfect - ref need a shot of humility

By Teresa Wipple

What a tragic waste.

Saturday night's State AAA basketball championship between Mercer Island and Shadle Park High Schools should have been one of those nights that make high school memories: a cheering crowd, competitive spirit, and the knowledge that the game was well-played, regardless of the outcome.

That script was followed to the letter - until the disputed finish, when a Shadle Park player took the six-foot baseline shot that changed a 65-64 Mercer Island advantage into a deficit.

One referee said the shot was fired after the game had ended. The other referee signaled it as good. From then on, it was a waste.

Laughter changed to tears.

Competitive spirit changed to frustration.

And cheers became hostile boos.

It was not even a victory that the supposed victor, Shadle Park, could savor. Angry Island fans stayed on the court for 45 minutes after the controversial call, forestalling an awards ceremony.

Yes, it was unfortunate. But so were other things.

Let's start with the element of human error present in all the competitive sports which employ trained officials to enforce the rules and judge the plays.

Since the advent of television replays, it has been argued that the referee's decision should be overridden if a replay shows that the official made a mistake.

This hits home for Mercer Island, because Islander coach Ed Pepple says he has videotapes of the game which show that the final basket was no good.

But all technological advances aside, the real burden of the decision belongs to the official making the call. And in the case of the Mercer Island-Shadle Park contest, the referee made a crucial mistake.

In the closing seconds or a championship ball game, when the call is close, the stakes high, the crowd deafening - and, in this case, the buzzer not working - no official should assume that he alone can make a correct call.

Chris Manolopoulos apparently assumed he was perfect.

Manolopoulos, the official who signaled from under the basket that the shot was good, should have checked with the official timer, Don Davis. Davis told two Islanders, assistant coach Bill Woolley and player Al Moscatel that the shot was fired too late.

Although Davis has the authority to rule on such a shot, he only does so if the officials ask him. Manolopoulos didn't ask.

And that was a waste.

The energy, enthusiasm, excitement, hours of practice, sweat and dedication were forgotten, overshadowed by the injustice of an official who hadn't the humility to admit he needed a second opinion, or the courage to admit he had made a mistake.

Now Mercer Island High School is appealing the decision to the Washington Interscholastic Activities Association (WIAA). Officials there have indicated the appeal doesn't have much of a chance, even with the video proof.

Pepple says, however, that "we're going to fight this thing as far as we can."

So, after beating the number 1 (Lakes), number 2 (Richland), and number 3 (Shadle Park) rated teams in the state, after proving to a skeptical press (which gave them 25-1 odds against winning) that Mercer Island has what it takes, Pepple and his team have to fight yet another battle with the WIAA.

Mercer Island High School didn't just deserve to win that basketball game last Saturday night - Mercer Island won. Yet, we might not be able to win this fight. And that would be a waste.

The flip side to Island's disappointment

There's a silver lining to the disturbing story of Saturday night's state AAA basketball fiasco. Police and television crews expected a riot. But Mercer Island didn't oblige.

Islander fans had already flooded the Coliseum floor, expecting the long-sought state championship trophy, when the score was changed. It would have been understandable had their exuberance converted to a destructive rage.

It is to the credit of Mercer Island school officials that an explosive situation was kept to a few brief scuffles.

Craig Currie, district superintendent, asked his staff to accompany him to the door. Currie said later his staff "did a masterful job of maintaining composure."

To the further credit of the Mercer Island student body, the show of anger was confined to verbal epithets.

And the greatest credit goes to head basketball coach Ed Pepple, who in his 14 years of coaching the Islanders finally felt the title within his grasp, only to have it jerked away after the game by a provenly-bad call.

During those confusing minutes, Ed, concerned for his students' safety, took to the microphone and told the crowd to leave the Coliseum and meet back at the high school. Miraculously, everyone complied.

Later back at the school Pepple stood before players, faculty, families and fans - estimated at 3,000 by then - and assured them that regardless of the score, Mercer Island was still the champion.

We couldn't have said it any better.

                                                            T.W.

Letters: Islander fans have their say

An 'outsider' looks at the state championship controversy

I've watched with great interest for the past week the large number of stories generated by the Mercer Island-Shadle Park basketball game.

I doubt that there has ever been a high school sports event to sustain such media attention as this one has. And not just locally. On the same night in the Memorial Coliseum in Portland, the Oregon Boys AAA Championship game was decided on a shot at the buzzer by the same one slim point. Yet when I was in Portland on Monday, the first news story on the sports radio was the Mercer Island-Shadle Park game, not their own state championship game. And the same was true in Portland's newspapers.

Why? Why so much attention? That's easy. Within 24 hours after the game, TV had videotapes of the final seconds and the papers had reported numerous first-hand views. They showed what most people at the Coliseum knew: that Mercer Island had won the game and that Shadle Park's final play (and it was a great play) came at least one second too late.

So, the stage was set. There was new suspense. Mercer Island would appeal. Would justice win out? Would Mercer Island get its championship trophy and Shadle Park accept its well-deserved runner-up trophy? Fat chance! Historically, at almost every level of sport the protest is nothing more than a salve that's used to cover the wound and ease the pain until it can begin to heal. This was to be no different.

And unfortunately, the following days were to become more of a gunfight than most western movies. Every day you could take your choice. The letters supporting the Mercer Island victory or the letters condemning the "temper tantrum," "riotous behavior" of Mercer Island students and fans.

There was even a call for the firing of Coach Ed Pepple, the five-year suspension of Mercer Island from tournament play, and the lifetime suspension of Mercer Island player Al Moscatel, a junior, from further action on the basketball court.

Obscured by this criticism and perhaps even unnoticed by some of the critics was the fact that Moscatel, perhaps not as fast nor as tall as his opponents, had been selected to the All-Tourney starting team. He did this by driving himself at 110 percent from the opening tip Thursday night until that final extra second on Saturday night.

And then for a moment he had been rewarded, he was a part of the State Championship team. Then someone said "no, it's not yours."

This boy (not a man) was at the high point of his life, and somebody stole it away. A Seattle sportswriter said it best: "he was uncontrollably upset." So were many. Only with Moscatel, he was still going at 110 percent and couldn't handle it. Tears weren't enough. He ran around pleading for help that was not to come. Condemn him for that? Hardly.

And fire Coach Pepple as someone suggested? For almost inciting a riot? The man has coached 24 years and finally brought an underdog team (which included his own son) to the ultimate spot for a high school coach, the State Championship. Only a mistake yanked it away. Should he have walked away? Or shouldn't he have looked for someone who had seen the same thing he had just seen, someone who could set it straight. And then it was he who got on the microphone and sent everyone back to the Mercer Island gym for a welcoming rally for the team. Inciting a riot? No.

The Mercer Island basketball team does not deserve criticism, nor do the fans. If you've ever competed in anything in life that reached a decision, then you know the feeling of winning or losing. But try to put yourself into a position of winning something very important and then having it taken away unjustly. How would you behave? Even Shadle Park's coach, after criticizing the scene at the end of the game, added that he wasn't sure he wouldn't have behaved the same. Who can be sure?

So please, remember a great tournament and the great play of eight excellent teams. And remember the championship game, whichever way that you feel it ended. And leave it there. Let the wounds heal. Mercer Island knows who won.

And I can't help but feel that there's an empty feeling in a lot of Shadle Park's fans, at least in the ones who saw the same clock I did, the clock that showed :00 with Greg Schmidt's hands still on the ball.

Gary Williams

P.S. If this sounds like just another Mercer Islander crying sour grapes, it isn't. The three tournament games were the first Mercer Island games I've attended. I've only lived here four years. I spent the first 35 years of my life in San Francisco, where my father has just retired after 40 years as the sports editor of the San Francisco Examiner and News-Call.

I grew up with all sports as a part of my life and did some sports writing. I know what it's like to lose (49ers-Giants) and to win (Raiders-A's), but no sports event I've ever witnessed reached me quite like this game. If you were there, you have some idea of what I mean. If not, it's probably very hard to understand.

Islanders number one in spirit

(To principal Larry Smith, Mercer Island High School, with copy to the Mercer Island Reporter)

I want to compliment you and your staff that was involved in the decision-making to open up the school late Saturday night for a pep rally after the championship basketball game was played.

Due to the circumstances of the outcome of the game, I have heard nothing but positive comments to the pep rally. The impression I am receiving is good; and our kids have a lot of school spirit.

Win, lose, or draw, Mercer Island High School will always be Number One with this kind of positive reaction.

Sue Israel

Tourney problem well-handled

The Mercer Island High School Parent-Faculty Board would like to commend School Superintendent Dr. Craig Currie's superb handling of the WIAA's 1981 AAA Boys. State Basketball Tournament.

What could have been a potentially dangerous situation was alleviated by the quick actions of school personnel.

We feel very fortunate to be associated with a caring and able staff.

Alison Clements, MIHS Parent-Faculty Club Board Secretary

Protest denied: *School to appeal WIAA decision*

by Teresa Wippel

Mercer Island High School administrators may have lost a battle, but they haven't given up the war to prove that the Islanders won the 1981 State AAA basketball title March 14 in the Seattle Center Coliseum.

School officials are preparing to appeal the decision made last Friday in Ellensburg by the executive board of the Washington Interscholastic Activities Association (WIAA), which disallowed Mercer Island's protest of game conditions and referees' procedures.

At issue is the final basket of the championship game between the Islanders and Shadle Park High School of Spokane. Mercer Island representatives contend that the clock ran out when the

Islanders were ahead, 65-64, and that a desperation basket by Shadle Park at the end of the game was too late.

The shot was put on the scoreboard, however, when referee Chris Manolopoulos signaled it as good, giving Shadle Park a 66-65 victory.

Mercer Island immediately protested the game's outcome, and the WIAA executive committee agreed last Wednesday, March 18, to hear the school's concerns the following Friday in Ellensburg. Also invited to the hearing were representatives from Shadle Park and the two referees who officiated the championship contest.

Mercer Island School District Superintendent Craig Currie presented the school's protest, which was based on game conditions and procedures followed by the referees. With Currie were MIHS Principal Larry Smith, the school's athletic director, Gary Snyder, and head basketball coach Ed Pepple. Charges included in the protest were:

- an obvious disagreement in signals between the two referees, based on observations of game spectators who said they saw one official, Dave George, signal that the shot was no good, while the other, Manolopoulos, indicate the basket counted. Curie added that after the protest was filed, newspaper accounts carried statements by George denying that he ever made a "no basket" signal. Island school officials have agreed to accept George's account, Currie said.

- the automatic horn which signals the end of each quarter was inoperative and was not connected to the scoreboard timer, making it necessary for the official timer to operate a manual air horn with one hand and the time clock with the other.

- the referees did not coordinate their efforts with the official timer, even though they knew the automatic signal horn wasn't working properly.

- the referees decided to allow the lead official (under the basket) to judge the final shot, when ordinarily the trailing official (at midcourt) makes that decision.

Mercer Island's major contention was a statement and diagram in the WIAA rule book which says a game ends when the clock reads double zero. Since the sounding device was being operated manually, the referees should not have depended on the final buzzer to determine the game's end, Currie said.

The rule book also states, Currie added, that if the signal is defective on a last second shot, the referees are supposed to consult the official timer.

INCLUDED IN THE Islander protest was a written statement by Don Davis, the official timer, who wrote, that at the game's end, "when I sounded the air horn, in my judgement the ball had not reached the hands of Greg Schmidt (the Shadle Park player who took the final shot)."

Brief statements were given by Manolopoulos and George, who were ushered inside in the middle of the hearing, then left hurriedly after their testimony.

George repeated his denial of any reports that he made a "no good" signal which contrasted his partner's indication that the basket counted.

"I concur wholeheartedly with Chris' judgement that the ball was released before the buzzer," George said.

Manolopoulos told the WIAA committee that he checked with George after he made the call. "I went up to Dave and asked if the shot was good. He said yes and I said, 'Let's get out of here,'" Manolopoulos testified.

SPEAKING FOR SHADLE Park were the school's principal, Jack Mathews, and the Spokane School District Superintendent Jerry Hester. Mathews and Hester argued that since both referees supported the call, Shadle Park was the rightful winner of the game. They added that is their opinion. The game does end with the sounding device, and that all coaches, players and referees involved in the championship tournament were aware of the manually operated signal and agreed to play under those conditions.

Shadle Park representatives concluded with a statement condemning the behavior of Mercer Island fans after the game ended as "a total mockery of good sportsmanship." Shadle Park cheerleaders had their poms and purses stolen, and students were hit with flying objects, said Mathews.

Both men asked the WIAA to launch an investigation into the Island fans' behavior, and if the school is found in violation, to put Mercer Island on probation.

After hearing all testimony, the WIAA committee met behind closed doors for more than an hour, then Executive Secretary Hank Rybus announced the decision.

"Based on the testimony received, it is the decision of the WIAA executive committee that there was no disagreement between the officials and that procedures used were appropriate for the situation that existed.

"The condition of the scoring device existed throughout the majority of the tournament and the hand-operated horn was the official signal to end the game.

"The outcome of the 22nd game of the state tournament stands. The vote was unanimous."

REACTION FROM CURRIE was immediate – "We definitely plan to appeal."

Coach Pepple said he was "very disappointed. We thought the evidence was clear. They must have had some other evidence that we didn't have."

Currie said Monday afternoon that the appeal, which goes before the same executive committee, would challenge that committee's ruling as "vague and incomplete".

"They did not respond to our contention of misapplication of the rules," Currie said, adding Mercer Island to answer with a yes or no to each of the school's charges.

He also said he is concerned that the committee's ruling represents the WAA's approval of what happened during the championship game. "Even if the committee can't say Mercer Island won, I'd like them to recognize that the procedures weren't correct, in the interest of sport and fair play, those things have to be changed so something like that doesn't happen again," Currie stated.

After the WIAA receives the appeal, the executive committee will have to decide if it wants to hold a closed hearing during its next regular meeting, April 23, according to Rybus.

April 1, 1981

WIAA appeal to wait until after spring vacation

Mercer Island High School officials will wait until after spring vacation to submit an appeal to the Washington Interscholastic Activities Association (WIAA), regarding the outcome of the State AAA boys' basketball championship between MIHS and Shadle Park High School March 14.

According to Ed Pepple, head basketball coach, school administrators are in the process of preparing an appeal of the WIAA's March 20 decision to disallow Mercer Island's protest of the championship contest. Spring vacation ends April 3, with school resuming April 6.

High school officials have 30 days from the date of the March 20 hearing to submit their appeal. The WIAA then has to make a decision as to whether it will hear the appeal, Pepple said.

"We think they will hear the appeal because we have not yet had a fair hearing," Pepple said.

The most logical date for the apparel to be heard would be at the WIAA executive board's next regular meeting April 23, Pepple said, although he hopes it might be heard earlier.

The coach said it has been suggested that a rules interpreter be present at the appeal. "Because of the incapability of the (WIAA) board members to look at the rule book, it might be wise for a rule clinician to come in and provide a ruling," he added.

April 29, 1981

WIAA decision no surprise; school district may take legal action

By Bob Ogle

It's getting tough to surprise Ed Pepple nowadays.

So, when the Washington Interscholastic Activities Association last week turned down Mercer Island High School's request for a hearing regarding the 65-64 loss to Shadle Park in last month's state AAA high school basketball championship game, the MIHS basketball coach had to regard the decision as "expected."

But the matter itself may be far from resolved.

"I'm not surprised," he said, following two separate WIAA rulings. One, delivered by the executive board last Thursday afternoon, denied the appeal. The second, delivered the following morning, placed an outright denial on further consideration of the matter.

In a scenario which is now familiar to most Mercer Island basketball fans, the Islanders lost the title game on a last-second shot by Shadle Park. While the official timer said the shot was delivered after time had run out, both game officials disagreed and counted the shot good. A game protest filed by Mercer Island was subsequently denied by the WIAA. Last week's request was an appeal of that decision.

Since that time, Mercer Island administrators have charged that WIAA operating standards were not properly followed during the game and that the WIAA has violated the district's right to dur process by not granting an opportunity for witnesses to be heard.

Mercer Island School District Superintendent Craig Currie said the denial was apparently based on a lack of evidence, which the

WIAA said was necessary in order to justify another hearing on the matter.

Friday's decision, Currie said, was just for clarification of the WIAA's stand. He was notified by WIAA executive board chairman Hank Rybus.

"They didn't want to mislead us into thinking we had a right of appeal now," Currie explained. "I told him (Rybus) that I'd appreciate having all this in writing. Until I can see it in writing, it's hard to reflect on where they are coming from."

Currie admitted that the options available to Mercer Island in the wake of the last week's mandates are simple – drop the matter of consider legal action against the WIAA. Such a decision, he said, could come sometime this week, after he has a chance to study the WIAA written decision. Rybus indicated that it would be mid-week before the documents will be delivered to Mercer Island.

Should the school district choose to go to court, Currie said, offers have been made to the district for "either service or means of providing service from private parties on the island," he said.

Pepple indicated he favored taking the matter to court, "either to get the right of appeal back or to have the entire matter decided."

If that course is eventually taken, he added, he hopes it will be the precursor of some changes in the WIAA.

"I hope what we do will have an effect on the foundations of the WIAA," he said. "If they gave one iota about the Mercer Island kids, they'd give us a fair hearing."

Since the game, Mercer Island has been hit with countercharges by Shadle Park, alluding to crowd misconduct following the bizarre post-game scene. That matter was tabled by the WIAA during Thursday's meeting.

"They said they tabled it because they didn't have enough letters to decide," Pepple said. "But I'd be willing to bet that if we were to drop this now, they'd drop that in a minute."

Rybus said Monday that he isn't sure "this is an issue that could go to court. I just don't know what's to be gained by doing so. I doubt if the score could be reversed.

"I'm pretty sure our board has gone as far as they feel they can go with this issue," Rybus concluded. "For the good of everybody, it should be over."

EDITORIAL COMMENT: WIAA intransigence denies due process
by Bob Ogle

High school athletics in Washington has been suffering ever since the state AAA high school championship basketball game.

By now, it's a familiar story. Mercer Island High School lost to Shadle Park 65-64 on a last-second (post-game?) shot. Half the state says the shot was not good because time had expired before the ball left the shooter's hands. The other half says that the ball did leave the shooter's hands on time, and that those who say otherwise are crazy.

What the referees said is obvious.

Until now, we have been faced with a simple issue - who won the basketball game? But the decision made last week by the WIAA not to allow Mercer Island another hearing, one which would involve witnesses called by both sides, has changed all that.

The issue transcends a simple basketball game. Suddenly, the issue has become due process. Mercer Island has a right to a fair hearing, to present all witnesses and testimony pertinent to the issue. The WIAA, with its decision not to discuss the matter any further, has derailed that right.

Has the WIAA given Mercer Island a fair hearing? Hardly. Mercer Island was able to present arguments, but only limited supporting testimony, during last month's protest hearing. The issue last week was whether such testimony would be heard, and the answer was given loud and clear. No.

Has Mercer Island dragged the issue out too far? Probably not. As Coach Ed Pepple says, "How can you quit when you haven't even had a chance to present your case? You can't allow that to happen. If that happens to us, it'll happen to anyone else who files an appeal."

What we have now is a game of freeze-out. Each side is trying to outlast the other and it has become the irresistible force versus the immovable object. Neither side is willing to compromise.

This must stop. The issue has gotten messy enough. Mercer Island has made charges, Shadle Park has made charges, and the WIAA has taken more than a month to make a decision which should have run its course and been finalized within three weeks of the championship game. There has been enough freeze-out, enough procrastination.

And now there is talk about legal action. The action that started in a basketball court could finish in a court where nobody likes to play.

To take this new issue to court would make the state championship game a mockery regardless of who wins and who loses. But if that is the only way for Mercer Island to receive a hearing by due process - a right guaranteed to individual and institution alike by the United States Constitution - then maybe that is what must be done.

The time has come to stop the game-playing, to stop the charges and countercharges and to stop the doubletalk. If the WIAA gives Mercer Island a fair hearing, complete with live witnesses, videotape and other testimony, then everyone's rights have been served.

If the WIAA presents a decision against Mercer Island after a public hearing, then the system has answered the question and Mercer Island has no right to appeal the game's out to a court of law. That would, indeed, be poor sportsmanship.

Ed Pepple has his doubts that the WIAA will observe the issue fairly and render an impartial decision. He says the WIAA already has its mind made up. That may be true. But one can hope that if WIAA officials do make a biased decision, there will be enough people and media representatives present to make them regret doing so.

There are already a number of coaches who are disgusted with the WIAA. Should these WIAA officials make a biased, irrational decision, it will come back to haunt them. It will weaken them as a group, giving them very little legitimacy. With this hearing, deciding on the basis of the evidence, they can reverse that slide.

I was not there the night of the game. I did not see the shot. I have to judge the case by the tangible, solid evidence presented by each side, free of prejudice. If the evidence says Shadle Park won the game, that the ball did leave the shooter's hands in time, then that must be the decision handed down, regardless of what side of the state you live on. If the evidence shows Mercer Island to be in the right, then that must be the decision of the WIAA.

The WIAA must grant this hearing, let the evidence be seen and heard, render a fair decision and put this matter to rest once and for all.

Before high school athletics suffers any longer.

May 20, 1981

WIAA puts Mercer Island on probation

by Bob Ogle

Ed Pepple thought it was "like rubbing salt in a wound."

Craig Currie said, "I wasn't surprised, but by no means am I conceding that we deserve it."

The Washington State Interscholastic Activities Association called it unsportsmanlike conduct and it meant a one-year probation for Mercer Island High School, beginning in September 1981 and extending through June 1982.

In anybody's opinion it all means the same thing - if Mercer Island is charged with a rules infraction or general misconduct during the probationary period, it will mean a loss of participation in post season play for any sport for an unspecified length of time. Otherwise, the school may continue as per usual all of its interscholastic programs.

The probation was handed down in the wake of Shadle Park High School charges of unsportsmanlike conduct during the melee which followed the Match 14 championship game of the state AAA high school basketball tournament. Shadle Park won the game 66-65, on a disputed last second shot and Mercer Island has appealed the decision to no avail.

According to a letter from WIAA Executive Secretary Hank Rybus to Currie, Mercer Island School District Superintendent, the probation came after "lengthy and careful consideration of the information" pertaining to the charges.

"We would like to have you understand that the Executive Board did not base its action solely on the conduct of Mercer Island at the time of the controversial basket but rather on conduct during the entire tournament," Rybus stated. "Among the items that caused concern were conduct of fans in the stands, lack of supervision on the part of Mercer Island adults and unacceptable conduct by the basketball coaches."

The document said the action was "not taken in a punitive manner but rather with the positive hope that it can help reinforce Mercer Island's efforts to direct its energies in a more acceptable direction. It is recognized that Mercer Island's spirit has come a long way recently, and if it could be oriented as more positive support for its own team with the elimination of derision of the opponent, Mercer Island's spirit would be outstanding."

Rybus did not elaborate on or specify any particular instances of misconduct against Mercer Island High School.

The probation left a bad taste in Mercer Island Coach Pepple's mouth.

"We not only lost our protest, but we didn't even get a fair chance for a hearing," he said. "Now, this, I think it's a little like rubbing salt into a wound."

Pepple said he believes the action was taken as retribution for Mercer Island's attempts to appeal the game's outcome.

"We dared to protest a decision, which we had a right to do," he said. "Consequently, we get put on probation."

Both Pepple and Currie are worried that the probation will put Mercer Island High School's athletics in a bad light.

"It makes us out as thieves, and low-class rioters," Pepple said. "It's an image thing, and it's an image which is not the truth.

"The penalty itself is toothless. But the aspersions cast by it are demeaning. They were not 100 percent Mercer Island incidents. Shadle Park had something to do with it too. Their coach, for example, called our kids a bunch of 'butts' and 'losers' right after the game."

Currie agreed with the damage to Mercer Island's reputation.

"But I'm less concerned with our image so much as with the fact that it could bring undue pressure on next year's student body. We can't always control the kinds of things that go on in scholastic activity. Other teams could possibly bait us.

"I just raise that as a question," he added. "I hope that won't be the case."

Currie said he was also disappointed that the WIAA based the decision on Mercer Island's behavior during the entire tournament. He said he did not feel the students' conduct during the first two games of the three-game tournament was unreasonable.

Currie declined to comment on whether Mercer Island intends to pursue the matter further, either in court or in front of the State Board of Education. That decision, he said, will be up to the Mercer Island School Board.

"I think the board feels now that the game is a moot point," Currie said. "What we would question now is the process that has been followed for the conditions surrounding the game."

"The probation creates an added dimension to the problem."

Students stage protest

A group of Mercer Island High School students waved protest signs and protested in a symbolic "hunger strike" for two hours in front of the WIAA building last Friday, following the WIAA's decision to put the Mercer Island School District on probation.

Jeff Price, organizer of the group, said the students decided to stage a protest because "we couldn't just sit and take it. We don't say this is going to change anything, but we just wanted to make it known we think it's (the probation) totally unfair."

The ten students carried signs proclaiming that "Probation Stinks", "Worthless Idiots are Always in Administration (WIAA)," and "Guilty Until Proven Innocent."

"It seems like we got a really raw deal," said Richard Tower, another protestor. "They (the WIAA) never even looked at our side of the story."

May 27, 1981

An interview with Hank Rybus

WIAA Secretary speaks to probation and protests

By Bob Ogle

The Washington Interscholastic Activities Association. For most people not associated directly with administration of high school sports, it wasn't a name that rang many bells – until last March.

The organization is in charge of coordinating athletic, forensic and music activities of Washington's junior high and high schools, and Hank Rybus is the body's chief administrator, technically called the Executive Secretary. He is in his 20th year with an organization which he says "was created because of a real need for a body to do such a job."

The body, normally mired in obscurity from the public, became well known last March during the fire surrounding the 66-65 Mercer Island loss to Shadle Park in the state AAA high school championship game.

Since the WIAA's Executive Board denied Mercer Island's protest of the game, denied any further consideration of the matter and then placed the Islanders on probation for the 1981 to 1982 school year, questions have arisen surrounding the WIAA's action regarding the matter.

Last Tuesday, Hank Rybus sat down for a two-hour conversation to clarify some of those questions, regarding a matter that he says, "should be put to bed once and for all."

This article is a partial, lightly edited text of that conversation.

There has been a lot of discussion centering around the malfunction of equipment during the final game of the tournament, particularly that the final buzzer wasn't in working order. How did this affect your decision regarding the denial of Mercer Island's appeal?

Rybus: It's unfortunate that the automatic sounding device wasn't operating properly. It was not operating properly for most of the tournament. There are a lot of games played during the regular season without an automatic sound device. So, for the tournament, we had to use a hand-held horn. People involved in the tournament know that's what was happening. It was being operated quite effectively by the person using it. We were doing the best we could under the circumstances. There was an attempt to have it fixed, but it just went out.

Everybody has to learn from a situation like this. You never know when something will break down, but you have to do the best you can.

At the end of the game, there was approximately a 30 second delay in acknowledging that the Shadle Park basket was good, 30 seconds in which Mercer Island fans thought they had won the game.

There was a delay in posting the final score. The timer explained that his vision has been blocked by players to the official. So, there was an error in clearing that up and that's also unfortunate. He was unable to see the signal from the official.

How do you think that affected the behavior of the Mercer Island fans after the game? Would their emotions have been warranted in such a situation?

It was a very emotional end to a game. I've never seen anything quite like it. You have to take that into account. But I think we have to learn to control ourselves and we can't use that as an excuse for unacceptable conduct. The executive board knows what kids are like. They took it into account when making a decision. Sure, it was all explained by people who were there. It certainly wasn't ignored. You can't say because it stopped short of being a riot that it was acceptable conduct.

A letter signed by you explaining the probation stated that the probation was on the basis of Mercer Island conduct during the entire tournament and not just during the championship game. Could you elaborate on this a little more? Many people have said they saw no difference between Mercer Island's behavior the first two nights of the tournament compared to that of the crowd supporting any other team.

In reading the material gathered from Mercer Island, Shadle Park and people responsible for the tournament, there was mention of enough things doing the tournament that the board said they wanted to analyze the whole thing, not just the emotional ending.

The board wanted to cause the school to look at other aspects of its behavior. I don't think they want to go on record to say Mercer Island was worse than any other school. Those schools could be subject to criticism also. It was part of a broad discussion about sportsmanship in general. We decided we had to be more aggressive about drawing up guidelines to promote better sportsmanship. The decision was made with the knowledge that Mercer Island isn't the only school that needs help. That's why we formed a committee to discuss sportsmanship in the state. It's first meeting is going to be June 3.

Taking everything into account, it (sportsmanship) was a real concern to us. There were some other areas that needed attention than just what happened at the championship game. The other schools weren't perfect. If they were, there would be no point in a committee.

There was also made mention in the letter of an improvement in Mercer Island school spirit over the past few years. Could you elaborate on that?

As far as support of the team is concerned, I've gone to other tournaments where Mercer Island has been involved and hardly anybody from Mercer Island was there.

It seemed like the thing to do was to not go to the tournament. Recently, Mercer Island has developed some really fine spirit, and by that, I mean enthusiasm. Now, there's an opportunity to direct that enthusiasm into channels supportive of their own team.

That's basically what probation means. They can continue their programs, but they have to correct these things. We've had other schools on probation before and, by the time the year was over, the administrators would tell us that it was the best thing that happened to them. It shouldn't be looked at so much as a punishment, but more as a challenge. All they have to do now is just avoid breaking the rules. I really wanted the letter to be helpful.

How did the board reach a decision regarding probation?

We took the overall information we had into consideration. The information was such that the board couldn't ignore it. The information came from Mercer Island, from Shadle Park, from people involved in the tournament – the officials, the scorer, the timer, the announcer, the ticket takers - and from letters from the Seattle police department.

Mercer Island principal Larry Smith mentioned that he received a letter from the Seattle police complimenting Mercer Island on his handling of the affair. Was that considered by the board?

Shadle Park also produced a letter from the Seattle police. The police were a little more specific in their letter to Shadle Park regarding specific behavior by Mercer Island. The Mercer Island letter seemed to be more like an acknowledgment that the police were glad it didn't get any worse than it was.

The possibility has been raised by some on Mercer Island that this leaves the school's athletic team subject to being goaded by other schools during a game, just to try to get Mercer Island to break probation.

That's possible. But I don't think it's very likely. The board is not so naïve to think that can't happen. We'd analyze it carefully before making a decision.

Has there ever been a violation of probation before, with the school violating the rules during the probationary period?

No, I don't think so. We've had some real turn around in some schools as a result of probation.

Let's move on and talk about the appeal process itself. Mercer Island officials have said they did not have the chance to present witnesses to the executive board.

The first hearing, in Ellensburg, was a good, open hearing. Mercer Island could've said anything they wanted to; Shadle Park could have said anything they wanted to. It was open to the public and the media was there. We didn't bring in the witnesses because it wasn't a court. That's the way we run our hearings. It's not a court and it's not a police station. It's just like we've done for other schools. We didn't want to make a circus out of it.

We told Craig Curry we work better just collecting written information. We didn't feel anything could be said that could not be put in writing just as well. If Mercer Island brought in witnesses, then Shadle Park would bring in witnesses and it could go on and on.

Why was Mercer Island's appeal for a new hearing denied?

We didn't feel there was any new information to justify having another hearing. There was a misunderstanding there.

Mercer Island said there was new information, but they didn't tell us what it was. The board believed they would be getting together to hear the same things all over again. It was kind of stressing the point to even have a hearing, since it was about a decision by the officials. You don't have a hearing on an official decision.

The hearing was granted because Mercer Island said they wanted to question other things. But at the hearing it bordered on judging the officials' conduct.

Do you feel the situation was handled in the best manner by Mercer Island officials?

If you mean, do I think they should have appealed it, I'd say no. Most administrators would've said, 'We lost the game. You lose some things in life.' It could've been a good learning situation for the young people right from the start.

But since they made the decision to appeal, which was their right, then I think they did a good job of presenting their side at the first hearing. The decision was made on good evidence, and they should've accepted that.

Frankly I was a little hazy as to what their case was. They had four points in the case and three of those points were based on the fact that the game officials disagreed on the call. When Mercer Island came to the hearing, they learned that the officials did not disagree.

Games can't be disputed because of a judgment call by the officials?

Of course not. That's the way sports are run. That's the way it has to be run.

When a game is protested, it is decided by the WIAA. When the decision regarding the protest is appealed, it is decided by the WIAA again. Doesn't this make the WIAA judge, jury and executioner?

That question is raised. For most groups, whether it's the WIAA or lawyers or doctors, the appeals process is an internal process. It's kept within the constituency. That's the way we do it.

Mercer Island Coach Ed Pepple suggested leaving the decision to a group of people responsible for making high school basketball rules. Why wasn't this done?

It was. We checked with the National Federation of State Associations, the group responsible for making the rules, and they could see nothing wrong with our decision. I sent everything Mercer

Island had submitted to that rule-making body and they supported the decision. Craig Currie should have a copy of their explanation.

Do you think it's possible this whole issue, which has taken more than two months to come close to settling, could have been solved more quickly?

It did go on way too long. We (the WIAA) moved fast for the first hearing. We wanted it all settled then. After that, I don't think you can hold us responsible for dragging it out.

And now it's just continuing to drag on. I don't think anyone will gain from that. The game isn't going to change. Why go on?

Because Mercer Island officials are questioning the decision-making process. Currie has said before that the game itself is now a moot point.

If anything in the handbook isn't satisfactory, all Mercer Island has to do is get support from four other high schools and propose an amendment that would alter what's in the book. If we can improve it, so everyone can understand it, we'd like to. If you can get support from four other schools, then the amendment is sent to league and to district officials for their appraisal. Then it comes to the WIAA office, where it is compiled with other amendments and mailed to each district. Then when our 35-member Representative Assembly meets each April, they can pass it by a two-thirds majority.

Mercer Island is going to take its case to the State Board of Education, which is the body you are answerable to (they did last week). What do you think will be the result of that?

We are responsible to the State Board of Education for matters of student participation. We have to submit a financial report to them each year and we also have to submit a report on appeals cases.

I don't know how the state board will look at this. It isn't really a matter of student participation, so it may not be in their jurisdiction. I might also add that the State Board of Education attorney had a lot to do with our decision.

The WIAA has come under fire from all different directions since last March. Also, many coaches from around the state have expressed their dissatisfaction with the WIAA. How do you react to this?

The WIAA is a good, grassroots organization. There is participation by a lot of different people. I think it's a well-respected organization in the nation.

I know there are some coaches who don't like the WIAA and I think I know why. The coaching situation has changed over the years. Years ago, one person at a high school coached almost all of the sports at that school. Since he had responsibility for all sports, he wanted a good balance between all sports. Our philosophy is that as many kids as possible should have as many good experiences as possible. That flies in the face of specialization and some coaches don't like that.

Getting back to the game and the appeal for a second, you sound as if you're a little weary of the whole issue.

Oh, I don't know if I'm weary as much as disappointed. It bothers me when we miss an opportunity to teach something to the students through this organization. I feel this has been a missed opportunity. There is still an opportunity, though.

The lesson is that this is a bitter pill, but life has its bitter pills, and they have to be accepted. Sport is an emotional thing. Some dramatic things happen. From it all, you should be able to teach some worthwhile things that apply to life. And unless something positive comes from all this, all of us will have failed. That includes the WIAA.

Do you think this incident has done a lot of damage to high school athletics?

No. I don't see where any great damage has been done. When I look at sports all over the state, I don't see great damage. What's being overlooked is that it was a super basketball game that night and it was a super year overall. If you could just wipe off this one blemish...

There's a lot of hurt connected with this for Mercer Island. That's part of sport. In time, it may become more memorable than winning the championship would have been.

What are your feelings towards Mercer Island right now?

I don't want to be harsh at all, and I don't hold any resentment against Mercer Island. They pursued what they believed was right.

Have you ever given any consideration to whether the shot that night was or was not good?

I've pondered it quite a bit. I pondered it that night. During the game, I was sitting on the end opposite from where the shot was taken, high up in the stands. I've seen a lot of last second basketball over the years and in almost every instance I've been able to say whether it was good or not. With this shot, I honestly did not know. I couldn't say. It was that close. And, with the scene after that, it was the damndest thing I ever saw.

July 1, 1981

Islanders win summer basketball tourney

Mercer Island erased a three-point half-time deficit to slip past Roosevelt in the championship game of the Nike Summer High School Basketball Tournament Saturday night at Bellevue Community College.

Kyle Pepple, starting guard for the Islanders last season, had the hot hand for MIHS in the final. Pepple netted 34 points, shooting 10 for 19 from the floor, and 14 for 17 from the foul line.

Pepple was named the tournament's most valuable player as Mercer Island went undefeated in eight games. The MIHS senior-to-be was also named to the all-tourney team along with teammates Al Moscatel and Eric Schwabe.

While Pepple was burning the nets in the final, Moscatel was controlling the boards with 19 rebounds. He also scored 18 points.

Roosevelt finished the tournament 6-2. The Seattle team beat Ingraham 58-50 to advance to the title game.

Mercer Island reached the final with a 70-58 semi-final victory over Bellevue High School last Friday. Pepple and Schwabe each scored 16 points in that game.

Bellevue cut the Islander lead to 54-53 with just over four minutes to play before Mercer Island was able to pull away.

In the quarterfinals, Mercer Island nipped Newport 60-57.

July 9, 1981

High school basketball players sharpen skills in summer camp

Two players from the state AAA finalist Mercer Island High School basketball team are in Milledgeville, Georgia today attending a Basketball Congress Superstar camp.

Kyle Pepple and Al Moscatel, both starters for the Islanders last season, were invited to attend the camp which Islander coach Ed Pepple calls "the eastern (United States) showcase for outstanding talent."

Coach Pepple also received an invitation and is attending the camp.

In August, the father and son will travel to Point Loma in San Diego, California to participate in a Sportsworld Superstar camp which features the premier players from the Western states.

That camp is expected to draw a large turnout from college coaches on the West Coast.

In July, 16 members of the MIHS basketball program will participate in a basketball camp in Salt Lake City, Utah.

Both Pepple and Moscatel are also playing for a Seattle-based All-Star team which has been invited to two national high school tournaments later this summer. Ed Pepple is coaching that team.

During the week of Aug. 3, the Seattle All-Stars will be in Provo, Utah, playing in a Basketball Congress national prep tournament.

That team will also play in a Las Vegas invitation tournament in August.

Pepple's squad has tuned up for the tournament with three wins in three contests over an Everett All-Star team, an MIHS alumni squad and a Marv Harshman Husky Basketball Camp team. The final contest was decided in the last moments, 103-102.

August 6, 1981

WIAA to hear appeal of probation today

Mercer Island School District administrators today will appeal a decision by the Washington Interscholastic Activities Association (WIAA) to put Mercer Island High School on probation for the 1981-82 school year.

The high school was placed on probation because of student behavior after MIHS lost the final game of the state high school basketball tournament. A group of MIHS fans refused to yield the floor to tournament officials after the controversial finish of the March 14 basketball game.

School administrators have responded to 36 charges made against the school. Administrators may choose to elaborate on those charges at a WIAA meeting being held today in Long Beach.

High School Principal Larry Smith said Friday he was pleased to get an appeal hearing with the WIAA, adding the school district does have a chance to reverse the probation decision.

"I always feel like there is a chance or I wouldn't be doing it," Smith said.

Other officials expected to attend the meeting include Craig Curries, school district superintendent; Gary Snyder, Jackie Hallett and Gary Bridgeman, high school vice principals; and Gretchen Illgenfritz, school board president.

The one-year probation does not affect the school's athletic schedule. "It is not a penalty. It's more of a warning to be careful," WIAA Executive Henry Rybus said last Friday.

The WIAA executive board voted during a May board meeting to put Mercer Island on probation. The vote was 8-0, with two members abstaining.

August 12, 1981

WIAA reduces probation period

by Eric Stevick

The WIAA last Wednesday voted to reduce the probation period for Mercer Island High School from the entire 1981-82 school year to the end of the high school basketball season.

At its meeting in Long Beach, the WIAA met behind closed doors for more than two and one-half hours before reaching its decision. The executive session followed more than two hours of testimony by six Mercer Island School District representatives.

The appeal hearing came nearly six months after Mercer Island fans and sympathizers refused to yield the floor for an awards ceremony following a controversial 65-64 loss to Spokane's Shadle Park in the final game of the State AAA basketball tournament.

Six days after the tournament, Mercer Island school district officials met with the WIAA in Ellensburg to protest the game mechanics used by officials in deciding to count a last second shot by a Shadle Park player. At that time, Spokane school district officials presented the WIAA with 36 charges against Mercer Island players, coaches and fans for alleged unsportsmanlike conduct during the tournament. Those charges lead the WIAA to place MIHS on a one-year probation March 11.

The WIAA executive board last week agreed with Mercer Island representatives that the high school sympathizers should not be judged on their conduct throughout the tournament.

"The board thought it would not be fair to single out Mercer Island for its behavior throughout the tournament and not judge any of the other schools," said Henry Rybus, WIAA executive secretary and spokesman.

"The greatest concern of the board was the prolonged action of the coaches (Ed Pepple and Bill Woolley). The board thought this had a mushroom effect on the players and fans," Rybus said. Pepple and Woolley spent 25 minutes after the game trying to resolve the conflict, according to Larry Smith, MIHS principal.

Rybus also cited a "lack of effectiveness" by school district administrators in restraining the coaches and players, and in turn the fans, as the other factor in influencing the board's decision.

Smith said Monday he was disappointed that the high school was not exonerated from the entire probation charge.

The WIAA had toyed with the idea of letting Mercer Island off on a warning only, Rybus said. However, since no such provision exists in the WIAA regulations, the board abandoned the idea.

School Superintendent Craig Currie and School Board President Gretchen Ilgenfritz said they would not comment until they saw the WIAA statement which explained the decision.

Smith said he did not see why the student body was penalized when the adults (coaches, officials and administrators) were responsible for the post-game action.

Smith also refuted the charge that the administration was ineffective in controlling the crowd after the game. "I can guarantee if we weren't effective, there would have been bloodshed there," Smith said.

At Wednesday's meeting, MIHS and school district representatives based their arguments on a June 10 letter from Smith to Rybus.

In that letter, Smith said the 36 allegations used to put MIHS on probation were "totally unfounded".

Smith concluded: "The only reasonable conclusion is the WIAA has placed us on probation not because of any legitimate finding of misconduct, but rather as retaliation for daring to challenge the outcome of the state basketball championship game and to be publicly exposing the inadequacies of your decision-making and appeal-processing abilities. We have dropped our pursuit of our game/result protest, and it is now time for you to drop this absurd, retaliatory probation."

School district representatives dismissed half of the 36 charges because they were either video or repetitious. Several charges assumed a Mercer Island fan committed an unsportsmanlike act - though no one was identified in connection with the allegations. Mercer Island administrators held that since the charges could not be proven, they should be dropped.

The Island contingent denied several other allegations, including a charge that Gary Snyder, associate principal in charge of athletics, did not seem willing to correct Mercer Island students for their misconduct.

Snyder said he was "perplexed, distressed, appalled, and confused" with the first charge. "At no time was I not willing to help," Snyder told the board.

In his letter to the WIAA, Smith placed the blame on tournament director Frank Inslee. Smith concluded: "It is incredible that the poor control, lack or organization and absence of direction on the part of the tournament director, Mr. Frank Inslee, has now been turned into an allegation with the blame for his foul-up being placed on the Mercer Island student body. And further it is difficult to understand why Mr. Gary Snyder was then blamed for not stopping it."

Inslee is also a member of the WIAA executive board. However, he was not allowed to vote at the meeting because of his direct contact with the tournament.

WIAA and school district officials appear to perceive probation differently. Rybus said Monday he thought probation could benefit MIHS by making the fans more conscientious, adding that probation is more of a warning than anything else.

Gary Bridgeman, vice principal in charge of activities, said student bodies from other schools could use probation as "a tool for retaliation" against MIHS.

PART II

1981-1982

"1982, they played with a vengeance... we had six players I felt were all capable of being starters... this team was literally intimidating defensively... their goal defensively was to have shut-out quarters, and they did it a number of times."

- Ed Pepple

November 25, 1981

'Last year was history'

Islanders determined to bring state title home this season

By Dave Thomas

And now for another chapter in that ongoing serial, "As the Basketball Bounces".

When last we left Coach Ed Pepple and his troops, they had just been turned away by the Washington Interscholastic Activities Association (WIAA) in a bid to regain the trophy that they believed belonged rightly to them.

In this episode, we see Pepple and his warriors starting on the only course of action that can truly resolve the controversy - they are preparing to open the 1981-82 season, determined to bring the state title home to Mercer Island.

As we open, Coach Pepple enters and says, "Last year was history. We don't think about what happened - except to use it as a springboard. The whole incident has made the team more resolved to play.

"We are determined to get back to the tournament this year and the only thing we want to do differently is not let the games get so close that something like last year can happen again," he added.

The Islanders' quest for the state basketball title last year ended with a one-point loss in the championship game to Shadle Park High School of Spokane. The winning shot was disputed for months after, as many officials, coaches, players and spectators believed that the last-second basket was shot after the clock had expired. The Mercer Island School District registered an official protest, but in a hearing held one week later, the WIAA ruled that the state title belonged to Shadle Park.

In addition, two months later the WIAA put Mercer Island High School on probation for unsportsmanlike conduct because of the behavior of students after the game ended. The probationary period runs through the basketball season and means that both players and spectators must abide strictly by WIAA rules until the season ends.

If Mercer Island is charged with a rules infraction or general misconduct during the probationary period, it will mean a loss of participation in post-season play for any sport for an unspecified length of time.

BUT VIOLATING THE PROBATION is only one of Pepple's worries. Besides trying to prevent emotions from taking over and affecting the team's play, he also has to work from a new angle - the top, looking down.

Last year, the team didn't expect publicity until it reached the postseason playoffs. Before that, news of the Islanders' talent had been overshadowed by publicity heaped on two rival teams - Juanita and Bothell.

This year, however, instead of gunning for the top teams, there will be teams looking to upset the mighty Islanders. It is a whole new perspective, but the added pressure doesn't affect the confident Pepple.

"I don't think we'll feel any pressure. In fact, maybe we will need it. I believe that is when this team plays the best - look at the tournament last year," he commented.

Despite Pepple's rosy outlook, he admits there is an area of concern that needs attention in order to prevent trouble. He doesn't have the bench strength he had last year.

Last year, Pepple said, he "never had a stronger bench." He had 12 players and he used all of them liberally. But he lost Tom Uczekaj, captain Chris Kampe, Doug Gregory, Erik Nordstrom, Mark Aldape and Scott Driggers through graduation and that has weakened the bench considerably.

"Right now, I only have 10 players on the varsity," he began. "If a couple of juniors and the inexperienced seniors come along, then we could be all right.

"If they don't, I will have to go with a seven-man team and make fewer substitutions. The only way that will hurt us is if we have injuries or foul trouble. Last year we were injury free. I hope we can stay that way again," he added.

J.D. STERN, TONY GROSSI and T.J. Yurkamin are the three seniors that Pepple hopes will add depth to the team. Their play, plus that of a couple of juniors, will be a key factor in determining how far the Islanders go this season.

Up front, Pepple has four returning players, including Al Moscatel, the team's leading scorer last year. The 6'2 senior averaged 12.2 points per game last year and, according to Pepple, "will score anyway he can".

Eric Schwabe is a 6'5 center who Pepple believes is the best shooter on the team. For defense and rebounding, Joe Thompson will fill the coach's needs. He is a 6'6 forward who has vastly improved his defense and board work. Pepple said Rich Dewey was the sixth man last year and his versatility makes him very important to the team.

The guard spots remain solid, with Paul Jerue and Kyle Pepple back to lead the way. Jerue is the off-guard and is aggressive and tough. Pepple returns to the point position and his passing and ball-handling skills help him "orchestrate the whole deal," the coach said.

One of the keys to the Islander attack is the fact that it is a team effort. The Islanders open with a pair of back-to-back non-league games and then head directly into the tough KingCo League, so they have no time to work out any kinks. The fact that they have been together and know what they want this year has helped eliminate the problem of being uncoordinated early in the season.

"They are just trying to get better. One player out in practice today was telling the others to keep working to get better.

"You don't have to hang anything in front of these kids - they know what they want," Pepple said.

THE TEAM OPENED with a Parents' Night scrimmage last night, and will host a jamboree with Lake Washington, Kennedy and Sealth on Dec. 1. On Dec. 4 they travel to Roosevelt High and then host Wilson of Tacoma Saturday, Dec. 5, to get the season into high gear.

Later in the month, the team will again travel to Las Vegas to participate in a tournament Dec. 23-26. This tourney attracts some of the top high schools in the country and this year is no exception. Participants include Calvert Hall, from Maryland, which is rated as the best high school team in the nation, and the number-one team from California.

So, December promises to be very busy for the Islanders, as they begin another long road to the Coliseum to be crowned as the rightful heirs to the state AAA basketball throne. And they want to be just as busy come March.

November 25,1981

Athletic gerrymandering puts KingCo teams into new Sea-King district

Some people may have been wondering during the fall playoffs why they didn't see some of the familiar faces from the North Puget Sound League (NPSL) competing against KingCo foes.

The reason was quite simple - Mercer Island and the rest of the KingCo league were the subjects of some athletic gerrymandering by the Washington Interscholastic Activities Association (WIAA).

Last year, the WIAA realized that the Seattle and Tacoma school districts were not involved in any kind of postseason district tournament. So, they decided to realign the West Central District Tournament and start a new district, the Sea-King.

The WIAA felt that the Seattle and Tacoma-area high schools would be better off in district competition after the regular season ended. So, they rearranged the league so that these schools would compete in postseason play, rather than just send some representatives to state tournaments.

This affects the KingCo - and thus Mercer Island - because the new set-up places KingCo schools in competition with those schools from Seattle's Metro League, rather than those from the NPSL. The Tacoma schools will enter the West Central to pick up the slack.

The WIAA had two main reasons for making the redistricting move. The first was that it was more equitable, according to Irene Halette of the WIAA.

"They (WIAA) were studying redistricting and trying to decide which was the best competition," Halette said. "They decided Metro was the league and that they had no district. So, they moved them into District 16 (Sea-King) and the Tacoma schools joined the West Central District."

The other reason was to help reduce travel expenses. Last year, the AA Seamount League had three divisions with schools ranging from Kent, Renton and Auburn, through Tacoma and out to the Olympic Peninsula. This year they split up into three separate leagues.

And the one that contained the schools in the Eastern Division are the schools that will compete in the Sea-King District - along with KingCo and Metro AAA and AA schools.

The state redistricting process sent a lot of people to a lot of different places, but one thing is for sure. The KingCo and the NPSL, two of the toughest leagues in the state, will no longer have to battle each other for the precious few state berths. That will make a lot of athletes in both leagues happy.

December 8, 1981

Islanders win two, open season against Bellevue

By Dave Thomas

Now that the practice is over, it's time to get down to the business at hand.

Mercer Island High School's boys' basketball team started and ended its preseason competition over the weekend. The Islanders open their league schedule today with a game at home against Bellevue – picked by many to provide the main competition for Mercer Island in the Crest Division of the KingCo League.

Last week the team continued a tradition that marked most of its season last year – winning. Friday, the Islanders traveled to Roosevelt High and came out with a 69-58 win. The next night, the team returned home and used a second-half sprint to capture an 82-45 win over Wilson High from Tacoma.

All that is now past history for Coach Ed Pepple, who has the task of preparing his troops for one of their many tough tests in the coming season. Pepple said that Bellevue, a third-place finisher in the Crest last year, is a team much like his Islanders.

"They have excellent shooters but not a lot of size. They are similar to us – they will pressure and use a man-to-man defense. I think we are stronger inside and will try to get the ball into (Joe) Thompson, (Mike) Williams, (Eric) Schwabe and (Rich) Dewey more," he added.

Pepple pointed to three Bellevue players his team will have to watch out for - forwards David Seeley and Paul Dammkoehler, and guard John Mittenthal. All three are excellent shooters, and the Islanders will have to take special precautions.

The varsity game begins at 8 p.m. in the Islander gym. The junior varsity team plays at 6:30 p.m.

During last weekend's contests, the best performance was turned in by Al Moscatel against Wilson. The senior forward, who led the team in scoring the past two years, poured in 32 points – 18 in the

Islanders 24-point third quarter which broke the game open. He also added 10 steals.

At the half during the Wilson game, Mercer Island held just an 11-point spread, but after the third period, the outcome was no longer in doubt and the Islanders rolled to the easy win.

Friday, the reverse was true. The Islanders built up a 45-29 half-time bulge and then held off a stubborn Roosevelt team to notch the first win of the year. Kyle Pepple and Schwabe led the Islanders with 16 points apiece.

December 15, 1981

Sports round-up: Hoop team continues winning streak
By Dave Thomas

What can you say? The Islanders game with Bellevue last Tuesday night was supposed to be close. Instead, Mercer Island jumped out to a 24-12 lead after one period and stretched it to 44-26 by the half as the Wolverines never got their footing in the contest.

Ten Islanders scored in the game, led by Joe Thompson's 16 points and 13 by Al Moscatel. Coach Ed Pepple said it wasn't that Bellevue played so poorly, but that Mercer Island played superbly.

The defense shut down Bellevue's big scoring trio of David Seeley, Paul Dammkoehler and John Mittenthal, holding them to just 22 points combined. On offense, the Islanders moved the ball well and found the open man enough to hit on 70.8 percent of their shots from the field. For the year, the Islanders are shooting 62 percent from the floor – that's better than their free throw percentage.

December 24, 1981

Islanders continue to dominate basketball foes

By Dave Thomas

The question that now seems to be popping up is not whether the Islanders will win the state title this year, but by how much.

The Mercer Island boys team continued its total domination of KingCo the last three games before traveling to Las Vegas for the Holiday Tournament. On Tuesday of last week, the team defeated Redmond, 96-54, and then on Friday beat the defending KingCo Champions from Bothell, 84-54.

To cap off the series, this past Tuesday, the Islanders went on the road against their closest opponent in the Crest Division, Interlake, and easily defeated them, 69-43.

Against Bothell, the Islanders jumped out to a 22-7 first-quarter lead and never looked back as they scored on less than 20 points in any quarter.

Five players scored in double figures, led by Eric Schwabe's 18 points. But the night really belonged to Kyle Pepple.

The senior backcourt man contributed 11 points, but even more important, dished out a school record of 16 assists. The previous high was 13. Leading scorers for the Islanders were Joe Thompson with 17, Al Moscatel, 16, and Rich Dewey, 10.

Against Redmond, the team continued its hot shooting from the floor. The Islanders hit on 62 percent of their shots, rolling to their highest point total of the year.

Moscatel led all scorers with 27, while Pepple and Schwabe added 14. Paul Jerue also reached double figures with his 10 points.

The Redmond game was fairly close at first, with the Islanders holding just a 46-34 lead at the half. But in the third quarter the Islanders decided to put the pesky Redmond team behind once and for all.

They registered their highest quarter point total of the night, outscoring the Mustangs, 29-6, and opening a 75-40 lead going into the final period.

The Islanders recovered from an early deficit against Interlake Tuesday and held a 25-12 lead after the first period. The lead stretched to 40-20 at the half and Mercer Island coasted in from there.

The Islanders were led by Moscatel with 18 points. Other players in double figures were Schwabe with 15 and Thompson with 13.

Now, the other KingCo teams can enjoy the holidays because the Islanders will be in Las Vegas from Dec. 26-31.

December 29, 1981

Islanders win first game in Las Vegas tournament

Not even jet lag and some of the best teams in the country can stop them.

Mercer Island High School's boys' basketball team got off the plane in Las Vegas at 3:30 p.m. Saturday, and at 7:30 that night, after a sluggish first half, ran away from McNamara High School of Forestville, Maryland, 75-57.

The game was the first for the Islanders in the week-long Las Vegas Holiday Prep Classic. The tournament features some of the top high schools from around the country. Included this year are Calvert

Hall, also from Maryland, the number-one ranked team in the country, and Verbum Dei, the top school in California and the Islanders' next opponent.

Mercer Island started slow but turned on its defense and turned loose Al Moscatel to rout McNamara. The defense held McNamara to just 35 points during the first three quarters and Moscatel hit a game high 38 points – including 16 in the second quarter when the Islanders started to find their rhythm. Moscatel also set two tournament records in the game Saturday. He broke the records for most free throws attempted (22) and the most made (20).

Mercer Island was able to stay in the game because of Moscatel's shooting and the strong play of Rich Dewey and Tom Williams off the bench, said Coach Ed Pepple.

The Islanders had an off-shooting night, hitting on just 43 percent of their shots, but did even better on defense, holding McNamara to just 37 percent shooting (19-for-51).

Dewey and Williams were the real keys in the defensive play. They were forced into action when starters Eric Schwabe and Joe Thompson got into early foul trouble and then later fouled out. The Islanders held Terry Graves, McNamara's scoring ace, in check as he got just 13 points and only five in the second half.

Mercer Island was scheduled to play Verbum Dei late yesterday afternoon, with results unavailable at press time. This is the same high school that produced David Greenwood, Roy Hamilton and Ray Townsend, all UCLA standouts and pro players. Last year's team was 17-9 and the school's record for the past 14 years is 355 wins, 44 losses.

January 5, 1982

Islanders take sixth in Las Vegas tourney

By Dave Thomas

It was sort of a mixed bag for the Mercer Island High School boys' basketball team when it played in the Las Vegas Tournament last week.

The Islanders proved they were capable of playing with and beating some of the best teams in the country. At the same time, the players and coaches were disappointed because, according to Coach Ed Pepple, they knew they could do better.

"I was very pleased with the team," began Pepple. "We proved we could play with good teams. Yet no one was satisfied - we all felt we could have played better."

After winning their first two contests, the Islander dropped the last two and finished in sixth place.

The highlight of the tourney for the Islanders had to be the second game, played Dec. 29. They faced a very good Verbum Dei team from California. This team is known as one of the most consistent winners in the country and has provided a pipeline of players to UCLA, including David Greenwood, now with the Chicago Bulls of the NBA.

Against Verbum Dei, the Islanders held their own for three quarters, but then fell behind. With just 2:41 left, Mercer Island trailed by 12. With 55 seconds, the Islanders still trailed by six. But with just 18 seconds left, Al Moscatel hit on a three-point play to tie the game. Moscatel was the leading scorer in the tourney with 105 points in four games and was a member of the all-tournament team.

In the overtime, it was Moscatel again as he hit a jumper from the corner with just one second showing on the clock to give the Islanders the upset win.

Unfortunately, Mercer Island had to play in the semifinals the next night and was unable to get its rhythm back until later in the contest against Valley, the defending champs in Nevada. The night before had taken too much steam out of the Islanders and they lost, 62-52.

ON THE FINAL night of the tournament, the Islanders faced the defending California champ, St. Bernard. On this night, Mercer Island's defense was tight, allowing the California champs just 34 shots, but they made 25 of them. The 74 percent shooting – it was about 84 percent in the first half, according to Pepple – put the Islanders in a big hole.

Mercer Island cut St. Bernard's lead from 36-17 to 59-55 in the fourth quarter, but the deficit was too big and the Islanders ran out of gas in the end, losing 69-59.

Now it's back to business for the Islanders in the KingCo league where they will tackle a major opponent right off the bat. Tonight, the Islanders have their first home game in five starts, facing Crown Division leader Juanita.

Both squads are undefeated in the KingCo, and Juanita doesn't seem to have been hurt by the loss of its two stand-outs last year, Don Sparling and Rodnie Taylor. Tipoff is scheduled for 8 p.m. at the high school.

January 12, 1982

Basketball team – number one and climbing

By Dave Thomas

The Mercer Island High boys' basketball team continued its total and ruthless domination of KingCo opponents last Friday with an 86-45 rout at Sammamish. The game again demonstrated the Islanders' control of their foes, as Mercer Island has won its five conference games by an average of 36 points. In fact, their closest contest was a 26-point win over Interlake.

Last week though, the Islanders appeared to be heading into some tough competition. But things didn't go quite that way. First, their big match with Juanita was postponed until last night due to the snow. Then they faced a tough Sammamish team that was 8-2 - the same record as the Islanders - on the Totems home floor.

Mercer Island waited until the end of the first period before making its move against Sammamish. The Islanders grabbed a 22-13 lead after one and stretched it to 14 by the intermission.

That was when the visitors turned on the defense. They allowed Sammamish just 20 points in the second half, and just nine in the fourth quarter. But the key was the opening of the second half.

If coach Ed Pepple lit a cigar like former Boston coach Red Auerbach did when he knew the game was won, Pepple could have been enjoying his three minutes into the third quarter. In that span, the Islanders used their press to create numerous turnovers and run off a 16-4 spurt, opening a 26-point lead.

Mercer Island's team play concept was clearly visible Friday. Despite having the team's leading scorer, Al Moscatel, held to 10 points under his season average, the Islanders were still able to run away with the game and have five players in double figures.

Leading the way was Joe Thompson with 18 points and 12 rebounds.   Two players who came off the bench to contribute extensively were Mike Williams with 12 and Rich Dewey with 11. Eric Schwabe added 13 and Moscatel had 11.

The Islanders faced Juanita last night, but results were not available at press time. Tonight, the team travels to Inglemoor for a game, and Friday they return home to play Newport.

January 19, 1982

What else is new? Islanders win 3 more

By Dave Thomas

I give up!

I'm throwing in the towel, running up the white flag, calling it quits.

I have run out of new things to say about the Mercer Island High School boys basketball team. Think I'm kidding? Look at the facts in the case.

One, they have yet to lose a game (in the state of Washington) this year. And that includes three just last week – 79-56 Monday against Juanita, 84-42 Tuesday against Inglemoor, and 82-43 Friday against Newport.

Two, they always win big – and I mean BIG. Their closest game this season was against Juanita when they only won by 23 – a cliffhanger for them.

Three, they always play the same. They use teamwork, crisp passing, balanced scoring and tough, tenacious defense.

Those are the facts. They always play like I've described above, and I always have to write about the same thing – only the opponents change.

Last week, the Islanders took the things they have done well all year and did them better. They held Newport scoreless in the entire second period – a stretch of 11 minutes and 9 seconds including the first quarter.

Against Juanita, they demonstrated how they earned their reputation as a streak team – running off large chunks of points on opponents. They opened up with a 15-0 lead and just coasted in from there. And the same was true with Newport. The Islanders trailed 13-12 with 3:09 left in the first period. By halftime, the Islanders had opened a 42-13 lead – a run of 30 consecutive points.

After the half, the Islanders came out and added a 10-2 spurt on top of the 30-pointer to open a 52-15 lead. It was at that point Pepple began his liberal substitution – something he's done all year.

And with the Newport win, the team helped coach Ed Pepple reach a milestone - his 350th win in his coaching career.

MONDAY'S GAME AGAINST Juanita was a make-up contest due to the snow the week before. The game featured the number one (Mercer Island) and three (Juanita) teams in the state rankings and promised to be the first – and maybe only – challenge to Mercer Island in the KingCo this year.

Unfortunately, promises are made to be broken. The only challenge came in trying to keep the team from burning itself out early and letting the Rebels back into the game. After jumping out 15-0, the Islanders had to make sure they didn't let down and lose the lead. They didn't let up, but pulled further ahead to erase any doubt as to who is the number-one team in the KingCo.

The next night, it was a basketball clinic from start to finish as Mercer Island had too many horses for Inglemoor. The Islanders jumped out to a 21-4 lead after one quarter, moved it to 45-19 at the half and jacked it up eight more, to 62-28, after three.

BALANCED SCORING was probably the team's strongest point last week, next to defense. In the three games, a different player claimed high scoring honors for the Islanders. Against Juanita, Al Moscatel led the team with 25. Joe Thompson claimed high man at Inglemoor the next night with 16. And Eric Schwabe laid claim Friday as he capped off a super all-around performance by canning 24 and controlling the defensive boards.

"They are a most unselfish group," began Pepple. "I usually don't know who has the most (points) until after the game."

This week's target practice for the Islanders will be in the Mercer Island shooting gallery – also known as the gym. Tuesday, Lake Washington ventures in and on Friday the Islanders are at home against Issaquah.

January 26, 1982

Islanders win 2 more; face hot Bellevue team

After winning all their conference games this year by whopping margins, members of the Mercer Island High School basketball team are getting anxious for some tough competition. Everyone except coach Ed Pepple.

"These guys want to get in and be tested. As far as I'm concerned, I don't care if I ever have a close game," he said after his team's "close" 80-52 win over Issaquah Friday.

That win came just three days after Pepple chewed his team out for a lackluster offensive performance in the first half of their game against Lake Washington. After that tongue lashing, the team responded with 50 second-half points and a 90-47 win over the Kangaroos.

Against Lake Washington, the Islanders played sluggishly in the first half, but came out in the third quarter and outscored the Kangaroos, 28-6, to put an end to the tip-toeing around. Al Moscatel led the Islanders with 17 points. Kyle Pepple and Joe Thompson added 14 apiece.

If the Islanders are really looking for a little tougher foe, they have to look no farther than their game at Bellevue tonight. The Wolverines were Mercer Island's first KingCo win – 31 – points but this game promises to be different.

Bellevue is the second hottest team in the league after beating Juanita last Friday by four points.

Also, with a win over the Islanders, Bellevue would be in a position to tie the Islanders for the Crest title and move on to the KingCo title game.

The game begins at 8 p.m. in the Bellevue gym.

Phenomenal '82 Islanders cap 14-year career
By Dave Thomas

They are the hottest team in the state. Undefeated in league play this season, rated number one in-state basketball polls, exercising total domination over all KingCo opponents, the 1981-82 Islander basketball team is the icing on 14 years of sweet success for Mercer Island High School basketball coach Ed Pepple.

Pepple, who has scored 352 victories in his interscholastic coaching career (stretching back 21 years, prior to coming to Mercer Island) is reaching the end of an era with this year's squad. It is the last time basketball will be a "family affair" in the Pepple household.

For Pepple, coaching and parenting have twice been intermingled in his years on Mercer Island. First, there was son Terry, who led the Islander offense in 1973-74, when the team was 22-0 during the regular season and finished third in the state tournament.

Now there is Kyle, who as a junior was part of the 1980-81 team which reached the state AAA finals, and as a senior, this year appears headed again, along with his teammates, for the state tournament.

Having a father who doubles as a coach has been known to put undue pressure on some athletes. They are thrust into the spotlight – forced to accept the role and perform perfectly in it. And the players are often resented by fellow players for the "special" treatment they might receive.

BUT ACCORDING TO PEPPLE and his sons, the father/coach-player/son roles never posed much of a problem.

"I thought it was easy. In fact, he was the best coach I ever played for. It was very enjoyable, and I wouldn't trade any part of it," said Terry, who is frequently seen at Islander games sitting behind the Mercer Island bench.

Pepple added he never felt any favoritism toward his sons, and insisted they had to be good enough to carry their own weight.

"They've got to prove themselves. They had to show that they deserved to be there – not just because they are the coach's sons," he said.

When it came to being a coach or being a father, all three Pepples agreed that the line was clearly drawn.

On the court, he was coach and at home he was dad, said Terry, who added that Pepple would yell at him on the practice floor just like all the other players, but when they got home it was forgotten.

Growing up with a basketball coach has its advantages, both Terry and Kyle said. The two were able to learn basketball skills all the time, not just when they went to the gym.

"It was he who got me started," Kyle began. "I loved it. I wouldn't be playing just because I was the coach's son. If I didn't like playing basketball, I wouldn't."

Terry agreed, adding that he learned more from his dad while growing up than he learned from any other coach he played for.

ONE OF THE REASONS both players were not under extra strain as the sons of the coach was that they weren't placed into the spotlight. Neither Kyle nor Terry was forced into the role of scoring star or had the entire team revolve around him. Instead, they were given equal value with their teammates.

Kyle is a perfect example. He is not known as a scorer, and his worth is determined by the number of assists and steals he collects in the game. It is his job to get the ball to the top scorers and let them put it in the hole.

But despite the equal treatment, neither Pepple son was isolated from the difficulties that go with being related to the coach.

In his senior season, Terry was suffering from stress fractures in both his feet. The doctor told him if he wanted to play, he would have to sit out the practices. His teammates felt there was some favoritism, Terry explained, but the situation was remedied with a team meeting where the doctor's instructions were made clear.

Kyle's problem was not so easily solved. When he was just a sophomore, he made the varsity team. This caused resentment on the part of some seniors who felt they should have that spot on the basis of seniority and were bumped because Kyle was the coach's son.

Kyle said he had to battle that situation by himself, working extra hard to prove that he deserved a spot on the team.

AS FOR PEPPLE, he wouldn't trade the opportunity to coach his sons for anything.

"Why should I trust anyone else with my kids when I think I can do a better job?" he asked. "It's better than having them play for someone else, where you don't get a chance to see them.

"Isn't that why you have kids? To enjoy them as they grow up? So far I have seen 450 assists (by Kyle) that I wouldn't have seen if he was playing elsewhere," he added.

Maybe there aren't that many pressures associated with being the coach's son after all. Terry recalls that during junior high and his first years in high school, he was known as "Terry, the coach's son," or "son of Ed Pepple." But when he entered his senior year, the tables turned a bit, and sometimes Ed was referred to as "Terry's father."

February 2, 1982

Islander round-up

Compiled by Dave Thomas

It turned out to be a real cliffhanger – for the Islanders, that is.

Mercer Island traveled to Bellevue in its only game this week and escaped with a 77-64 win. It was the closest game for the Islanders since they defeated Roosevelt by 11 in their opening game of the year.

Actually, the game was not really as close as the score indicated. Mercer Island had the game in control in the first half but let up considerably after the halftime break and almost let the Wolverines back into the game.

The Islanders jumped out 20-4 in the first period as Eric Schwabe hit for 12 points. They extended that to 48-23 at the half as Al Moscatel joined in the scoring with 16 of his team-high 24 points. After the intermission, however, it appeared that the teams switched jerseys.

Bellevue shut down the Islanders, cutting the Islanders' lead to 11 by the fourth quarter – but the Wolverines could get no closer. Paul Dammkoehler triggered the spurt with 15 of his game-high 26 points in the second half – 13 in the fourth quarter.

This week, the Islanders are on the road again with two contests. Tuesday, they play at Redmond and Friday at Bothell. They defeated Bothell by 30 points earlier this year and Redmond by 42. Tipoff for both games is 8 p.m.

February 9, 1982

Islanders play last regular season game tonight

It's just a matter of time now.

The Mercer Island High School boys' basketball team is going through the motions of finishing its regular season, getting ready to move into the playoffs.

Last week, the team added two more victories to the long list of wins, beating Redmond 74-57 on Tuesday, and Bothell 62-40 on Friday. Tonight, the Islanders finish the regular season with a contest against Interlake on their home court.

The going will definitely become tougher as the Islanders play the Crown Division winner for the KingCo title next Tuesday followed by the Sea-King district tourney and unless the roof caves in the regionals and the state tournament.

But first, the Islanders must get by Interlake, which may be tougher than it seems. As coach Ed Pepple said, it is tough to get up to play an opponent whom you've beaten by 40 points this year.

The team seemed to have some problems getting ready to play Redmond and Bothell last week. The usually fast-starting Islanders stumbled out of the blocks a little against Redmond and started even slower against Bothell.

At Redmond Tuesday, the team struggled to a six-point lead after the first period but opened a 17-point spread in the second. The Islanders maintained that spread through the second half to defeat the pesky Mustangs.

IF REDMOND WAS PESKY, Bothell was downright stubborn Although the Islanders held as much as a 10-point lead in the first half, it took a Kyle Pepple jumper to hold a slim two-point lead at the intermission.

The Islanders quickly slammed the door in the second half, however. After surrendering 28 points in the first two quarters, Mercer Island's defense allowed Bothell only eight points in the third quarter and just four in the fourth as they ran away for their 13th KingCo win of the season, 17th overall.

Rich Dewey, down with pneumonia, missed the Redmond game but was back for the Bothell match. Mike Williams missed both games and will be out until possibly the KingCo title game, having undergone minor knee surgery to have torn cartilage scraped off his knee. He is back shooting and doing some jogging.

Al Moscatel picked up the scoring slack as he hit 15 of 23 shots for 36 points against Redmond. Friday, he followed it up with 20 points, on 8-for-12 shooting. Joe Thompson added 16 against the Mustangs and Eric Schwabe helped out with 13 against Bothell.

IN THE FOOTSTEPS of the varsity, the junior varsity will be trying Tuesday night for an undefeated season. If they can defeat Interlake's JV, the Islanders will end the year 20-0.

Tipoff for the JV game is 6:30 p.m. The varsity will follow at 8 p.m.

On February 16, 1982, the Mercer Island Reporter produced "The Winning Road", a special insert dedicated to the team. What follows are the stories included in that section.

1982 squad a coach's dream: '24-hour-a-day team' heads for state title!

By Dave Thomas

After a season unmatched in local basketball annals, the Islanders tonight play Juanita on their first step toward a long-sought state title. Tonight's game, at 8:30 p.m. at Hec Edmundson Pavilion, is for the KingCo Conference championship.

In Tuesday's win over Interlake, 75-48, Mercer Island took the Crest Division championship and kept clean its 14-0 record for its first undefeated league season since 1974.

This season's bombshell has been the consistent margin of victory. The Islanders outscored their KingCo foes by a total of 421 points, with average per game margin of 30.1 points. They defeated four teams by 40 or more points, and their closest game was a 77-64 win at Bellevue.

Except for two losses in the Las Vegas Holiday Prep Classic to the nation's top prep teams, the Islanders demolished all before them from the moment the season began, unlike the 1980-81 squad that peaked late in the tournament. That tale will help explain the killer instinct of the 1982 team.

LAST YEAR as the number-three team from KingCo, the Islanders were hardly given a second glance. Local teams to watch were Auburn with their seven-footer Blair Rasmussen, and Juanita with their standout, Rodnie Taylor.

But when the dust had cleared from the West Central District and regional games, Mercer Island was still going after that state title.

Came the semi-finals. The Islanders were still the surprise team, with six juniors, five of them starting. But as others fell by the wayside, even Juanita and Auburn, Mercer Island suddenly found itself in the state title match.

Enter Shadle Park. East vs. West, Shadle Park with Mark Rypien, their all-everything athlete, against a team of no-names. The Islanders held a one-point lead as a Shadle Park player dropped in a shot at the buzzer, or after? That, and the confusion afterwards, led to two protests to the Washington Interscholastic Activities Association, a counter protest, and Mercer Island's being placed "on probation" for this season. The second-place trophy has never been given to Mercer Island, nor do the Islanders want it.

SO THEY CAME out fighting last December. Virtually all the same players, apparently determined nobody's going to get close enough for a disputed finish.

Besides determination, the team fortunately has talent which makes up for the lack of height. Returning principals, now seniors, are guards Kyle Pepple (6-1 ½) and Paul Jerue (6-1), forwards Al Moscatel (6-2) and Eric Schwabe (6-5 ½) center Joe Thompson (6-6), and sixth man Rich Dewey (6-3).

For the bench, Pepple conferred with his six starters and the decision was unanimous to keep three seniors and let the juniors reap experience on the JV. "Their wisdom proved right," said Pepple. "Instead of sitting on the bench, the juniors played a 20-0 JV season. And the senior reserves proved totally supportive, accepting their roles and providing leadership from the bench."

Senior reserves are J D. Stern (5-10), Tony Grossi (6-1), and T. J. Yurkanin (6-5). Stern, quarterback on the 1981 Islander football team, is backup point guard, "an unselfish player who gets the ball to his teammates," said Pepple.

Grossi, reserve inside forward, "is an excellent rebounder, very strong and aggressive," according to Pepple. "When he's in there, he brings a lot of enthusiasm to the game."

Yurkanin is backup center, "a very aggressive, hard-working player who does everything well, particularly rebounding, and who maintains the same kind of enthusiasm as the starters," said Pepple.

The fourth reserve is the Varsity's only junior, Mike Williams (6-3 ½). Called by Pepple "an outstanding shooter and scorer, a good jumper who rebounds well," he has fit in extremely well and gives the group some continuity into next season.

Only 2 ½ weeks ago Williams underwent arthroscopic surgery to repair a knee cartilage torn in the second Bellevue game. He has, according to Pepple, made a remarkable recovery and by late last week was again working out with his teammates. Pepple expects Williams to see action in the playoffs.

For the two additional reserves, Pepple draws on the JV, rotating different players. "They're the nucleus of next year's Varsity," he said, "and we expect them to help us go on from here."

AS THE SEASON started Dec. 4, the team found itself in the limelight because of the tournament fiasco. But it quickly won its own place in the sun, beating Roosevelt 69-58 then trampling Wilson of Tacoma 82-45.

The Islanders' opening KingCo match was touted as a barnburner with Bellevue. Instead, Mercer Island burned Bellevue 85-57.

In its next four matches before the Christmas break, Mercer Island won by 42, 30, 26, and 41 points.

As the only Seattle-area team ever invited to the Las Vegas Holiday Prep Classic, against some of the nation's best high school teams Mercer Island wound up sixth. They defeated McNamara of Forestville, Maryland, and Verbum Dei of California, one of the country's most consistent winners, before losing their last two, to state champions Valley of Nevada and St. Bernard of California.

The losses reminded the Islanders they were not invincible. Back home, they came down hard every game.

In what was supposed to be a close match with Crown Division leader Juanita, it was Islanders 79-56. From there on they mowed down each opponent in turn by from 20 to 43 points.

Tonight's game launches the postseason playoffs' that will culminate in the state tourney in March. Both Pepple and assistant coach Bill Woolley think the Islanders have the talent and motivation to reach the top.

Woolley says he hasn't seen a team that can stay with the Islanders for an entire game, but he has some worries. "The only things that can stop us are injuries or severe foul trouble. It is hard to officiate aggressive teams. Once we get into the later rounds of the tournament, we may get an official from east of the mountains or down south that hasn't seen us play, or who has called nothing but slow down offenses – he may take one look at us and get whistle-happy," Woolley said.

Pepple doesn't let any of this faze him. He believes only a bad breakdown can defeat his team. On the other hand, he suggests, out there somewhere might be another team like last year's Islanders: underrated, slow to start, that gets its act together in time for the tourney.

THE BREAKS OF the game might decree otherwise, but at the moment fans and the press polls all favor the Islanders to win the state championship. They appear to have the talent and they certainly have the drive. And they have already virtually dismantled the record book.

So far, the team is shooting 55.5 percent from the field, and five players are shooting better than 50 percent. Al Moscatel leads with 64.1 percent. The other forward, Eric Schwabe, has made 61.7 percent. The other three are Rich Dewey, 59.5, Joe Thompson, 59.2, and Kyle Pepple, 52.6. A sixth player, Paul Jerue, finished just under the magic 50 at 48.5.

Scoring was just as balanced. It is rare for a school to have more than one or two players who average more than 10 points a game. Mercer Island has three: Moscatel, 20.3; Schwabe, 12.7; and Pepple, 10.2 with Thompson just missing at 9.9 a game.

The starting front line of Schwabe, Moscatel and Thompson were the workhorses on the boards. Moscatel was the leading rebounder with 136. Schwabe and Thompson followed with 118 and 101, respectively.

In the backcourt, Pepple and Jerue teamed up for 241 assists (178 by Pepple) and Pepple and Moscatel led the club in steals with 89 and 52, respectively.

These numbers are just what this team can do on paper, but they don't play on paper. Hard to quantify are the intangibles: an extrasensory perception that tells each player where his teammates are and what they are going to do. The principals have played together since the fifth grade, which might help explain their extraordinary chemistry.

But the Little Dribbler program has been going since Pepple inaugurated it in 1968, so many, many Mercer Island youth have grown up playing basketball together. And Pepple has had many very, very good teams.

This one, no doubt, is something extra special. "They really care about each other," Pepple said. "They're friends off the court as well as on."

The 1982 Islanders are any coach's dream. Pepple calls them "a 24-hour-a-day team!"

Ed names program 'built on pride' his main achievement
By Dave Thomas

Before basketball coach Ed Pepple came to Mercer Island High School in 1967, he turned down the job via telephone. Fortunately, somebody in the school district lost the message and by the time Ed was asked again, he had changed his mind and decided to accept.

The rest is history. Eight KingCo Conference championships in Ed's first 14 years here, three seconds and a third; even trips to the Washington State AAA tournament with two third place finishes and one – uh, what Ed calls – "uncrowned state championship." His 1981 team, a modest third place in KingCo, caught fire in the playoffs, reached the finals and, many believe, won the title. After the final buzzer, the score was changed – but that's another story, not yet finished. Currently, after a persistent protest denied just as persistently, the Island cagers are on "probation," the Washington State Interscholastic Activities' Association's way of saying "Go away, stop bothering us."

Now Ed seems headed for a state title with the all-around strongest – and undoubtedly the most unusual – team of his career. Without a single "big man" star, he's got a squad of players who each can do it all: block, assist, pass, rebound – and certainly shoot. Consistently.

ED'S INITIAL turndown was to University of Washington coach Mark Duckworth, who called Ed one Tuesday in 1967 to ask if he wanted to coach Mercer Island.

Ed said no. "I was in my first year as head coach at Mark Morris in Longview, and I felt committed to stay and put their program onto a successful track," he said last week.

Duckworth's message to Tag Christiansen, then Mercer Island athletic director, never reached its mark. Two days later Tag himself called Ed and asked if he wanted the job.

By that time, Ed had talked it over with his wife, Shirley, and decided to at least talk about it.

"That Saturday, I was taking a class on a field trip to the Seattle Repertory Theatre. I had my interview on a park bench at the Seattle Center," he recalled.

Why did he change his mind? For one thing, Mercer Island had an established program which, while it had won no championships, was already competitive. Ed was getting a little tired of building from scratch. But mainly, it was a special challenge.

People had told him not to take the job, that there would be too much pressure.

"I understood the last coach had left under some controversy," he said.

Nevertheless, when he arrived at Mercer Island High Ed found the "pressure" had been highly exaggerated. Although the athletes were moderately successful, they in fact had "a loser's attitude," he said.

"There were people in the community who wanted the teams to win, but there was not the pressure you find today."

It was the kids themselves that had a negative attitude, he found.

Ed immediately embarked on an attitude-rebuilding program, finding and developing talent and psyching his athletes on to victory.

He considers the change in spirit his prime achievement, creating a sports program "built on pride."

ON-COURT ACHIEVEMENTS are hard for Ed to recall, because he prefers "only to look forward."

His first year, Mercer Island won the KingCo Conference championship, defeating a Newport team that finished second in state the year before.

He remembers all too well the incident that was at once the best and worst time of his career: last season's controversial loss to Shadle Park in the State title game, when the Islanders were State Champions for a minute and a half – the time it took to change the score and the outcome of the game.

"In the span of 1:30, we had our highest and lowest points," he said.

He remembers the 1972 team that lost players to injuries, illness and disaffection, but still made it to the state semifinals. At the time that year, he only had seven players on the squad.

Breaking Richland's five-year home-court winning streak in 1973, and the Las Vegas Tournament – particularly wins over the Arizona state champion in 1979 and Verbum Dei of California in this year's tournament – also are high lights.

ED'S LINKS to basketball go all the way back to his high school days and beyond. As a senior at Lincoln, his team finished second in the state. From there, it was on to college, where he continued playing. He spent two years at Everett Community College and that produced the biggest changes in his life.

While at Everett, he decided to give up business as his major and turn to coaching for a career. It was also where he met Shirley, who eventually became Mrs. Ed Pepple.

Ed transferred to the University of Utah where he used up the last three years of his basketball scholarship.

His senior year at Utah was memorable. The team went 24-4 and entered the West Regionals of the N.C.A.A. tournament. In its first game, Utah went up against a University of San Francisco team on its way to an unbeaten season, led by a fellow named Bill Russell. The next night Utah defeated Seattle University, 105-85, and the 105 was an N.C.A.A. record.

After graduation, Ed entered the Marine Corps and continued to play basketball, for the camps where he was stationed and for the national Marine team.

Out of the Marines, Ed went into coaching in 1958 in Fife, where he stayed six years. He moved to Meadowdale for three years, then to Mark Morris. While they were moving around Shirley gave birth to their four children, Terry, Jill, Jody and Kyle. Recently Ed and Shirley became grandparents of Matt, whose present form indicates football rather than basketball. "Maybe he will become a tight end," Ed suggested.

WHAT NEXT? College coaching, maybe?

"If I make a move, it can't be horizontal," said Ed. "It would have to be an improvement, and I don't know of any high school job that is better than this one. The administration is the best. I couldn't ask for more supportive people – they stayed right by us even in the difficult times last year. If I moved, I would be taking a chance," he said.

Ed doesn't think college is his cup of tea. He didn't get into coaching for fame and fortune, and the road trips and recruiting jaunts away from his family don't appeal to him.

"Life is to enjoy. Right now, I enjoy going to work – I would hate like the devil to get into a job I hated. I consider myself a Mercer Islander, even if I did come late," he concluded.

Meanwhile, quite a few people in the community are glad to have him around.

RETURNING STARTERS

Al Moscatel

"He is the supreme competitor. He refuses to lose." – Coach Pepple.

Al has been the offensive spark plug for the Islander team the past two years. He has led in scoring, and when they need two points, they look for their 6' 2 forward.

With the team being acclaimed as "unselfish," epitomizing the concept "team sport", it is a tribute to Al's scoring talents that the others so frequently look for him to put the ball in the bucket.

His talent was spotlighted earlier in the season. When the team travelled to Las Vegas to participate in a national tournament against the best high school teams in the country, Al was leading scorer in the entire tourney, and was named to the All-Tournament team for the second year in a row.

When Al was in fifth grade and Ed Pepple and his teammates were going to Texas for a tournament, Moscatel's math grades kept him at home. From that point on, Al has been determined never again to miss his chance.

For the first time this year, Al played on the high school golf team. Otherwise, he concentrates on his studies and basketball. He hasn't thought much beyond this season but intends to go to college next fall and study either psychology or business. College basketball is a possibility.

Paul Jerue

"He is at his best when the game is on the line." – Coach Pepple.

That clutch ability of Paul has been his key contribution. That isn't to discount his other skills, but when things are tight, he knows what has to be done, and gives it his best.

After playing with Kyle in the backcourt for so many years, Paul also has developed a knack for knowing where to be and what to do. He can help Kyle with the press or pick up the offensive or defensive end while Kyle is doing something else. His versatility on the floor is another of his key attributes. He is a tenacious defender and can also score when needed. He can pick up a sluggish offense with clutch hoops or swing the tempo with a key steal or another defensive play.

Despite his basketball prowess, Paul is probably better known for his football skills. He was a defensive back and flanker on the football team last year, where he also showed his worth in the clutch. Several times he would make a key play both on offense and defense to help the team.

Paul has been a resident of the island all his life and has been active in basketball since he entered the Boys Club and Little Dribblers programs at the age of eight like almost all the Varsity players year after year. At school, he is a member of the Student Council and Honor Society. Outside school, he enjoys water skiing and tennis.

Next fall, Paul plans to enroll in a college where he can play football. He says he probably will go to the University of Washington and try out as a walk-on for football.

Joe Thompson

"He is the anchor inside. He takes tremendous pride in his defense – begs to guard the toughest man." – Coach Pepple.

Inside is where the Islanders like to find Joe, whether it is to receive a lob pass for a lay in or clear out the lane to grab a rebound. The tallest member of the team at 6'6', Joe is the key to the Islanders' inside game. He controls the boards and is the intimidating factor on defense, while on offense, he is the man people like Kyle look for when trying to get the ball inside.

Basketball, as it turned out, was almost abandoned by Joe at an early age. Between eight and ten, he was a member of the local A.A.U. swimming team. In his last year - at ten - his team represented Washington at the A.A.U. West Regional and the team come home victorious. It was then a tough decision - basketball or swimming.

Due mainly to his fast growth as a child, Joe chose basketball, fortunately for Islanders fans.

Joe was born at Walter Reed Hospital in Washington D.C. in April, 1964. Joe and his parents, Dr. Gale and Catherine Thompson, moved to Mercer Island as he was ready to start kindergarten.

From that point on, school has been a big part of his life, and right now, he has sent out pre-med applications to Stanford, Dartmouth and San Diego Universities. He wants to continue playing basketball, and the Dartmouth coach has expressed an interest.

Joe enjoys the outdoors, particularly kayaking, hiking and fishing.

Rich Dewey

"He is the perfect sixth man. He is an offensive and defensive spark."— Coach Ed Pepple.

When talking about the ingredients of a perfect sixth man, you can put Rich in almost all of the categories. He is an extremely quick and aggressive defensive player, while on offense he can come off the bench cold, make things happen and put the ball in the hoop.

It is the versatility that makes a player effective in the difficult role of sixth man. To be successful, a player has to be able to play any position and fill a need on the court. That is what Rich does so well. At 6'3", he plays both guard and forward and can change the tempo of the game with either his offensive or defensive play. His tough defense allows him to fill in and fit in with either guard on the floor, and his alertness inside and talent lets him be either a defensive or offensive player at forward.

Rich was born in the Seattle area March 7, 1964, but his family soon moved to Portland. That didn't last long, and the family was back on Mercer Island by the time Rich entered the third grade. In the fifth grade, he was playing basketball and had already started playing with most of today's teammates.

Rich concentrates on studies and basketball. In his free time, he enjoys water skiing and drawing.

College basketball is on Rich's mind and if he does play, it will probably be at Occidental College. He hopes to study marketing or advertising.

Eric Schwabe

"He is a gifted offensive player who makes the game look easy – smooth." – Coach Ed Pepple.

No other Islander on the front line blends all aspects of the game as smoothly as Eric. Coach Pepple stated at the beginning of the year that Eric was "the best pure shooter on the team". Throughout the season, he hasn't been proven wrong. The 6'5 forward has an easy way about him, and he makes it look like he is under no pressure at all – with foul-line jumpers as well as muscling the ball past two or three opponents under the basket.

What makes him especially valuable is that he is just as graceful and talented at the other end of the floor, rebounding and playing defense. He can take charge at either end of the court, depending on what the team needs.

Eric was the last player to join the present troupe. He arrived here already in the seventh grade, and he quickly fell in with some fast company – sports wise. At South Mercer Junior High he met Kyle and Al and moved into the fast lane of basketball.

When not playing basketball, Eric goes in for more relaxing sports like golf and tennis. This year, he played on the golf team at the high school.

Now, he is concentrating on the season at hand, and will wait and see what develops afterwards. He says he hasn't made any commitment to a college, but he will be going to one. Scholarships, or even getting a chance to play somewhere, are still in the back of mind.

Kyle Pepple

"He is the guy that makes everyone else better." – Coach Ed Pepple.

When Kyle reaches the top of his game and brings out the best in the others, it's obvious why the Islanders have been so successful this season. As a point guard, Kyle has no equal. His passing abilities and defense are keys to making the entire team hum. He is the player who creates situations that turn the tempo of games around.

On defense, he spearheads the full court press that has created so much havoc for opponents. When he gets his hands on the ball, he controls the flow of the offense, and his sharp, crisp passing has been the key to many easy Islander hoops. When things get clogged up inside, Kyle shoots the ball himself. His dead aim from outside often is overlooked because his other skills are so impressive.

The 6-foot senior guard was born in Everett and January 19 celebrated his 18th birthday. He is also a stand-out in football and track and participates in other school activities like DECA and Student Leadership classes. The son of Ed and Shirley Pepple, Kyle has been exposed to basketball all his life. With a father who's a coach and an older brother who played basketball, Kyle's exposure to the sport has been extensive and his love for the game is evident in his performances on the court.

After graduation this spring, he plans to go onto college, although he isn't sure which one, and study business or social work, and maybe play a little basketball.

Tortuous route begins tonight

Tonight, the Islanders begin their quest for the state title that eluded them last year, facing Juanita in the KingCo championship game at 8:30 p.m. at Hec Edmundson Pavilion on the University of Washington campus.

Next stop will be the Sea-King District meet, which will begin this weekend.

If the Islanders beat Juanita, they will play at Sammamish Friday, February 19. If they win that first game, they will play at Sammamish again Tuesday, February 23. Winning that, they will be in the winners' bracket games of the tournament, which will wind up on Friday and Saturday, Feb. 26 and 27, at Hec Ed.

If the Islanders lose their first game, they will play at Bellevue on Feb 23. If they win that game, they will travel to Hec Ed Feb. 26 and 27 in the consolation bracket.

If they lose to Juanita, Mercer Island will open play at Garfield Feb. 19. If they win that, they will play at Ingraham Feb. 23 and then at Hec Ed. If they lose the first game, they stay at Garfield for a game Feb. 23 and then move on to Hec Ed.

The SeaKing is double elimination, and if the Islanders lose two of their first three games, they will be out of the tourney.

If Mercer Island qualifies for the Regionals, they will either play at Cascade High School in Everett or at Renton High School. That will be determined by their finish in the SeaKing Tournament. The number one and three teams will play at Renton, while the number two and four teams in the SeaKing will go to Everett.

Confused? Why not. Somehow, we have confidence Ed Pepple's Islanders will find their way.

For the record: 1982 Islanders rewrite the book

The 1982 Islanders reveal their special qualities not only by their records, but by their attitude toward records as well.

After the third or fourth game last December, they asked coach Ed Pepple to interrupt his 15-year tradition and stop posting records after the games. "It's not important," they told him, "Who gets what. What's important is how we play, whether we win or lose."

"They don't want individual credit," said Ed. "They don't want to be talking about each other's performances, either.

"So, all I post is the free throws."

Nevertheless, this year's players have been smashing record after record.

Kyle Pepple's career assist mark is the most amazing. The previous career high had been 372 by Paul Bain set from 1977 to 1979. At the end of the regular season, Pepple had 454. He's hoping to get 500 by the end of the playoffs. He also holds the single-season assist record, 202 last year, and the single-game mark, 16 earlier this year.

Pepple has also smashed the career steals mark. He has amassed 220, to this point breaking the old mark of 158 set by Doug

Gribble who graduated in 1974. This year he also broke his own single-season mark by claiming 89 thefts so far – six better than the mark he set last year.

Indicative of the teamwork involved are the marks of Al Moscatel. Despite Pepple's demolition job on the record book, Moscatel will still finish third or fourth on the all-time steals list, and even more remarkable, fifth on the assist ladder – despite Pepple's passing ability.

Moscatel will land near the top in two other categories as well. He will finish in the top all-time ten in rebounds, and either second or first on the all-time scoring list. Coach Pepple says he will definitely finish second and has an outside chance at first – he is about 167 points shy right now of Jeff Hawes' 1968-70 record 1267 points.

Another individual mark on the verge of being broken is season free throw percentage. Joe Thompson has hit 83 percent of his charity line shots this year ahead of the 82.5 standard Mark Morgan set in 1973.

As for team records, marks are dropping like flies. The team has already broken the team steals record and is on the verge of breaking at least five more. Their points-per-game average of 76 is ahead of the 72-per-game record set by the 1968 team led by Steve Hawes, now with the NBA.

The previous high for field goal shooting, 49.7 percent set in 1979, has been left far behind by a team making an incredible 55.5 percent of its shots.

If the Islanders continue to hit the averages, they will break records for field goals, assists, steals and total points. These team marks are the greatest tribute to the awesome talent and abilities of this team. In just one year, they have literally rewritten the school record book, and they aren't quite finished yet.

Both Varsity and JVs undefeated in league: Varsity goes for KingCo championship at UW tonight

Two undefeated Mercer Island boys' basketball teams finished the regular season last Tuesday, Feb. 9. The Varsity defeated Interlake, 75-48 to end KingCo season play at 14-0, in first place in the Crest Division. The team will play Juanita at 8:30 p.m. tonight (Feb. 16) at Hec Edmundson Pavilion, University of Washington for the KingCo championship. Tickets are available at the gate, with no pre-sale.

Earlier the night of Feb. 9, Bill Woolley's Junior Varsity defeated Interlake's JV 73-47 to wind up 20-0 for the year. With a 15-point lead midway through the third quarter, the JVs pulled a technique out of the Varsity's playbook. As the quarter wound down, the JVs put on a spurt to widen their lead to 30. After that, it was a breeze as Woolley's boys easily dominated the Saints.

Main attraction as usual was the unparalleled Varsity. The only time they stood still was when they presented roses to their parents in a pre-game ceremony. After that it was all work and a lot of pleasure, as the team continued its steamroller trio through the KingCo.

Interlake stayed with the Islanders, the state's number-one-ranked team through the first quarter and trailed by just one point.

Opening the second period, Mercer Island ran off 17 consecutive points to open a 29-11 lead. Interlake struggled back but trailed by 14 at the half.

"We came out and were a little flat tonight," began head coach Ed Pepple.

"I don't think the undefeated thing entered their minds," he said.

It may not have been on their minds to start with, but by the end of the game, they had become the first Islander team undefeated in KingCo since 1974. (Incidentally, that was the year another Pepple, Terry, was a senior Islander.)

Tuesday night the Islanders' prime senior playmaker, Kyle Pepple, controlled the game's tempo and "ran the club well," according to his father, Ed Pepple. The third quarter saw the team slowly build on their lead and ice the win. They extended the margin to 62-35 very early in the fourth quarter, and it was all over for Interlake.

Once again, the balance made the difference for the Islanders. In the second quarter, Eric Schwabe picked up the scoring slack. In the third quarter it was Al Moscatel, and then Schwabe again in the fourth. Schwabe ended up with a game-high 22 points and Moscatel added 16.

Pepple spread 14 points out through the game and added seven assists. Coach Pepple said Kyle might have had more assists, but when he would get the ball inside, his teammates would be fouled. Indirectly, Pepple accounted for about 15 more situations that led to free throws.

Tonight's title game is just that, for both Mercer Island and Juanita have already qualified for the Sea-King District Tournament which gets under way this weekend at various sites.

But the game is something more for the Islanders, and this team in particular. The starters have been playing varsity ball since they were sophomores and have not won a KingCo title. Even though the real goal is a state title, Pepple says this team wants to win so they can hang a banner in the gym saying "KingCo champs, 1982."

Pepple says they will have to stop Juanita's two scoring leaders, Mike Haney and Erv Kuebler. And they can't let J.D. Taylor get going. In league play against Juanita, the Islanders ran out to a big lead early and then coasted home with a 79-56 win.

Pepple says his team doesn't plan any surprises, just the same brand of basketball they have played all season long. He adds that Juanita had better come ready to play tonight.

Ticket prices are $3 for adults, $3 for students without an A.S.B. card, $2 for students with an A.S.B. card and $2 for students in grades K-6.

Assistant Coach Woolley: He's not a Pepple clone, but ability's there

That tall player who sits next to Ed Pepple on the Mercer Island bench – who looks a little older than those on the floor.

That's assistant coach Bill Woolley.

Bill, who's also coach of the immaculate 20-0 Junior Varsity, was one of Ed's early players, dating back to the days of Steve and Jeff Hawes, Greg Jack, and the legendary turn-of-the-decade leaders whose records are only now being broken.

Woolley's jeans, work jacket and "longer" hair contrast sharply with the formal style of Pepple. (Those who know him doubt Pepple would wear his hair longer even if he had it to wear.) Woolley looks more like a basketball player than Pepple, over whom he towers, although appearances are deceiving – Pepple, as well as Woolley, once was an excellent basketball player too.

Both know whereof they coach, and they coach much alike. Woolley says he owes a great debt to Pepple, "one of the biggest influences of my life."

Ed helped Bill get his first teaching job, at South Mercer Junior High, and his first coaching job. Woolley's teacher all along, the two men think very much alike, and suggestions move both ways, says Woolley.

In the fall of 1967 Pepple became Mercer Island High School head basketball coach and Bill entered the high school as a sophomore from South Mercer. Bill played basketball in high school, the last two seasons under Ed on the Varsity team. After he graduated, Bill spent two years at the University of Puget Sound and the last two at the University of Washington where he got his teaching degree and majored in psychology and minored in math.

Bill had tried coaching his first summer out of high school, and like Ed, he enjoyed it so much that was it.

Ed told Bill of a possible opening at South Mercer, and a job coaching. Bill was hired as a junior high teacher, and as things worked out, became high school JV coach in 1978. This season, his team finished a perfect 20-0 year by beating Interlake Tuesday, Feb. 9.

Playing for Ed, Bill says he learned the fundamentals, when to make the right move or decision. As Ed's assistant, he began learning the inside aspects of the game.

"When I became a coach, I learned how to deal with the players. I learned about things like team morale and attitudes – all the intangible things. I learned the X's and O's as a player and the rest from coaching," Bill added.

Ed's influence on Woolley has left the younger coach feeling fully prepared to move out into his own program. Bill has said that for the past two years he has felt ready to become a head coach, and all he needs now is a chance.

Before he goes anywhere, Woolley wants to make sure the situation is right. He says being the assistant at Mercer Island is better than some head coaching jobs.

He hasn't looked too hard. Having coached the present team since they were Little Dribblers, he feels especially attached to the 1982 Islanders, and has wanted to see the season through.

Woolley faces the specter of teacher layoffs, brought about by budget cuts and state parsimony. All teachers in the district with less than eight years are being notified their jobs are in jeopardy. With just seven years, Bill is on the list. He says it helps him job-hunt a little harder.

This year's Islanders should certainly improve his stock. A coaching candidate who guided the JVs to a 20-0 season and assisted on what might become the 1982 state championship AAA team would be difficult to overlook.

February 23, 1982

Islanders take KingCo title; face Garfield

By Dave Thomas

It was just what the doctor ordered.

"Doctor" Ed Pepple felt the Mercer Island High School basketball team's 89-72 Sea-King District win over Bellevue last Friday was just what the team needed, as it began the final journey toward the state AAA title.

"This was the first game where we haven't run out to a big lead and then coasted in," he began. "This was a good game because we needed to get used to playing close games."

Close wasn't the word for it. The mighty Islanders, who had defeated the Wolverines twice during the regular season, had all they wanted from a Bellevue team that wouldn't roll over and go away. The game was, to borrow an old cliché, closer than the score indicated. With only four minutes left in the game, Bellevue had cut the Islanders' once nine-point lead to five and had a chance to cut it to three. But when it got tough, the Islanders pulled themselves up and played like the machine that swept to a KingCo championship last Tuesday, 73-42, over Juanita.

"WE MADE MANY MENTAL mistakes and created opportunities for them. But we tightened it up when we had to," Pepple said.

After the game, the loudest cheer came from the Islander locker room when it was learned the Islanders will play Garfield, which beat Sammamish in the playoffs, tonight.

"We're finally out of the KingCo," shouted senior forward Al Moscatel.

The Islanders had been hoping to face different opponents, so they could try some other styles of play. Up to this point, they have played only KingCo schools. But there was also the matter of sacrificing variety for proximity.

"You give up one thing for the other," said Rich Dewey after the Juanita game. "You have the option of playing different teams or staying close to home. Last year we played three nights in a row at Auburn. The traveling wasn't bad, but it was hard for our fans to get there. I would rather stay close to home – I don't care who we play," he added.

Playing close to home, at Sammamish High School, has certainly allowed the fans to come out in droves – too many for the tight confines of the Sammamish gym, the site of tonight's 7:30 p.m. match-up. So many fans were waiting to get in to last week's games that, despite a Washington Interscholastic Activities Association rule to the contrary, 300 tickets were sent to Mercer Island High School for pre-sale for tonight's contest. Fans can contact the high school to see if any tickets are left.

THE BELLEVUE GAME was a fan's game, and just about anything that could happen, did. The referees wore out two whistles calling fouls – a total of 57 were called and 72 free throws were taken, 42 by the Islanders.

Bellevue had three players with four fouls and two players – David Seeley and Marc Eilers – fouled out. Mercer Island had five players – Paul Jerue, Moscatel, Dewey, Eric Schwabe and Joe Thompson – with four fouls each. Thompson had four fouls in the first half and Schwabe three. But despite the trouble, no Islanders fouled out.

The free throws are what made the game closer – not that Bellevue made many, but that the Islanders didn't. Mercer Island shot just 27-just-42 from the line and point guard Kyle Pepple hit on only six of 12 on the night.

THE ISLANDERS PLAYED at Sammamish Friday after defeating Juanita Tuesday in the KingCo Championship game. The KingCo match-up was an all-Mercer Island affair as more than 4,000 people looked on in Hec Edmundson Pavilion on the University of Washington campus.

The Islanders opened up a 10-point lead at the end of the first quarter and never looked back. The closest Juanita got after that was nine points as Mercer Island rolled to its first KingCo title since 1977.

"We missed it (the KingCo title) for a few years," said Pepple after the Juanita victory. "It was nice for this team, especially the seniors."

An arial view of Mercer Island (looking south). Below, the exterior façade of Mercer Island High School, home of the Islanders.

An early image of Coach Pepple in the locker room with his team.
Below, future NBA player Steve Hawes goes for two.

Chris Kampe (30) pulls down a rebound in a game against Redmond.

Al Moscatel (32) takes flight over a Bellevue defender.

1975 Mercer Island Boys' Club Traveling Tens Team

left to right, front row: Eric Nordstrom, Al Moscatel, Joe Thompson, Chris
Kampe. Harold Friebe, Paul Jerue. Second row: Andy Winterbauer. J.D.
Stern, Kyle Pepple, Jason Craig, Bill Givan, Skip Galvin;
in back, Coach Dr. Larry Jerue

1980-81 Mercer Island Islanders

left to right, starting with back row: Coach Pepple, Doug Gregory, Eric Schwabe, Scott Driggers, Joe Thompson, Eric Nordstrom, Mark Aldape, and manager Scott Swanson; kneeling: Kyle Pepple, Paul Jerue, Rich Dewey, Al Moscatel, Chris Kampe, Tom Uczekaj.

Above, Islanders celebrate their victory over Lakes in the 1981 state semi-finals. Right, Kyle Pepple and Doug Gregory can't believe their eyes when the scoreboard is changed in the Shadle Park game. Below, Coach Pepple consoles Gregory after the game.

Clockwise from top: Mercer Island students protest outside the WIAA
offices in Bellevue in 1981; Hank Rybus, Executive Secretary of the WIAA;
Coach Pepple directs his team.

Kyle Pepple (22) dribbles past a Juanita defender. Below, Paul Jerue (30)
comes up short on a steal in a loss against Roosevelt.

The Islanders campaign for a state championship in 1982 comes to an end.
Below, Coach Pepple and son Kyle share a laugh.

Quin Snyder as a promising young sophomore in 1982. Coach Pepple
predicted he would become an "all-time" player.

1982-83 Mercer Island Islanders

Front row: (32) Paul Dammkoehler, (50) Rob Mitchell, (42) Brian Schwabe, (52) Scott Lammers, (30) Jorgan Light, (24) Mike Hubbard.
Back row: Coach Ed Pepple, (22) Sam Moscatel, (34) Scott Norwood, (40) Peter Lyon, (44) Lazlo Bedegi, (10) Quin Snyder, (20) Rick Hodge, Trainer Tom Spencer.

6'8 sophomore Brian Schwabe (42) makes an impact for the Islanders in the 82-83 season.

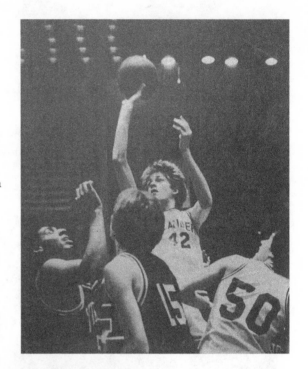

Bellevue transfer Paul Dammkoehler (32) goes up for a rebound with some help from Rob Mitchell (50).

Coach Pepple calls the play. Below, guards Quin Snyder and Sam Moscatel during an interview with the press.

5'9 Sam Moscatel pulls up over a Bellevue defender. Below, Pepple during the 1984 matchup featuring two nationally ranked teams from the KingCo conference: #10 Juanita and #12 Mercer Island.

Seniors Quin Snyder (top) and Brian Schwabe (below) entered the 1984-1985 season with high expectations and national attention.

Quin Snyder became a McDonald's High School All-American in 1985 before heading to Duke.

Islanders celebrate their win over Curtis in the 1985 AAA state championship game at Seattle Center.

Above, the 1978 Little Dribblers with coach Bill Woolley. Quin Snyder (21) is third from left in the back row, Brian Schwabe is third from left in the front row. Below, the 1985 AAA State Champions (Schwabe and Snyder are posed next to the trophy, shaking hands.)

Coach Pepple with wife Shirley. Pepple was inducted into the
Washington State sports hall of fame in 2012 and to this day remains
the winningest high school basketball coach in state history.

February 23, 1982

Island fans on best behavior at basketball games

By Bob Ogle

A well-behaved crowd is as important as a good basketball team if Mercer Island High School wants to make it into the state tournament this season.

Because of the high school's probationary status, stemming from last year's loss to Shadle Park in the final seconds of the state championship game, the behavior of Mercer Island fans will play an important role in helping the Islanders to win a state title.

It's not hard to see how last season's loss and the probation status that followed have complicated the game of basketball on Mercer Island.

The Islanders lost to Shadle Park, 66-65, on a last-second shot of questionable character. Claiming there were irregularities in tournament procedures, Mercer Island appealed the outcome to the Washington Interscholastic Activities Association.

The WIAA not only denied the appeal, but also placed Mercer Island on "probation," stemming from what it called "unsportsmanlike conduct" during the tournament by Island partisans.

Thus far, observers agree that Mercer Island's crowd has been, at the very least, a typical basketball crowd. All that remains are the playoffs, which began last week. Continued good behavior during the playoffs means probation will likely be lifted by the WIAA.

Sportsmanship has been the watchword for the WIAA this year, Rybus said, and not just at Mercer Island. All schools are being watched carefully, now and during the playoffs. During the state AAA finals next month, the WIAA will stress coordination of security of forts by all schools involved.

Rybus said he believes Mercer Island officials have seen probation as a positive thing, as he predicted they would at the outset.

"I think Mercer Island has now settled into accepting that," he said. "I haven't seen them play, but I've heard reports regularly from Gary Snyder showing the planning they've done.

"I commend Gary on the steps Mercer Island has taken. They've done a good job reminding the students and the fans about good sportsmanship."

So Rybus still sees it as a positive action, Snyder still thinks it was unnecessary, and Mercer Island coach Ed Pepple still has a bad taste in his mouth from the whole deal.

PEPPLE'S COMMENTS now are nearly a replica of what he said when the Islanders were put on probation last year.

"I can't speak for everybody," he said, "but I think it was something that was done because we protested. I look at it as a joke. I can't look at it any other way."

Of course, crowd control isn't a huge part of Pepple's job. His concern in the team, and he said he's never been concerned about his players behavior, then or now.

"Our team didn't do anything wrong," he said. "There are no teams around that are better to officiate. We don't allow our kids to go off the deep end, I've never been worried about our team being out of control or our crowd being out of control."

Even if the taunting continues, he said, he's not too worried about trouble.

"What has happened (in some games) this year is 10 times worse than anything we've ever done," he said. "People like that are just showing what they're made of. Our kids are aware, and hopefully they won't react to that."

There is one more important similarity between the 1981 and the 1982 basketball seasons. Both Mercer Island and Shadle Park are members of high school basketball's elite corps again this year. It's not unlikely they will meet again before it's all over.

Neither Snyder nor Rybus has much to say about a potential Mercer Island-Shadle Park matchup. It's tough to speculate about anything like that anyway, since there's no telling what could happen.

Surprisingly, Pepple doesn't have that much to say on the subject either, "Last year," he explained, "is history.

"Our total energies are on this year," he said, "We did everything we could to get a wrong righted last year. Since then, we've worked hard at it, and we've done everything they (the WIAA) wanted us to do."

He admitted that revenge isn't his main concern, and neither is getting out from under probation.

"Our goal is to win the state championship. That's all we're thinking about."

March 2, 1982

Whew! Islanders take SeaKing title in overtime

By Dave Thomas

Mercer Island High School's boys' basketball team better hope it doesn't run into Juanita again this season.

In the third meeting between the two teams last Saturday night at Hec Edmundson Pavilion, the combatants were involved in a hard-nosed, knock-down, drag-out fight that saw technical fouls, blood – both real and bad – and a remarkable 52-47 overtime win by the Islanders.

The win gave the Islanders the SeaKing District Title and sends them to Renton High School this Friday at 9 p.m. for a match-up with the Curtis Vikings in Region 11 of the State AAA playoffs.

The regional pairing is not the dream game that many people were hoping for. Kentridge – the state's second-ranked team going into last weekend – lost twice, 53-51 to Foss Friday and 63-58 to Rogers Saturday. But an early Mercer Island-Kentridge match-up is still possible. If the Islanders lose to Curtis, they will have one more chance to qualify for state – against the winner of the Roosevelt-Kentridge match, which opens the Region 11 slate Friday. The Saturday game will be at 8 p.m.

The Islanders earned their third shot at Juanita when they routed Garfield, 72-59 last Tuesday.

Moscatel led the Islanders against the Bulldogs with 22 points. Joe Thompson, who was effectively shut down against Juanita, added 19 and Pepple had 17.

TWO FACTORS LED to the incredible finish in Saturday's Juanita game. First, the Rebels, after losing twice before, know what they had to do to stay with the Islanders. Second, Mercer Island was complacent.

"We came out thinking that we could win without doing anything," began last-minute hero Al Moscatel. "We can't ask for a better lesson than the one we learned tonight."

"We weren't totally prepared to play tonight. It was a good thing we learned the lesson where it wasn't a loser out game," said coach Ed Pepple.

For Mercer Island, things started bad and got steadily worse. The Islanders fell behind 16-6 in the first quarter, struggled, but could never take control. They didn't take the lead until Moscatel hit two free throws with 4:45 left in the third quarter, but that didn't last long as Juanita quickly regained control of the game.

With less than three minutes left in the game and the Islanders trailing 45-40, Juanita's J.D. Taylor came down court on a 2-on-1 break. He took the ball to the hoop against Kyle Pepple, and the two collided.

Taylor's elbow met Pepple's head, cutting a muscle and causing a deep gash. Trainers and doctors got the bleeding stopped and took Pepple into the locker room, where he was given 15 stitches. He returned to courtside in the over-time to lead the cheers for his teammates.

THAT INCIDENT WAS the turning point for the Islanders. They worked inside for two Eric Schwabe lay-ins, but a pair of Dave Burt free throws left the lead at 47-44, Juanita. The Rebels had the ball and just 1:30 was left on the clock. At that point, Juanita suffered its own loss when Taylor was whistled for two fouls – his fourth and fifth of the game.

The Islanders had two chances to cut into the lead, but Schwabe and Joe Thompson missed the front ends of one-and-ones. But the Rebels also suffered from cold shooting at the foul line. With 56 seconds left, Juanita's Brian Webster missed his one-and-one and later, Mike Haney missed two free throws with 18 seconds to go.

In between the Juanita misses, Rich Dewey sank one free throw and Moscatel hit a jumper to tie the game at 47. But with six seconds left, Dewey missed a pair of charity-line tosses that would have won it for Mercer Island.

In the overtime, it was all Mercer Island. Moscatel hit a jumper to give the Islanders the lead and they held it from there. Juanita stayed cold as Haney missed two jumpers and a free throw. The Islanders, meanwhile, added three free throws – two by Moscatel and one by Schwabe – to clinch the win.

"Juanita could see they (the Islander players) wanted this game. They were determined to win it – they played with reckless abandon at the end," said a tired but happy Pepple.

That reckless abandon was what had Juanita coach Bob Anderson livid throughout the game and particularly at the end. Midway through the second quarter, Anderson picked up a technical foul and then his chair as he almost jumped through the gymnasium ceiling.

"THERE AT THE END they (Mercer Island) were jumping all over us – it's a bunch of crap," began a frustrated and angry Anderson. "All year they have gotten away with it, and they still did tonight. J.D. (Taylor) got raped on his fifth foul and he gets called for it."

After the game Pepple said his team played just about as bad as it can, and Juanita was the main reason.

"We had to earn everything we got tonight. We couldn't make our field goals or our free throws and there isn't a lot left after that.

"Juanita also did an excellent job on the boards. Their defense forced us to shoot from the outside, we weren't making them, and we weren't getting any second shots inside," he added.

THE BIGGEST SIGH heard after the game was not that the contest was won, but that it appears Mercer Island is out of the KingCo rut. In their four post-season games, so far Mercer Island has played Bellevue once and Juanita three times.

Juanita assistant coach Ken Broches indicated the Rebels felt the same way, when he wondered aloud if "there were any other teams in the state playing basketball."

Mercer Island will have a chance to find out this Friday night.

Besides overtime win, Islander season has lacked excitement, Pepple says

By Bob Ogle

Prior to last Saturday, Mercer Island High School basketball coach Ed Pepple had expressed mild displeasure at meeting the Juanita Rebels for the third time this year.

The teams had played once during the regular season and again for the KingCo championship, and both had been convincing Mercer Island wins.

Saturday's game for the Sea-King District championship was expected to be a rerun, but Pepple was thinking about the law of averages.

"Sooner or later, it's got to catch up with you," he said before the game, referring to playing Juanita twice before. "You have to lose some motivation. It just isn't as exciting."

Saturday night, Pepple had all the excitement he could handle, and certainly more than he wanted. Mercer Island won 52-47 in overtime, thereby preserving status as a fugitive from the law of averages.

One can reliably assume Juanita learned something from the first two losses. But whatever Juanita Coach Bob Anderson learned, he sure wasn't talking about it.

UNLIKE ANDERSON, Pepple had something to say after the game – once he started breathing easier.

"We're 3-0 against them now," he offered. "I guess the law of averages hasn't caught up with us yet."

But he acknowledged that beating Juanita badly in two previous outings didn't help the Islanders take them seriously a third time. All his players wanted was a look at somebody they hadn't beaten yet.

"It was obvious we weren't totally prepared to play tonight," he said. "When you play a team three times, that'll happen. But we're just happy to be playing in Renton next week."

Juanita wasn't the only scenery familiar to the Islanders during the tournament. First-round opponent Bellevue had also played Mercer Island and lost twice before.

Second-round opponent Garfield had been a change of pace, but the result had been the same as ever – MI 72, Garfield 59.

Pepple was less than pleased at having to cover the same old ground to get to regionals, but he wasn't complaining much. Before this year, Mercer Island had traditionally played in the West Central District, traveling to garden spots like Puyallup and Auburn to play teams from throughout Western Washington.

THIS YEAR, the new Sea-King changed that. All Mercer Island had to do, it seemed, was keep beating the same teams they beat during the regular season.

Of course, there was one advantage compared with this year.

"In the West Central District, we played different teams than during the season," Pepple said.

"It doesn't put us at any disadvantage, other than it's been boring. We're just tired of playing the same teams. We enjoyed playing Garfield. Playing Juanita is enjoyable, but it's just not the same."

He was right. Saturday night playing against Juanita just wasn't the same.

All-KingCo honors

Winning on the court has brought added recognition to the Mercer Island High School boys' basketball team. Kyle Pepple and Al Moscatel were both named to the first team of the Eastside Journal American's All-KingCo selections for 1981.

Pepple and Moscatel were joined by Tim Nicholas of Newport, Mike Haney of Juanita and Paul Dammkoehler of Bellevue on the first team, which was selected by the sports staff of the Journal.

Eric Schwabe and Joe Thompson were selected on the second team, while guard Paul Jerue made it a clean sweep for the Islander starters as he was given honorable mention.

Friday game tickets limited

Only 600 tickets will go on sale tomorrow (Wednesday) at Mercer Island High School for the regional championship game against Curtis of Tacoma Friday night, Mar. 5.

The game will be played in the small Renton High School gymnasium, 400 South 2nd, Renton. Another 600 tickets will be available at the door, but with the first game scheduled for 7:30 p.m., early's the word for those hoping for game-night admission. The Islanders play at 9 p.m.

Islanders head coach Ed Pepple expects a noisy evening. "Curtis is the talk of the West Central District," he said yesterday, "and the fans are known to be wild and vociferous. Almost as enthusiastic as Mercer Island fans. This," he concluded, "could be a battle of the fans."

March 9, 1982

Tourney-bound Islanders beat Curtis for 2nd shot at state title

By Dave Thomas

Mercer Island High School basketball players were jubilant after their 50-42 win over Curtis last Friday because it earned them a second straight trip to the state tournament and a shot at the title.

Mercer Island fans were jubilant for two reasons. First, because their team won, and second, because they know they wouldn't have to cram into the Renton High School gym again to watch the Islanders play.

In the small gym selected as the site for the AAA Region II finals, which was filled beyond capacity with Mercer Island Curtis fans, the spectators got treated to another Mercer Island "clinic", as the Islanders showed yet another team the meaning of team basketball. And they left no doubt that they are the team to beat in the state tournament beginning Thursday in the Seattle Center Coliseum.

Mercer Island came prepared to meet its first non-KingCo opponent since it beat Garfield more than a week ago and played as if reading the script from a three-act play.

The first act found the Islanders slowly inching away from their opponent - in this case, Curtis - and the suspense builds. The action occurs in act two, when Mercer Island spurts forward and runs up a big lead, this devastating its foe.

The final act is the celebration scene, where the Islanders hold off their victims and win the contest. As with many of the other scripts used by Mercer Island, the Islanders began the final act midway through the third quarter.

IN THE THIRD period Mercer Island turned on all its burners, expanding a 23-18 halftime lead to 36-22 with two minutes left in the quarter. This explosion surprised Curtis coach Don Huston, who thought his team was very much in the scene at intermission.

"I felt good at the half. We had some plays that didn't go well, we missed some free throws, but we were still down by only five. I thought we had a chance in the second half," Huston commented.

The chance turned out to be somewhere between slim and none. The Vikings came out to start the second half and found that they had not only their free-throw shooting ability in the locker room, but now their field goal shooting was there as well.

During the game, Curtis made just 39.4 percent of their shots from the field - 13 for 33 - and were only slightly better, 47 percent, from the foul line.

"You have to shoot free throws. You can't shoot like that and beat a team like that," added Huston on his team's 16-for-34 night from the charity stripe.

Huston also gave credit to the Islanders for helping his team shoot so poorly.

"Mercer Island played well. I underestimated them. They are better athletes, and their press is better than I expected.

"We handled their press well, but we didn't take good shots once we got down there," he added.

DEFENSE WAS ALSO on the mind of MI coach Ed Pepple, who felt his team's defense turned the game around.

"We did a heckuva job defensively all game. We just kept it going," he said.

Another reason for the Islander's success was the play of the big men inside. Eric Schwabe played a tremendous all-around game, while Joe Thompson was a stalwart on defense despite playing in foul trouble most of the game - he fouled out with 1:43 left.

Schwabe and Thompson combined for 15 rebounds - Curtis collected 20 as a team - and Schwabe also broke loose for 16 points, the team high. Al Moscatel and Kyle Pepple added 14 points apiece to lead the balanced Islander attack.

Curtis was also hurt by the loss of Brian Roberts early in the fourth quarter on fouls. Roberts had led the team with eight points at the half, but that was all he got as the Islanders shut him down completely in the second half.

The game was close through the first half, but Mercer Island opened up the second half with a 13-4 spurt which soon became a 36-22 advantage. Leading the way was Schwabe, who scored seven of the 13 points. From there it was just a matter of holding the Vikings away from the door.

The Islanders opened a 56-33 lead late in the contest, mostly due to free throws - those made by Mercer Island and those missed by Curtis. But at that point both coaches cleared their respective benches, officially closing the matter of the game's outcome.

Curtis was knocked out of the tourney the next day, losing to Roosevelt, 60-59 in overtime.

State tournament preview: Stage is set for a Shadle Park rematch

by Dave Thomas

Will there be a Mercer Island versus Shadle Park rematch for the state AAA high school basketball title this Saturday night in the Seattle Center Coliseum?

That could be one result of a draw held Sunday afternoon to determine the first round of play for the state tournament to be conducted this Thursday through Saturday March 11-13 in the Coliseum.

The Islanders are now just three victories away from claiming the state title they thought they had last year, when they lost to Shadle Park of Spokane on a controversial last second shot. But before they claim the top rung on the ladder, they must get by three of the top eight teams in the state.

Joining the Islanders this year are Everett and fellow KingCo member Juanita from Region I, Roosevelt from Region II (Mercer Island's region), Fort Vancouver and Foss from Region III, and Davis and Shadle Park from Region IV.

In the draw held at the Washington State Interscholastic Activities Association office Sunday, Mercer Island selected Davis from Yakima as its first-round game. The Islanders also drew an eight out of the hat, which means they are the eighth game on the schedule Thursday, with tip off at 10 PM.

The other first round AAA matches will pit Shadle Park against Roosevelt at 1 PM, Fort Vancouver against Juanita at 2:30 PM, and Everett against Foss at 6:30 PM.

Friday's matches will have the losers of the Shadle Park-Roosevelt and Fort Vancouver-Juanita games playing at 10:30 AM with the winners playing at 4 PM. The winners of the Everett-Foss and Mercer Island-Davis matches will face off at 8:30 PM that night with the losers pairing off at 10 PM.

Saturday's championship final will begin at 9 PM following the AA championship game at 7 PM. Both of those contests will be televised live on KING TV, channel 5.

Obviously, the favorite in the AAA class has to be Mercer Island. The Islanders have stormed through their regular season unblemished – except for losses to Valley, the Nevada state champ and St. Bernard, the California state champ at the Las Vegas prep tournament during the Christmas break.

Only two things might work against them as they enter the tournament. The first is that they have not played many teams outside of the KingCo conference.

The other hurdle is Davis from Yakima. Islander coach Ed Pepple said he knows absolutely nothing about his first-round opponent.

Of course, it works both ways. Davis Coach Gene Rostvold said in a phone interview Sunday afternoon that the only thing he knows about the Islanders is they are supposed to be an excellent team and probably the team to beat in the tournament.

And it sounds as if Davis wants to be the one to do it.

"The team wanted to play Mercer Island in the first round," began Rostvold. "They play well under pressure, and they rise to the occasion.

"If you want to win the title you have to beat the best and I feel it's better to play them right off and get it out of the way," he added.

After listening to Rostvold describe his team, it sounded much like Pepple describing his Islanders. Davis is a small team which makes up for its lack of size with quickness. The team likes to pressure at both ends of the court and can "do whatever is necessary to win."

Davis, like Mercer Island, is an experienced team due to a large number of underclassmen returning from last season. Last year the team was 20 and three and played five sophomores and two juniors. This year the Pirates have just five seniors on the team.

Rostvold starts 5'11 Junior Todd Stottlemyer and 6'2 senior Joe Harris at guard, a pair of 6'1 junior brothers, Lonnie and Montie Phillips at forward, and 6'6 senior Jim Oakes at center.

Harris and Oakes, co-captains, lead the team in scoring, averaging 14.5 points apiece per game. Montie Phillips added 10.9 points a game while Lonnie averaged 9.3.

When Rostvold looks to his bench he searches for three main people. Senior Mike Mitchell is a 6'1 swing man who plays at either guard or forward. Mike Vincent and Dale Moore are both 6'2 forwards that have some weight to throw around inside.

The game promises to be a matchup of two teams with very similar styles – quick and high pressure. Two factors give a slight edge to Mercer Island. First, the Islanders have been to the tournament before and know the kind of pressure involved. Davis is making its first trip and may be a bit awed by it all.

Second, Mercer Island is a team-oriented club. If there is a team in the state that works better together, it hasn't shown up west of the Cascades, yet.

Next for the Islanders will be either Foss or Everett. Foss has to be considered a bigger mystery than the two teams from east of the mountains. In the West Central tournament, Foss defeated Kentridge – which was still undefeated at the time - but then lost to Curtis, which was eliminated from the playoffs.

Foss relies mainly on two players. Co-captain Billy Velizis, a 6'2 senior who leads the team in scoring, averaging 16.5 points per game, while 6'4 postman Ron Jenkins averages 10.3 points a game. The unpredictable Falcons cause concern for Everett Coach Joe Richer.

Richer said he has heard that Foss is a completely different club from the one his Eagles defeated earlier this season. But despite the concerns, Everett is favored to beat Foss.

The Seagulls, 21-1 this year, have several of the players back from the team that Mercer Island eliminated in the regional playoffs, 51-49, last year.

The team is one of the biggest in the tourney and has used size to its advantage all season. The big man in the attack is Mike Champion, the 6'9 senior pivot. Champion leads the team in scoring with 17.4 points a game and is the catalyst of the Gulls inside attack. At the other end is point guard and captain Dave Hutt.

Hutt, a foot shorter than Champion at 5'9, runs the Everett attack and also averages 13.8 points a game. The third offensive leader is 6'4 Chris Chandler. Chandler averaged 13.4 points a game and helped Champion inside.

If the Islanders get by two of these opponents, they will then face one more for the title – either Roosevelt, Fort Vancouver, Juanita or Shadle Park. The Islanders have beaten Roosevelt and Juanita already this year – Juanita three times - and have a good idea of what to expect.

Of these four teams, Roosevelt might be considered a dark horse. The Roughriders lost five times this year, but in the last two weeks have begun to put things together and may be peaking just in time for the final sprint to the finish.

They are led by the inside-out attack of Gary Gardner and Demetrius Carter. Gardner leads the team in scoring this year averaging 18.6 a game while Carter – who almost single-handedly beat Kentridge in the first game of the regionals - averages 12.6. The quick 'Teddys' also had Craig Jackson and Brad Smith average in double figures for the year at 12.5 and 10.1 respectively.

If there is any team in the final eight that knows more about the Islanders than Mercer Island, it is Juanita. The Rebels lost three times to Mercer Island and would like nothing more than another shot at them. The Rebels are led by seniors Mike Heney and Erv Kuebler and sophomore J.D. Taylor.

But first, Juanita must get by Fort Vancouver. The Trappers are a fairly big team, but they are also young – five juniors grace the roster. Two of these juniors, John Campbell and Mike Merlino, lead the Fort Vancouver offense during the year. Campbell averaged 19.1 points and Merlino 11.4. Senior center Rich McKee provided the experience and 13.1 points a game.

Finally, there is Shadle Park. Coach Dave Robertson has done a remarkable rebuilding job with the defending AAA champs. With only one player returning off last season's team and not much size inside, Robertson said he never imagined the team would do this well.

He attributes their success to a lot of pride on the part of the players, the ability to come together and play as a team, and the flexibility to play many different styles of basketball – whatever type of tempo is dictated.

Leading this year's version of the Highlanders is Jeff Schmidt, the only returning player from last year's squad, and Randy Richards, a transfer from Medical Lake. But as Robertson points out, there really isn't any big star on the team and if they get the job done, it's because of a strong team effort.

As for the possible rematch in the title game, both Robertson and Pepple agree it doesn't matter who is there, as long as their own teams make it.

"The kids would like to play Shadle Park," began Pepple, "but not in the losers bracket. We would rather play someone in the winners bracket than Shadle Park in the losers bracket."

Playing in the winners bracket is the goal of all the coaches and players in the tournament. Staying on the highroad is the only way to claim the state basketball title.

Moscatel nominated to All-American basketball team

Al Moscatel, Mercer Island High School senior, has been nominated by Islander coach Ed Pepple to the 1982 McDonald's All-American Basketball Team.

A team of 25 high school basketball stars will be selected later this month from among the 1,2000 nominees.

Players and their coaches will participate in the McDonald's All-American game in Chicago on April 10.

March 16, 1982

22-points rout propels team to finals

By Bob Ogle

By all rights, last Friday night's state AAA semifinal game between Mercer Island and Everett should have been one of the best games of the tournament.

Nothing of the sort. It started out a tight contest and ended up just short of the worst route since Little Big Horn as the Islanders rapped the Seagulls, 66-44, to return for their second try at the state championship in two years.

It was supposed to be a good game because Mercer Island and Everett were ranked first and second in the state, respectively, and because the Gulls had a history giving Mercer Island a run for its money. Everett had lost to the Islanders in regionals the year before, but only by a 51-49 count.

The Islanders had also looked a little ragged in the first round against Davis, winning 55-53, and there were whispers that they might not be that good after all.

Any whispers were not lost on Coach Ed Pepple.

"After the Davis game," Pepple said, "there wasn't the jubilation in the locker room you'd expect. That was because of our performance."

Pride took over against Everett, he said.

"The fans tonight got to see the Mercer Island team I know and love," he said. "We thought we proved we were pretty good."

Part of the problem against Davis was the lackluster play of guard Kyle Pepple. Ed called it the worst game his son had played all season.

After Kyle pumped in 14 points and added six assists against the Gulls while spending most of his time running their guards to near-death, Dad knew things were okay.

"You can't keep him down for more than one game in a row," the elder Pepple said. "They've all got a lot of pride.

It was evident from the beginning. The Islanders canned five of their first nine shots from the field, finishing 12 of 20 for the half. They ran up a 14-8 first-quarter margin and dragged that out to a 29-17 edge at the half.

In the second half, the bulge never got smaller than 10 points. Getting into the AAA title game had never looked any easier.

Of course, when your opposition shoots only 33 percent from the field (14 of 42) while you're hitting a whopping 64 percent of your own shots (22 of 34) it ought to be easy.

Ed Pepple said the ease wasn't really to his credit.

"The credit for the game plan goes to the assistants," he said, referring to Bill Woolley and Terry Pepple. "They were the ones who scouted Everett. We just wanted to make them work for everything they got."

Everett boasted three scorers averaging double figures, 6-8 center Mike Champion (17.4), 5-9 guard David Hutt (13.8) and 6-4 forward Chris Chandler (13.4).

Mercer Island found an easy way of solving those three problems. Islanders Eric Schwabe, Rich Dewey and Joe Thompson battled Champion underneath and held him to 12 points. Al Moscatel drew Chandler as a defensive assignment and responded by holding Chandler to 13 points, his lowest output of the three-day tournament. As for Hutt, Kyle Pepple got that job, and he did it well. Hutt finished with eight points, his lowest total of the tournament.

Conversely, the Islanders placed three scorers in double figures. In addition to Pepple's 14, Moscatel nailed 18 points and Schwabe added 16.

Everett Coach Joe Richer said before the game he had been looking forward to playing Mercer Island and setting last year's account. He didn't have much else to say after the teams left the court.

On Saturday, March 13, Mercer Island squared off against Roosevelt High School of Seattle in the state AAA championship game at the Seattle Center Coliseum.

State tourney: RHS 58, MI 52

'Our poorest game ever'

By Dave Thomas

Two things can account for Mercer Island's 58-52 loss to Roosevelt in the State AAA high school tournament finals Saturday night. One was that things went wrong, and the other was that things didn't go right.

For the second year in a row, the boys' basketball team reached the tournament finals at the Seattle Center Coliseum. And like the year before, when the Islanders lost on a controversial last-second shot to Shadle Park, they came out on the short end of the stick.

The loss was harder to take than last year's though, because the Islanders had nobody to blame but themselves this time around. It was as coach Ed Pepple stated, the worst time to play your worst game of the year.

"We played hard. It was a total team effort. Nobody did not contribute to the loss – and that includes the coaches. It was not our night – it was our poorest game ever," he stated.

Anyone in the stands who had seen the Islanders play before certainly wouldn't argue with Pepple. The team had one of those nights when everything they touched turned to lead – particularly their shooting. After hitting 58.3 percent against Davis the first night and 64 percent of their shots against Everett in the semifinal game,

Mercer Island could connect on only 33 percent against Roosevelt, hitting 17 of 52 shots.

An example of this frustration was evident on the face of senior Al Moscatel, who couldn't buy himself a basket in the first three quarters. He hit only 8 of 20 shots – after shooting 7-of-9 against Davis and 6-of-10 against Everett in the first two games of the tournament.

THE COLD HANDS even went with the Islanders to the foul line. They could make only 18 of 32 free throws, but more importantly, they had Roosevelt in foul trouble most of the second half but could not hit the crucial one-and-one chances.

"When you can't make field goals and you can't make free throws, there isn't a whole lot left. It was obvious the only thing we had out there tonight was courage," said Pepple.

Courage and emotion were the two deciding factors in the game. Roosevelt had just a little bit more of each – especially when it counted. The main cog in the Teddies' damaged machine was Gary Gardner. The 6'3 senior was forced to step in and assume the role of team leader and ball-handler after Craig Jackson and Demetrius Carter went to the bench.

Jackson went out in the first two minutes when he took a charge from Moscatel and suffered a mild concussion. Carter exited at the 7:09 mark of the fourth quarter with five fouls – he followed Islander playmaker Kyle Pepple and Joe Thompson who picked up their fifth fouls in the third quarter.

But even with Jackson and Carter on the bench, the Islanders were unable to get over the hump in the second half. Early in the third quarter, the lead was cut from 27-17 to 28-24 and it looked like the Islanders had put their first-half slump behind them. But all of a sudden, they let up and Roosevelt took off and stretched the lead to 10, 34-24. It was at that point that Pepple picked up his fifth foul on an offensive charge.

IN THE FINAL quarter, with Carter and Jackson out for Roosevelt, the Islander pressure became much more effective, and they began forcing the Teddies into numerous mistakes. But again, they couldn't take advantage of them.

Al Moscatel's jumper made it 46-43 with 3:09 left, but that was as close as Mercer Island could get the rest of the way.

"We were out of control all night. I don't know what happened," began Pepple. "We made the big plays and still could've won—we had plenty of opportunities."

Seven-year itch for state title ended Saturday for Islanders
By Bob Ogle

Mercer Island High School finally got what it had wanted for so long – another chance to stake a claim as the best prep basketball team in the state.

When it was over Saturday night, there was nothing left but a jubilant Roosevelt High School team and a 58-52 Islanders loss. The time came for the Islanders to back up the claim for the final time, they couldn't make it happen, and so ended the 1981-82 basketball campaign.

But when the final second ticked off, it put the wraps on more than just a basketball season.

It closed the door on one of the most successful basketball years in Mercer Island history, the loss to Roosevelt notwithstanding.

It ended a 17-game winning streak, dating back to the Las Vegas Holiday Tournament last December.

And it ended a long relationship between a group of seniors who have played basketball together for years, many since they were "Little Dribblers" in fifth grade. Starters Kyle Pepple, Al Moscatel, Joe Thompson and Paul Jerue were part of that program, while fifth starter Eric Schwabe joined soon after. They and others on the team, including seniors J.D. Stern, Rich Dewey, T.J. Yurkanin and Tony Grossi, have been a close-knit bunch on and off the court.

It was that brotherhood, for lack of a better term, which had sustained them through most of the return trip to the Seattle Coliseum, and which darn near brought them back to beat Roosevelt in what all parties acknowledged was Mercer Island's "worst game this year."

"It crushes my heart to see this happen to them," Coach Ed Pepple said after the game. "They were on the threshold of doing what they wanted to do. It goes deep for them. It cuts all the way to the core."

When both Thompson and Kyle Pepple fouled out midway through the third quarter, it would have been easy to fold. But the Islanders didn't, and Paul Jerue provided the reason – the bond between the players.

"We had two guys foul out and we still gave 100 percent," Jerue said. "We never quit. We push each other, and we let each other know we want it."

That kind of character also leads to a certain type of confidence, almost a cockiness. Jerue acknowledged that might have been a problem, but he wasn't sure.

"I thought we might have been a little overconfident," he said. "But we're always like that, so you can't tell."

THE WAY THE Islanders lost symbolized the way they won – as a team. All the players made mistakes at one time or another against Roosevelt, and collectively, they all led to the loss.

Losing the ball game hurt all of the players deeply. It has to hurt any time you travel a long way and come up empty. But, for the seniors, knowing they would not play another high school game together both intensified the pain and made it easier to bear.

"It doesn't bother me that much, just because we're so close," Jerue said of never being on the court with his friends again. But he does admit it will be tough to stay in touch, since he plans to attend the University of Washington while many of the others want to attend college out of state.

"I guess it's basically going to be a phone-call type of thing," Jerue said. "But we all know that when we do get together, we'll have good times."

Moscatel felt a little differently.

"The thing that hurts me the most isn't the game," he said softly. "It's knowing that we're never going to play together again. It's not just a team. It's a bunch of friends."

Moscatel recognizes that the natural course of events dictates that people - even old friends - grow up and move on. High school days only last so long - a fact that is sad but true.

"I'll go on, and everybody else will go on," he agreed. "But it just won't be the same."

MI's 'money player' finishes high school career in style

By Bob Ogle

Albert Moscatel has traditionally filled a lot of roles for the Mercer Island High School basketball team.

He has been a scorer, a rebounder, a ball-handler, a cheerleader and generally one of the most talented all-around individuals to ever play ball at Mercer Island. Certainly, he is one of the most talented players in the state this season.

But what has set Moscatel - Al, if you please - apart from most of the other talented players is his knack of being able to do just the right thing at just the right time. When the Islanders have needed help at any given moment, Moscatel has generally been the guy to offer assistance.

Last weekend, he finished his high school career in grand style at the state AAA basketball tournament. After averaging 20 points a game during the regular season, he averaged 19 points per game in the tourney, with 19 against Davis, 18 against Everett and 20 in a losing cause against Roosevelt. Such a tournament requires such a performance, and Moscatel delivered his best effort, as always.

His performance was enough to get him named to the all-tournament team, along with teammate Kyle Pepple. In fact, Moscatel earned the most votes of any player on the all-tourney squad, with 26 sportswriters in favor. Others in the group included Chris Chandler of Everett, Joe Harris of Davis, and Demetrius Carter and Gary Gardner of Roosevelt. Gardner was named tournament MVP, an honor generally reserved for a member of the championship squad.

MOSCATEL'S CONTRIBUTION went far beyond statistics. He donated the big effort when it was needed, whether it was a three-point play against Everett to provide a little breathing room, 12 of Mercer Island's first 15 points against Davis, or a 13-point fourth-quarter performance against Roosevelt which spearheaded a comeback drive.

And in between heroics, he was full of enough adrenaline to keep the entire population of Mercer Island fast breaking for a year.

Such has been the career of the 6-2 forward, who is still deciding which college will get his skills. He is being recruited by several, both locally and out of state.

Moscatel maintained his tournament performance was really not much different from standard operating procedure.

"I always play the same way," he said. "As far as getting excited, that's just me. I get excited because it gets me going. When the other guys on the team see me happy, it gets them going too."

Now that Moscatel is graduating, Coach Ed Pepple must be wondering who is going to give the clutch performances in the future. Any praise Pepple delivers now has all been delivered before.

"Al is our money player," Pepple said. "The tougher the game, the tougher he plays."

June 8, 1982

Islanders in summer tourney

If you thought summer was a time for the Mercer Island High School basketball team to slow down, forget it.

The team, minus graduating seniors, is now in the middle of the 12th Annual Bellevue Community College-Nike Summer Tournament. The event, which takes place at BCC, began two

weekends ago with a jamboree and will run through the end of the
month with the championship game on Saturday, June 26.

Elimination play got underway this past weekend with 28
teams in four divisions facing off against each other. The Islander
squad opened play with two victories Saturday - against Kings and
Roosevelt. Roosevelt was the team that defeated Mercer Island for
the state AAA title in March.

"They didn't have anybody back from last year's team, we
didn't have anybody back, and the game wasn't really that close," said
Mercer Island coach Ed Pepple of Roosevelt. "This means we've beat
them four of the last five times - but we lost the one that really
counted," Pepple added.

Mercer Island has competed in this tournament each of the
13 years and has won it twice, including last year when the Islanders
beat Roosevelt in the final game.

The other teams in the Islanders' division besides Kings and
Roosevelt are Monroe, Ballard, Sammamish, and Lakeside. Mercer
Island will play Monroe, Ballard and Sammamish this Sunday, and
then face Lakeside Saturday, June 19.

Play is continuous at the college on Saturday and Sunday and
runs from 11 am to 4:30 pm both days.

June 22, 1982

Dynamic duo: MI's Pepple, Moscatel lead all-star team

Mercer Island's dynamic basketball duo, guard Kyle Pepple
and forward Al Moscatel, sparked the State Team to an upset 104-100
win over the highly favored City All-Stars in a June 15 game in
Yakima.

The contest, the first of the two-game series sponsored by the Washington State Basketball Coaches Association, was played at Eisenhower High School before a crowd of 2,500.

Moscatel was named most valuable player, scoring 32 points, pulling down 12 rebounds and handing out seven assists.

As he had done for the Islanders, Kyle Pepple was the floor leader who orchestrated the offense and helped State protect a narrow lead with a key steal and some stellar late-game ball handling.

With only 45 seconds remaining in the game, Joe Harris of Davis had a breakaway lay-in with the score 102-100 in State's favor. Pepple came from behind, stole the ball and enabled the State team to run 38 seconds off the clock before Al Moscatel was fouled. Moscatel hit the two clutch free throws to wrap up the victory with seven seconds remaining. The Islanders were assisted by 6'2 Jim Beeson of Chelan, who tallied 28 points.

The second game, played in Tacoma, was a City victory from start to finish and was not as close as the 100-91 score would indicate. Dwayne Scholten of Lynden Christian was the game's MVP as he tallied 18 points to help the City team even the series.

High-scoring honors, however, went to Mercer Island's Kyle Pepple, as he hit 10 of State's first 12 points, and finished the contest with 19 points, six rebounds and five assists. Moscatel got into early foul trouble, but sparked State in a late-game comeback along with Pepple, which helped cut a 20-point City lead down to only nine.

"I was extremely proud of both of our players," said State Coach Ed Pepple of the Islanders. "On paper the state team appeared hopelessly outclassed, but in Yakima Al was fantastic and Kyle played a key role even though he was in foul trouble. Without our guys the state team wouldn't have been in the game. They simply refused to lose and impressed a lot of people.

"In Tacoma, the city team proved just too strong, but Kyle played a superb game and Al was outstanding defensively. Mercer Island was well represented in the All-State games."

Moscatel and Pepple were two of 20 state AAA and AA high school basketball players chosen by the Washington State Basketball Coaches Association to play in the series.

PART THREE

1982-1983

"1983 was a season of last-second shots, either to tie games, win games or send us into overtime. It was heartburn for the coach, but it was really exciting for the fans."

- Ed Pepple

November 24, 1982

No losers disease: Basketball team has winning attitude

By Mike Westby

Of course Islander basketball coach Ed Pepple has a talented team.

Most coaches are drooling over the players this man has the luxury of parking on the bench. But it has not always been that way.

When a considerably younger Ed Pepple came to Mercer Island High School 16 years ago, his first job was to cure what was then known as Mercer Island-itis, i.e., "the losers' disease."

Pepple explains: "Mercer Island-itis was basically an attitude around the league that Islander kids had so much money they were spoiled and not willing to work hard. Everyone thought the Islanders were losers. The problem was that they thought like losers.

"If we were ahead, the kids had the feeling that they would eventually lose. If we were behind, they felt they couldn't come back," he said.

The "losers' disease", as Pepple calls it, was a real problem that first season, but the coach quickly treated the malady.

"It's simply a matter of the right attitude," Pepple explained. "I haven't heard the word Mercer Island-itis used since that first year."

And for good reason. Ed Pepple has amassed a 294-82 record by coaching the right attitude. It's a first-class act, from the military haircuts to the maroon-blazer road trips. "This is a team," said Pepple. "First and foremost, we are a team."

THE TOTAL TEAM CONCEPT has been an important and successful weapon in the Pepple basketball arsenal, annihilating all 14 of the Islanders' KingCo opponents last season enroute to a KingCo championship, a District title and a Regional crown. It ended in a bitterly extracted 58-52 win by Roosevelt in the state finals.

As for this season, Pepple says, "the mood is optimistic.

"We lost some people off of a highly successful team, but we have some fine players coming into the system."

Pepple lost nine seniors off last year's squad, including all-leaguers Kyle Pepple and Al Moscatel, second team all-leaguers Eric Schwabe and Joe Thompson, and honorable mention selection Rich Dewey.

Other seniors lost to the robes of graduation were Paul Jerue, AI Moscatel, Tony Grossi, J.D. Stern and T.J. Yurkanin.

"I think we have as talented a group as we had last year," Pepple estimated. "We might even be a little deeper than last season. We do lack experience though."

This group might well lack varsity experience, returning only one player from last year – forward Mike Williams – but the basketball experience they do have is not all that bad.

"We're taking on some players off the undefeated JV team," grinned Pepple. "I expect to see some good things from these guys."

SOPHOMORE GUARD QUIN SNYDER is one of the young men in whom Pepple places high hopes.

Snyder will be the playmaker in Pepple's fairly sophisticated motion offense, a role that will take some learning.

"The whole key is taking these talented players and teaching them a system. Quin has the talent. I think that he could be an all-timer. He could be all-league this year as a sophomore."

And, perhaps most important to Pepple, "He's a highly coachable kid," who's learning the system.

Bellevue transfer Paul Dammkoehler will play the off-guard spot for the Islanders with Williams at small forward.

"Paul and Mike are very similar in their style of play," Pepple said.

"They both move well and have good leaping ability. They're also the most experienced players on the team."

Williams, of course, played a part in the Islander fireworks last season, while Dammkoehler provided some sparks of his own, chipping in 20-points a game at Bellevue.

At 6 foot 7 inches, Scott Lammers looms heavily as the top candidate for the center spot, with the power-forward role going to one of three other players.

PETER LYON, a 6-3 finesse player with a deft touch from the perimeter, is battling for a fifth spot on the starting roster with Brian Schwabe, a 6-8 sophomore; Jorgan Light, and Bellevue Christian transfer Rob Mitchell, who Pepple describes as "the enforcer."

"It's still wide open at that spot," Pepple claims. "Any one of those guys could make it."

Pepple will be expecting some big help from a bench which he anticipates will get liberal use.

Sam Moscatel is the heir apparent at point guard. "Sam is the best defensive player we've got. He absolutely harasses the opponents."

Moscatel could be called on to rejuvenate the awesome defense that got the Islanders as far as the finals last season.

"If we can end up playing with half the defensive intensity we showed last year, we'll be fortunate," said Pepple. "That bunch could play defense."

FORWARDS MIKE HUBBARD and Laszlo Bedegi will be called on to contribute as well, according to Pepple, as will off-guard Rick Hodge.

"Everyone on this team will have an opportunity to help us," Pepple said. "And I believe that everyone can help us.

The Islanders take on Blanchet in a home game Dec. 4.

"It'll be a good one to watch," promises Pepple.

And the winner?

"I never make predictions," he said.

November 24, 1982

Transfer of athlete was 'family decision'

When 17-year-old Paul Dammkoehler and his family decided to move here from their Bellevue home so Paul could attend Mercer Island High School, they had no idea it would create so much flack.

"I guess when your son is a good athlete, people feel they have a right to know why his family is moving," said a weary Nancy Dammkoehler last week. "But they don't. It is our family's decision."

The Dammkoehlers have been besieged with questions since last summer, when they announced their plans to move from the Bellevue School District to Mercer Island.

Their son, Paul, an all-star basketball player as a junior at Bellevue High School last season, is considered by many the best guard in the KingCo League.

"Paul was not happy at Bellevue High," said Mrs. Dammkoehler. "It was not just a single issue, but a variety of issues. I can't discuss the details," she added. "We have agreed with Bellevue High that no one would discuss the matter."

WITH THAT AGREEMENT, Bellevue High released Paul Dammkoehler for transfer.

"The important thing for us was that Paul would have a happy and productive senior year," Mrs. Dammkoehler said, "so that he would be ready for the next four years."

Paul told the Reporter that his problems with the Bellevue athletic program were beginning to affect his academics as well.

"I talked about it with my parents, and we all felt that I should look for a more positive environment. Athletics are pretty important to me," he said, "and I guess the situation was getting me a little down."

He indicated that his family had been impressed by the academics and athletics at Mercer Island High School.

"It looked like a very good place for Paul to be," Mrs. Dammkoehler explained. "I think Bellevue has a fine academic program, but Paul was just not happy there."

So, the Dammkoehlers moved to an apartment on Mercer Island, and that is a key point to them.

"It's important to emphasize that we moved," she said. "I don't want to sound picky, but we have had a pretty rough time with this whole thing, and I want people to understand it wasn't just a case of Paul's transferring." The Dammkoehlers and Paul now live on Mercer Island. The only other member of their family, a daughter, is in school in the East, said Mrs. Dammkoehler.

THE DAMMKOEHLERS are meeting requirements of the Washington Interscholastic Activities Association, she emphasized. "The only important public information is whether or not we're legal, and we are."

A spokesperson for the WIAA said he saw no problems with the Dammkoehler transfer, which he described as "in accordance with all the rules."

Mercer Island basketball coach Ed Pepple, despite his well-known appetite for outstanding players, had nothing to do with the Dammkoehler transfer, according to Mrs. Dammkoehler. "I'm sure he was as surprised as anyone else here when Paul applied for admission," she told the Reporter. They've had no regrets, she added. "The administration, Ed, the kids, have all been fantastic. Paul feels really welcome."

Paul said he is eager to put the controversy behind him and contribute to Mercer Island High both on the court and in the classroom.

Dammkoehler headed the list of all-league selections in the KingCo League last season, averaging 20 points per game.

"He'll be a factor on this team," Pepple said. "Paul is a good jumper, he has a nice shot and he is capable of playing some fine defense."

For the Islanders, Dammkoehler is expected to start at the off-guard position.

December 7, 1982

Dammkoehler stars in Islanders' 74-65 win over Blanchet

It was fitting that senior guard Paul Dammkoehler buried the Blanchet Braves hopes of a last-minute comeback Saturday night with a picturesque and explosive one-hand slam-dunk.

Fitting because Dammkoehler had been picturesque and explosive all night long, especially in the opening period when he almost single-handedly blew the Braves out of the game. He hit the bucket five times off the floor and twice from the foul line for 12 first-quarter points and smoothed the way for a 74-65 win over a frustrated Blanchet entourage.

"I felt pretty good," Dammkoehler grinned after the game, "I was loose and shooting well, and everyone else was really doing their job. This was an important win for us."

The win sets the stage for a clash in Bellevue tonight at 7:30 p.m., a game that Dammkoehler and company are eagerly awaiting.

"The win gives us a good mental edge heading to Bellevue," he said.

Of the Blanchet game, Dammkoehler commented that the officials were calling an "unbelievably close one," which partially accounted for his five personal fouls – three in the first half.

HAD DAMMKOEHLER not gotten into early foul trouble, he might have been able to improve on his 21-point evening, though it's doubtful he could polish his 90 percent shooting percentage. Nevertheless, with the Bellevue transfer on the bench, Islander mentor Ed Pepple had to look elsewhere to preserve the playing edge that his Islanders maintained through-out the contest.

He did not have to look far.

Noted for their tremendous depth, the Islanders offered up several other hero candidates, among them sophomore guard Quin Snyder.

Snyder ran the point position to near perfection, tallying a team leading five assists and 14-points.

"For a young guard to come into his first varsity game and play the way he did tonight is truly outstanding," lauded Pepple. "This young man is going to be all-league if he continues like this."

Snyder didn't want to talk about his own accomplishments after the victory, but rather spoke of team contributions.

"This team is really coming together. This was a good test, and we really came through to pass it. We showed some people what we've got tonight."

SNYDER also got into early foul trouble, drawing two quick second-quarter calls, and joined Dammkoehler on the bench near the end of the first half as seniors Jorgan Light and Sam Moscatel came on in relief to hold onto a 36-26 halftime lead.

"Having Snyder and Dammkoehler on the bench is like (Seattle Supersonic coach) Lenny Wilkens playing without Gus Williams and (Jack) Sikma. But I can't say enough about our bench.

Sammy Moscatel, Jorgan Light and Rob Mitchell really did a job out there," Pepple said.

Light contributed five points on the night, while Moscatel and Mitchell poured in a bucket apiece.

Mike Williams quickly returned to last-season form, ripping the twines for 14 points with a 7 for 9 shooting night.

Scott Lammers and Brian Schwabe each had four blocked shots, a rather remarkable defensive stat made more significant by the fact that the duo also led the Islanders in rebounding with four boards apiece.

Dammkoehler and Light each had four rebounds, as the Islanders took a 28-24 edge in total rebounds for the game.

Mercer Island was unable to stop Blanchet's Chris Murray, who led all scorers with 28 points.

"Murray is just a sensational player," Pepple said of the senior guard. "We had gone to a zone defense pretty early because of the foul trouble, but he just had a typically good game."

The Islanders shot 31-45 from the floor, and 12-19 from the line.

December 14, 1982

Victory in Victoria for Island Cagemen

By Mike Westby

The regular season is far from over, and the Islander cagers are already champions.

The Islanders returned from Victoria, B.C. Saturday after scoring a Friday-night blowout victory over Mt. Douglas, 96-47 in the championship round of the Canadian tourney.

The schedule provided little difficulty for the polished Islanders. But while dribblers north of Washington may be singing the praises of Ed Pepple et al, the Islanders will have to convince a frustrated but scrappy Redmond squad of their true talents when they tangle with the Mustangs on the road tonight at 7:30 p.m.

Victoria is already more than convinced.

Senior guard Paul Dammkoehler led all scorers with 24 points in the Mt. Douglas game, followed by Brian Schwabe who had a career high 19 points.

Forwards Mike Williams and Jorgan Light each hit in double figures as did point-guard Quin Snyder.

Williams poured in 11 points while Light and Snyder came up with 10-point efforts.

Scott Lammers and Rob Mitchell had 5 and 3 points respectively. Rick Hodge and Sam Moscatel scored a bucket apiece.

The potent Islanders advanced to the championship by thrashing Nanaimo in the semifinals, 73-43.

Snyder, Dammkoehler, Lammers and Schwabe combined for 62 points to lead the Islanders in the victory.

In earlier tournament action, Pepple's troops marched over Kitsilano, 74-47.

The Islanders strung together 19, 20 and 21 points scoring blitzes to waltz away with the easy victory as Dammkoehler netted 16 points and Lammers rifled 12.

In Mercer Island's only league contest this season, the Islanders cruised past Bellevue 59-42.

Lammers dominated his inside post position, stretching his lumbering 6'7 frame to the boards for seven rebounds and leading the scoring with 12 points.

Williams scored 11 points in Bellevue, while Dammkoehler and Snyder chipped in 10 each.

The Islanders, 4-0 overall, will be looking to take over first place with a win in Redmond tonight. The Mustangs are 0-2 heading into the contest.

On December 14, Mercer Island defeated Redmond 70-51 in a game played at Redmond High School..

December 21, 1982

Cagers fight tough match but lose 52-48

By Mike Westby

Prep hoop fans packed into the tiny Bothell gym fully expecting to see a very fine basketball game; they came away seeing two.

Unfortunately for Islander supporters the one that eventually went in the record books was Bothell 52, Mercer Island 48, a loss that drops the previously unbeaten Islanders to 2-1 in league play (7-1 overall) as they prepare to face Interlake at home tonight at 7:30.

Game number one in the Bothell clash was played in the first half. It was a contest of speed, which the Islanders dominated.

MI point guard Quin Snyder gunned at will in the opening periods, shooting holes in a frustrated Cougar man-to-man defense. The wiry sophomore netted 12 first-half points and gathered a handful of assists as the Islanders battled to a 35-29 lead heading into the locker room.

That lead vanished in the third quarter, however, when Cougar coach Bob Morris abandoned his man-to-man defense and opted for the 1-2-2 zone.

"We had no choice but to go to the zone," Morris said after the game. "They had us pretty worried in that first half and we had to do something to shut them down."

The zone did that, holding the normally explosive Islanders to a meager four points in the third quarter, and allowing the Cougars to climb back into lead at 40-39.

"I think that Bothell really learned to respect us in that first half," MI coach Ed Pepple said. "They got us in the second half, but it was not because of the offense we were running, it was the way we were running it. If you hang back on these guys (the Cougars), they'll physically overcome you because they're so big and strong."

Despite the absence of three key players - Mike Williams (back), Rick Hodge (knees) and Scott Lammers (flu) - Pepple's cagers bruised their way back into the contest, rattling off seven unanswered points to chase a 46-39 deficit and tie the game with 2:13 on the clock.

You couldn't have heard a bomb drop as Paul Dammkoehler toed the penalty stripe to attempt the tying baskets. But without a flinch, Dammkoehler coolly squeezed off the crucial shots, quieting at least one side of the capacity crowd.

Teammate Pete Lyon repeated the feat with 32 seconds left in the game, this time bringing the Islanders back to within two at 48-50, and Snyder's theft of the Cougars' in-bounds pass offered Dammkoehler a 20-foot opportunity to send the game into overtime.

It's a comeback scenario that Ed People has directed many times in his coaching career. But on this night, it was not to be, as Dammkoehler's errant launch bounced off the bracket and Lyon's tip-in attempt located down into the waiting grasp of Bothell's Steve Morris. Nine seconds later, it was over.

"We're a young ball club and we'll learn from this," Pepple said. "We made some mistakes in judgment tonight that are bound to happen when you're inexperienced. But for us to come out here and play this close a game with them on their own court is something I can be proud of. We'll definitely be ready for them the next time."

Snyder, who wound up with 14 points on the evening, issued a similar warning to Bothell as he departed the gym.

"We showed a lot of heart out there tonight," he said. "We wanted that game, and we're gonna want it even more the next time."

Dammkoehler and forward Brian Schwabe were the only other Islanders to enter double figures as they tallied 10 and 11 respectively.

The Cougars' 6'7 Curt Brott led Bothell scorers with 14 points. Morris had 12, while reserve center Mike Hoffman poured in nine.

The two teams will meet again on Friday, Feb. 2, in the Mercer Island gym.

"I hope we both keep playing well so that the game really means something," Pepple said.

THE JV'S MEANWHILE had little trouble with Bothell turning back the Cougars 36-32 in the evening's earlier battle.

Scott Norwood led the Islander assault with 15 points, followed by Troy Carter with eight, and Jeff Patrick who had seven.

Coach Bill Clifford's club is now 2-4 and on the way back up with a two-game winning streak.

December 28, 1982

Islanders take Interlake in a breeze, 66-48

By Mike Westby

The Mercer Island High School "Animal Band" played accompaniment Tuesday night as the Islanders waltzed their way through Interlake to a 66-48 victory.

Mercer Island coach Ed Pepple called the steps from courtside as his Islanders darted out to a 14-4 lead, never to look back.

"It was pretty routine," Pepple said of the latest victory. "But even with the win, I can't say that I was pleased with the way we played."

Pepple indicated he was troubled by the Islanders' lack of enthusiasm. Which he attributed to the team's "poor physical condition."

"We're just in terrible shape," the coach said, "and that can really dampen your enthusiasm. Of course, Mike Williams and Rick Hodge are still out. And then we have Scott Lammers, Quin Snyder, Sam Moscatel and Paul Dammkoehler all playing while under the weather." All are recovering from the flu.

Dammkoehler came up with his usual numbers – 19-points and six rebounds – but was, according to Pepple, not at 100 percent.

"I could tell that Paul wasn't in his classic form. We'll take a few days off before returning to practice for the O'Dea game (Dec. 29), and hopefully, we can get everybody healthy and playing healthy."

Forwards Jorgan Light and Pete Lyon came up with sterling performances, netting 12 points apiece, a statistic not wasted on Pepple.

"I'd say that Light and Lyon had the biggest games of their careers Tuesday night. I was very pleased with the way they played. They were outstanding."

Scott Lammers, 6'7 center, provided the hub of a spectacularly tight defense that held the Saints to eight first-quarter points and only two offensive rebounds in the first five minutes of action.

Lammers, meanwhile, hawked the boards for a game-leading 11 rebounds and chipped in six points.

Pepple is counting on Lammers for a similar effort in the O'Dea game, which he predicts will give a good test to his defensive middle.

"O'Dea is a small, but very quick team," said Pepple. "We are bigger and slower, and we'll really have to rely on our size in the middle to win the game."

O'Dea features two fine players in Troy Miles and Eric Nelson.

Nelson, a solid 6'4 post, is what Pepple describes as a "banging type of player."

"Nelson's a fine athlete. He's very physical," said Pepple, "and a good shooter as well."

Tip-off time for the home game against O'Dea is 7:30 p.m.

January 4, 1983

Islanders fall to O'Dea; break home win streak

By Mike Westby

A blocking foul 40 feet from the basket by a player who was defending a one-point lead with barely a tick left on the clock is no way to lose a basketball game.

But that's exactly the way Ed Pepple's Islanders fell to O'Dea Wednesday night.

The Islanders, who led comfortably throughout the game until the last 43 seconds, took what appeared to be a game-winning 55-54 advantage on Paul Dammkoehler's clutch baseline jumper from 12 feet out with seven seconds remaining. But in attempting to draw a charging foul on the next Irish possession, MI drew the whistle, placing the contest's leading scorer, Troy Miles, at the penalty stripe for his 27th and 28th points of the evening.

Miles, who had scored at will all night, netted the pair to nail down the victory for O'Dea, simultaneously dropping the Islanders to 8-2, as they now ready for an away game at Juanita on Tuesday at 7:30 p.m.

"There is no way that we should have lost that game," said Pepple after watching an eight-point fourth-quarter lead erased by a series of Islander mistakes. "We were in control from the very beginning. We just made some mistakes in judgment at the end. I'd say we had at least 15 opportunities to win that game, but we didn't."

Pepple said that he does not blame any one individual for the loss and credited a fine performance by Miles for the Irish win.

For the Islanders it is the first loss at home in 18 games, a winning streak that trails back two campaigns to a 69-64 loss to Inglemoor in the 1979-80 season finale.

MI jumped out on top of the Irish 16-10 at the end of the first quarter and continued to outgun the AA team in the second, swelling the margin to nine points, 33-24, at halftime.

Despite giving some ground, the Islanders held on to the lead until the final 43 seconds, when Miles connected on two from the foul line to give O'Dea a 54-53 edge.

MI failed to score on the next trip down court and quickly fouled Miles with 16 seconds left.

Miles missed the front end of a one-and-one, Sammy Moscatel hustled the board and fed Dammkoehler for the pull-up jumper that put the Islanders back on top, setting up the last foul on Miles and the 56-55 defeat.

"If we are going to lose games," Pepple said solemnly, "losing them in non-league situations is the place to do it."

Dammkoehler led Mercer Island scorers with 28 points, firing 9-17 from the floor and hitting on 5-6 from the line.

Jorgan Light was next in scoring with 10 points, while Quin Snyder, who joined Scott Lammers in fouling out in the final period, had four.

O'Dea out rebounded the Islanders 35-32.

JUNIOR GUARD RICK HODGE, who has been sidelined with sore knees is expected to be back in action when the Islanders face Juanita tonight.

Mike Williams, on the other hand, is still out until at least the Sammamish game on Jan. 7 with a back injury.

The senior forward is the only returning MI letterman on the squad.

"We could definitely use Mike in there (against Sammamish)," said Pepple. "But we won't play him until he's ready, that's for sure."

The Islanders, according to Pepple, face two very tough KingCo League challenges this week from Juanita and Sammamish.

The Rebels will dribble a seven-game win streak into their Tuesday-night clash with Pepple's cagers, and Sammamish presents a formidable threat with its heavily-recruited big man, 6'11 Todd Anderson.

January 11, 1983

MI's Jorgan 'Lights' the way to week of win

By Mike Westby

Islanders basketball coach Ed Pepple left the Light on last week following his club's victory over Juanita Tuesday night, and the Sammamish Totems were not amused.

Senior forward Jorgan Light flashed on to score a career-high 20 points in the Islanders' 55-44 win over Juanita Jan. 5 and was still burning bright when Pepple sent him into blind Sammamish two days later. Light sparked a second-half fireworks display that blasted the Totems 38-27 in the final two periods as MI posted the 56-45 decision.

"Where have they been hiding him?" Juanita coach Bob Anderson quietly questioned after his team fell to the "Light Brigade" Tuesday.

"We've known what we had in Jorgan all along," answers Pepple. "I've always been aware of his special talents. I've just been waiting to see them in a game."

And Light couldn't have picked a better set of games to show them in.

"I was hoping for a split going into this week," Pepple said following the Sammamish win. "But I'll settle for this."

The ninth-ranked Islanders (now 5-1) will most certainly improve their position in the state basketball polls with last week's performances, especially the triumph over Juanita which debuted last week at number three.

Senior Paul Dammkoehler netted 14 points in the Juanita contest, collecting a game-high 10 rebounds.

THE ISLANDERS CAME out cold against Sammamish, scoring only one bucket in the opening frame, while yielding to the scoring whims of the Totems' 6'10 center Todd Anderson. Anderson hooked his way to eight of Sammamish's 10 first-quarter points, ending the evening with 23 points and game-high honors.

Light began to hit his jumper after intermission, opening the inside game to point guard Quin Snyder's deft passing.

Pepple lauded the defensive efforts of Rick Hodge, Scott Norwood and Rob Mitchell: "They were the real key to this win," he said. "They hung in there and just played a solid, tough defensive game."

The Islanders will play Inglemoor tonight at the Mercer Island gym before embarking on a string of three away games. Tip off for tonight's game is at 7:30 p.m.

January 18, 1983

Islanders in first place after 2 wins

By Mike Westby

Senior guard Paul Dammkoehler found the scoring groove again last week. After a two-game absence from leading the team in hoops, Dammkoehler, the Islanders' top scorer this season, netted a game-high 20 points to pace Mercer Island past Inglemoor 93-56 Jan 11, and pumped in another 16 to top the scoring in the Islander's 63-54 win over Newport Friday night.

The two victories – coupled with last week's loss by Bothell to Juanita – put the Islanders in first place in the Crest Division of the KingCo League.

Dammkoehler, who has been averaging over 14 points a game, is the sixth leading scorer in the KingCo League and did nothing to hurt his average last week as his combined performances earned him 17-25 stats from the floor for an 18-point average.

Senior Pete Lyon also played an instrumental role in the Islanders' two victories, as the sharpshooter fired 9-11 from the line enroute to a 13-point effort against Inglemoor and netted a pair of key baskets in the Newport contest.

The Islanders shot an efficient 50 percent from the floor to stroll past Inglemoor, taking a 36-23 lead at half time and outscoring the victors 57-33 in the last two frames for an easy win.

Point guard Quin Snyder dished out four assists on the evening while scoring seven points to aid the cause.

THINGS GOT A BIT stickier in the Newport contest as the Knights, down 57-36 after three, refused to roll over and nearly rolled over the Islanders in the late going with an 18-point surge that came nine points short of catching Mercer Island.

"I never felt that we would lose the game," coach Ed Pepple said afterwards, "But I'm sure the fans had some real concerns."

The Islanders will defend their first place standing at Lake Washington tonight. Tip-off is at 7:30 p.m.

On January 18, Mercer Island defeated Lake Washington, 69-50. Paul Dammkoehler scored 19 for the Islanders, bringing their record to 8-1.

January 25, 1983

Victory again: Islanders down Indians, 75-45

By Mike Westby

The Islanders basketball second team came off the bench Friday to outscore the starters 39-36 and embarrass Issaquah 75-45.

Pete Lyon, Sam Moscatel, Rob Mitchell and Brian Schwabe stripped off their warmups to enter the fray and returned from the hardwood with a total of 33 points.

"Instead of us putting guys in and the team slipping," said Mercer Island coach Ed Pepple, "we were able to maintain the degree of intensity throughout the game. The bench just did a super job Friday night. It was our best sustained effort in a long time."

Schwabe replaced a foul-troubled Scott Lammers in the opening period to net four quick buckets and lead the Islanders to a 19.8 first-quarter advantage.

Likewise, Lyon left the bench to ignite a 10-point scoring burst that sent the Indians down 42-24 at the half.

Starting forward Paul Dammkoehler was the only starter to render double digits for the Islanders, hitting 6-12 from the floor for 12 points.

Dammkoehler led the scoring in the Islanders' 69-50 victory over Lake Washington in the week's earlier action.

"Both games were simple," said Pepple, "But that is not the way we look at them coming in."

"We have to make sure that we don't catch ourselves relaxing against teams that have poor records," he said. "Our goal is to go into the Bothell game (Feb. 4) tied with the Cougars. Now, a loss to a team with a poor record is going to be just as devastating as a loss to a team with a good one. We just can't make any mistakes at all."

Mercer Island plays three of its last four contests at home, including the pivotal Bothell clash, which could decide the top spot in the Crest Division.

"We have been very pleased with the support that we have received from our fans. We've appreciated their attendance of the away games, and we'd like to think that we're a much tougher team at home because of the support we get there."

The Islanders will look for that home support when they take on Bellevue tonight at the Mercer Island Gym.

February 1, 1983

Islanders face Bothell to battle for top spot

By Mike Westby

It's been a week of big contests for the Islander athletic squads.

The wrestlers stunned Issaquah; the swimmers dunked Lake Washington; and now it's up to basketball coach Ed Pepple to ice the cake with a win over Bothell Friday night, Feb. 4. The Islanders and Cougars have battled all season long for the top spot in the KingCo's Crest Division, spending the majority of the time knotted in the first-place spot.

Bothell (11-1) heads into this week of action with a half-game lead over the Islanders (10-1), who were idle over the weekend. The Cougars had to struggle to get by Bellevue 43-35 on Friday to stay atop the standings.

Mercer Island trounced Bellevue 70-39 earlier in the week, led by Jorgan Light's 17 points.

Bothell and Mercer Island met last on Dec. 17, when the Cougars turned back the Islanders 52-48, in a split-tempo game that featured a first half dominated by MI's young point guard Quin Snyder, who netted 12 first-half points and gathered six assists.

The sophomore repeatedly took advantage of the Bothell defense, deftly firing scoring strikes to the likes of Paul Dammkoehler and Brian Schwabe, enroute to a 35-29 half-time lead.

"We just stopped attacking in the second half," Snyder said of the final two periods which saw a 12-point swing in the score that ultimately lost the game for the Islanders.

Cougar coach Bob Morris credited the turnabout to his change in defensive strategy, from a man-to-man to a zone defense.

"The zone took away their inside passing game," Morris claimed.

"It allowed us to use our size and power and shut their game down."

Islander coach Ed Pepple agrees that the Cougars are impressive in stature but does not foresee a repeat of the December conflict.

"Sure, they're big," said Pepple, "but we stayed right with them. And that was without some key people on the floor. We'll have some of those players back for this one."

Pepple guided a group of walking wounded into the Bothell gym for that first game. Rick Hodge and Mike Williams had been sidelined with knee and back injuries. Scott Lammers was out with the flu, and at least a handful of others, including Dammkoehler, were suffering from milder forms of the bug.

Of that group, only Williams, who is out for the season with back problems, will not suit up.

Snyder has been dealing with some back aches of his own, but otherwise the Islanders appear to be in top physical shape for the game.

"They'll be playing a different team Friday night," said Pepple.

"It should be a great game."

The contest will feature several interesting matchups, not the least of which is the battle of the middle to be fought by MI's Scott Lammers and Curt Brott.

At 6'7, BOTH PLAYERS cut imposing figures in the middle, though Brott outweighs his island adversary by a hefty 25 pounds.

"Brott may be the best offensive center in the league," said Pepple, "but I don't think that there is a finer defensive center in the league than Scott Lammers. I may be a little prejudiced, but Lammers has proven to me this season that he has no equals in the league defensively."

Lammers is coming off an impressive defensive showing against Bellevue in which he totally intimidated the inside, blocking six shots.

Brott faced Schwabe, the sophomore back-up, in December and was held to 14 points, a bucket under his season average. Against Lammers, Pepple is looking for Brott to become even less of a factor.

Brott has been more than simply a scoring machine this season, though, menacing his share of would-be scorers, and gathering a reputation as an enforcer.

His expansive frame is only the most visible sign of his intimidating style of play. Harnessing the power to bench press most KingCo backcourts, Brott could give Lammers the true test of how far his defensive abilities extend.

IN THE BACKCOURT, the Islanders' top scorer, Paul Dammkoehler, will pair off with the Cougars' Steve Nohr.

When they last met, Dammkoehler and Nohr were stalemated, but the Islander guard had been under the weather, Friday's rematch will provide each with a chance to showcase some exceptional scoring talents. But look for Dammkoehler to prevail. Nohr has been averaging just over 10 points per game this season, while Dammkoehler has hit a steady 14.

"And he could be scoring more," said Pepple. "This is a team-oriented offense, so Paul doesn't score as much as he could (he scored 20 points a game at Bellevue last year) but he does other things that help the team. He has become a more well-rounded ball player, though I'll look for him to score more points in the big games ahead."

THE SHOWDOWN AT point guard pits Snyder, a sophomore, against Steve Morris, a 13 points-per-game scorer and liaison to the muscular midsection of the Cougars game, Brott and Joe Petridge.

Snyder has come on so strong in his first year as the trigger man of the Islanders' potent offensive weapon, as to draw regional acclaim as an up-and-coming all-leaguer. Pepple calls Snyder "a great talent with all-timer potential."

Snyder seems to have overcome his early tendency to force the ball in the middle – a trait that could prove fatal against the Cougars – and has begun to settle comfortably down into his role as MI's leading assist man.

PETRIDGE DRAWS THE unenviable Light, who surfaced a few weeks ago to score a career-high 20 points against Juanita.

Light has since hit games of 14, 8, and 17 points.

"Jorgan is playing much better than he was in December," said Pepple. "I'm sure he'll make it interesting."

Pepple said that he loves close games like this one. "I prefer it to being favored by 16 points. That's not much fun."

"We played well enough last time to win it if we had had all of our players," the coach said, "and now we do."

The Islanders face a challenge from Redmond tonight before taking on the Cougars.

Both games are at the Mercer Island Gym and begin at 7:30 p.m.

February 8, 1983

Islanders cork season in overtime win against Bothell

By Mike Westby

Very few so-called "title games" live up to the expectations of the ticket-buying public. Media-hyped games are a dime a dozen, but a true championship contest is as rare as a bottle of Chateau Lafite Rothschild, '53.

The sour-grapes expression on Bothell coach Bob Morris' face Friday night said it all: it's been a good year for the Islanders.

In fact, the standing-room-only crowds of 2,500 who savored the Islanders' overtime triumph over Bothell might be enjoying coach Ed Pepple's '83 basketball squad even more than last year's would-be state-champion crop.

"It's a different type of team," says Pepple, whose club avenged its only KingCo setback this year by downing Bothell in a 42-40 rematch. "This team does what it has to win. They play with a lot of presence. Last year's team didn't have to do that to win games."

This year's team has done it often with a feisty group of over achievers who make up for a certain lack of experience – no returning lettermen – with scrappy efforts and plain hard work.

"They really worked for this one," lauded Pepple in the locker room just minutes after Islander guard Paul Dammkoehler swished a 20-foot jumper with four seconds left in the first overtime period to break a 40-all score and lift MI (19-2) into first place in the Crest Division.

"They played a heckuva defensive ball game. When you hold a club like Bothell to just 40 points," he explained, "that's really saying something for your defense."

Forward Rob Mitchell and center Scott Lammers were able to handle the Cougars' bruising tandem of Curt Brott and Mike Hoffman quite effectively in the game, although Brott finished the evening with a game-high 18 points, four of those coming from the penalty stripe late in the fourth quarter.

"I thought that Rob Mitchell was a real key to this win," commented Pepple. "He really made Brott think about what he was doing out there. Everything that Brott had, he earned. Mitchell was exactly what we needed out there."

Mitchell, who replaced Lammers in the middle after the Islanders center got into foul trouble, had no points for the game but came up with eight rebounds, all of them at seemingly key moments, and played menacing defense on the league's best offensive center.

BOTH CLUBS GOT off to poor starts, hitting under 30 percent from the floor in the first half, as the Cougars stretched out a 7-0 lead early in the first frame, and closed the period on to 11-8.

The tight nerves and forced shots continued throughout the following stanza with the Islanders managing to climb back to within one at 16-17 by intermission.

"When you can't shoot the ball well," Pepple said, "you have to do something to get it going."

That something for Pepple involved a perimeter, ball-control offense that attempted to bring the Cougars out of their bread-and-butter zone and open up the middle.

Pepple went to the slowdown tactic with 6:07 remaining in the third quarter and a one-point (20-19) lead. He credits the change in strategy for the victory.

"That was the difference," he said. "It really won the game for us… we got some big buckets while we were in that offense."

In bringing Bothell's big men out from under the hoop, the Islanders were able to regain the tempo of the game, according to Dammkoehler, who indicated that the Cougars had dictated the style of the contest up to that point.

"I think that we were playing their type of game in the first half," Dammkoehler said. "No question. But we were playing it our way later in the second half."

Unlike the Islanders' Dec. 17 loss to Bothell (52-48), the local boys dominated the boards this time, out-rebounding the bigger and stronger Cougars 37-22.

"I didn't expect that," Pepple said. "We had emphasized rebounding this week, because we knew that we would have to do well on the boards. We didn't expect to win (the game) under the boards."

The Islanders, plagued with 17 turnovers and only four visits to the foul line, wound up relying on the rebounding of Mitchell, Lammers (6), Dammkoehler (7) and Jorgan Light (5) to ultimately swing the game in MI's favor.

"I think that we're a lot better rebounding club than people think," said Pepple. "We only got out-rebounded by Bothell 36-34 the last time we played them. And they were without Lammers."

The clubs ended regulation play knotted at 38, and were again tied at 40 when Dammkoehler buried the ball from the top of the key. The Cougars hurried the ball up the floor and Steve Morris let fly with a 28-foot boomer that air balled five feet short of the rim.

Mercer Island closes out the season at Interlake tonight and faces Juanita at Hec Edmundson Pavilion Feb. 15 to decide the KingCo championship.

February 15, 1983

Islanders are in it again; championship game tonight

It wasn't just a case of Mercer Island grabbing another division championship when the Islanders dismantled Interlake 76-52 last Tuesday night.

In addition to sealing another Crest Division title and a chance at Juanita at 8 p.m. tonight (Tuesday) in Hec Ed pavilion, the game served as a benchmark of sorts.

Scott Lammers used the occasion to break the Mercer Island record for career blocked shots. The senior center's whopping 76 rejections surpasses the mark of 74 set by former Islander, Husky and Portland Trailblazer Peter Gudmundsson.

Lammers, a 6-foot-7, 200-pounder, was within one of tying Gudmundsson's record heading into Interlake.

MI guard Paul Dammkoehler, meanwhile, used the occasion to mark the scoring of his 1,000th high school career point.

Dammkoehler, a senior transfer from Bellevue, has been averaging over 16 points a game this year and ends the regular season with 1,003 total career points.

Ed Pepple marked his 387th career win as a high school basketball coach – his 315th at Mercer Island.

Tonight, he hopes to mark his ninth victory in a Crest Division Championship game.

"It's what we've been looking forward to all year," said Pepple. "We're excited about playing and we're ready to have a good game."

The Islanders are sporting a healthy roster with the exception of starting point guard Quin Snyder, who has a twisted ankle.

"His status as of Friday," said Pepple, "is he can't put weight on it. But we hope to have him back. We'd definitely miss him."

Juanita may, or may not, have the use of their leading scorer J.D. Taylor. Taylor, who has been averaging 19.1 points a game, has a bad knee.

"We have to assume that J.D. will be playing," said Pepple. "That is how we'll prepare for the game. J.D. is a great player and I'm sure if there is any way he can be in there, Bob (Juanita coach Bob Anderson) will play him. Either way," he predicted, "It's going to be a great game."

The winner is the number one seed in the Sea-King Tournament. The loser is the number two seed and will face Metro's number two team.

That night, Juanita overcame Mercer Island in the last second to beat the Islanders 68-67 and capture the KingCo Conference title. J.D. Taylor led the Rebels with 23 points, with Jorgan Light contributing 20 and Paul Dammkoehler 16 for MI.

The Islanders entered the Sea-King Tournament as a #2 seed, set to face off against Garfield of the Metro Conference.

February 22, 1983

Islanders book a room at the Heartbreak Hotel

By Mike Westby

It doesn't get any closer than it was in Bellevue Friday night. Or any better.

Mercer Island and Garfield – rated second and third respectively in the state's AAA basketball poll – fought through two over-time periods before the Bulldogs finally escaped with a 74-73 victory in front of 1,700 bedazzled fans at the Bellevue High School Gym.

The Islanders' next bout is with Sammamish at 8 p.m. tonight (Tuesday) in the Garfield gym.

Friday night, senior guard Paul Dammkoehler knocked down a 15-footer just ahead of the final buzzer to give the Islanders a 68-68 tie at the end of regulation play, aping a last-minute comeback that saw MI erase a five-point deficit in 22 seconds.

Dammkoehler, who led all scorers for the evening with 25, leveled the score again with 13 ticks left in the initial overtime on a breakaway bucket.

Teammate Jorgan Light gave the Islanders a one-point lead at 73-72 on a hat trick, but Garfield's Jeff Woods put the Bulldogs up for good with three seconds left, popping out from under the hoop for an easy basket.

"I've been waiting for that basket all my life," Woods admitted gleefully. "I would have preferred a jumper, but I'll take it, I'll take it."

Garfield advances to the district semi-finals against Blanchet at Ingraham High School (8 p.m. tonight), while Mercer Island enters the losers' bracket against Sammamish at Garfield.

If the Islanders win the Sammamish contest, they will face the loser of the Franklin-Inglemoor game at the Seattle Center Arena Friday.

"We're not thinking about that yet," said MI Coach Ed Pepple, whose club lost another heartbreaker earlier in the week to Juanita 68-67 on an at-the-buzzer tip-in. "We're concentrating on Sammamish. We aren't out of this (the tournament) yet. This just means that we have to win the next eight in a row if we want to win the state championship."

Considered by many to be the premier team in the state, Garfield moved out to a 5-0 advantage over Mercer Island, only to be buried in the wake of an aggressive Islander attack that blitzed the Dogs 21-6 in the last seven minutes of the opening frame to close the period on top 21-11.

"We thought that they might have underestimated us," Pepple explained. "Our game plan was to let them know right away that we weren't going to hold back at all. We were going to take it right at them."

A typically awesome rebounding club, Garfield stumbled under the boards in the first half as Scott Lammers and Rob Mitchell dominated the key, giving the MI backcourt ample opportunity to light up the scoreboard.

Needless to say, Bulldog coach Al Hairston was not a happy man in the first half as Mercer Island mounted a 21-16 lead mid-way through the second quarter.

"We just weren't executing well at all," Hairston recalled after the game. "That's why I called that time out."

The Garfield mentor stopped the action at 2:32 in the second, down 14 points.

The Bulldogs immediately gunned off six unanswered points to close the gap to seven, 32-25, but the Islanders came up with a pair of buckets in the final minute to pull back out to a 36-27 half-time cushion.

Down 42-31 in the third quarter, Garfield swung the tempo, recapturing the control of the rebounding battle and holding the Islanders scoreless through a seven-point scoring spree.

Bulldog Glen Tinned rocked the gym with a stylish jam that brought Garfield to within four at 38-42; Pete Lyon responded with a clutch jumper at the other end and a big defensive board on the ensuing Garfield possession, but Woods netted a bucket at the end to tie the score at 36 heading into what appeared at the time to be the final period.

Garfield took command of the fourth and led 64-59 with 32 seconds left in the game.

What transpired in the next half minute was almost unbelievable.

Garfield's Eric Briggs missed the front end of a one-and-one opportunity. Schwabe gathered the rebound and was fouled.

Schwabe buried number one to make the score 64-60. He missed the second, Dammkoehler got the rebound but missed and Sam Moscatel collected the board and scored, making it 64-62 with nine seconds remaining.

Moscatel quickly wrapped up Tinned, sending him to the foul line where he again missed; outlet pass Paul Dammkoehler – tie ball game.

"We have real confidence in Paul to take that last shot," Pepple said. "We have other guys who can take it as well though."

Light made the free throw that put MI up by a point in the closing moments of the last overtime, but 28 seconds was too long to hold the Bulldogs as Woods finally steaked open for the winning layup.

Both coaches agreed the game was as good as any they've coached.

"That was the best game I've been involved in as a coach," proclaimed Hairston. "We wanted to play Garfield," responded Pepple. "We knew it would be a great, great game, which it was."

It was also a great game that almost never was, as academic violations by Garfield forced a last-minute juggling act in the tournament seedings.

Garfield, which forfeited five games because a reserve player had reportedly falsified his grades, dropped from Metro number one to Metro number three. The change made Blanchet the new top seed and put Franklin in the number two spot.

Garfield found out about the violation and notified Metro Athletic Director Barbara Twardus, who met with SeaKing Chairman Don White and decided to keep the tourney pairings as they were.

The two reportedly made the decision to avoid creating a turmoil in the tournament but had not foreseen the turmoil that was soon raised by Sea-King coaches and athletic directors, all of whom maintained that, if Garfield was no longer the number one Metro representative, it should not be seeded as such.

Finally, the Sea-King officials met to vote on the matter and decided to change the seedings.

"I am not disappointed that we played Garfield (as a result of the change)" said Pepple. "I'm disappointed that two people got together and decided to arbitrarily make the decision without consulting anybody. That is not the way to do things. The least that could have been done is to talk to the various representatives. Ideally, they should have talked to all the schools to see how we felt about it."

In the end, however, Pepple said that the right choice was made.

"It was the only thing to do, he said. "If you have a system, then you have to go by that system. The tournament is for the kids, not for the convenience of the coaches and administrators."

Matching up against league rival Sammamish on February 22, the Islanders entered the fourth quarter of their second game at the Sea-King Class AAA District tournament down 51-36 to the Totems. Guards Quin Snyder and Paul Dammkoehler quickly turned on the heat, helping Mercer Island tie the game 60-60 with 30 seconds left.

Coach Pepple called a timeout and set up the final play, where Dammkoehler drained a 17-footer with three seconds left on the clock for the Islander win.

After the game, Pepple addressed the fired-up team in the locker room, as reported by the Seattle Times. "Don't you guys ever tell me that anything's impossible," he said. Later, he turned his attention to the press, calling the game "one of the greatest comebacks in basketball history" and saying that the rally didn't really surprise him. "I told the kids at the end of the third quarter that if they hung tough and kept the pressure on, that they had a chance."

Quin Snyder led the fourth quarter surge with 10 points and finished with 14 for the night. Dammkoehler finished with a team-high 15, and Scott Lammers added 11 for the Islanders.

The next night, in a loser-out game, sophomore forward Brian Schwabe led the Islanders in their rout over Inglemoor, 67-51, putting up 21 points, including 10 in the second quarter. Paul Dammkoehler added 20 of his own before Pepple took him out of the game for good with 4:17 left to play.

The win gave the Islanders that chance to compete for third place in a matchup against Blanchet the following night, at Seattle Center Arena. "It's a great matchup. We're very similar teams," Pepple told reporters. "I think it's going to boil down to who wants it most, and who's executing and shooting."

March 1, 1983

Blast that buzzer: Blanchet 50, Islanders 48 in MI's finale

by Mike Westby

Blanchet coach Steve Segadelli said he beat one of the best coaches in the state when his club knocked off Ed Pepple's Islanders 50-48 on a last-second shot at the Seattle Center Arena Saturday night.

Pepple, meanwhile, feels the Segadelli-led Braves beat one of the best teams in the state.

They're both probably right.

The Islanders, now 20-5 and out of the playoff picture, dropped yet another contest in the final second, as Blanchet sophomore Charlie Wickstrand sent up an eight-foot prayer that was answered at the buzzer.

"We've lost five games this season by a total of seven points," Pepple noted ruefully after the game. "I've never had a season with so many at-the-buzzer finishes. We've won some of them, and we've lost some of them. I just wish we wouldn't have given them (Blanchet) the chance to shoot that shot."

The Islanders, who scripted a similar finale against Juanita in the KingCo championship game – losing 68-67 on a Brian Bischoff tip-in - took a 48-46 lead over Blanchet with 26 seconds remaining on a single Paul Dammkoehler free-throw.

Wickstrand sank a 12-footer to knot the game at 48 with 14 seconds left.

"We wanted (Jorgan) Light and Dammkoehler down court to receive the ball on that last play," Pepple explained of the game's final 14 seconds. "Quin (Snyder) was to bring the ball down."

But that's not exactly what happened.

Light fired the inbounds pass to Snyder, who was pressured and unloaded back to Light. Light then proceeded to win his way down court with the ball where he got trapped by Blanchet's Chris Murray and Jeff Zenier.

Zenier made the steal and exploded down court to attempt the winning basket. The shot came hard off the glass and Wickstrand managed to snare the ball. He turned and fired the game winner as the last second disappeared from the scoreboard.

"When Zenier took that shot, we all went to the boards pretty hard," recalled Wickstrand later. "Murray went for the tip but it hit his hands and came to me. I was just hoping it would go in before the buzzer and it did. I've been dreaming about putting us in the state with a basket like that ever since I came to Blanchet."

Pepple's only regret was that Wickstrand had the opportunity to send up that "dream shot."

"We made some mistakes at the end that gave the ball game away," said Pepple. "I have to accept the blame for that. I guess I just didn't communicate what I wanted them (the players) to do. Blanchet is a good team, but I don't think they are better than us. We had that game. "

Blanchet was set to key heavily on Dammkoehler during the final Islander possession, Zenier said in describing his steal of a Jorgan Light pass that set up the winning shot.

"Coach Segadelli just told us to get in his (Dammkoehler's) face and not let him shoot the ball. But then we saw that Light had the ball and we knew he was not that good a handler. We knew he would have to put the ball on the floor. I just overplayed him and made the steal."

Dammkoehler's hot hand gave the Islanders an early command in the Sea-King tournament game, as the 6–3 guard buried his first four attempts to net eight of MI's 14 first quarter points.

And things were looking bleak for Blanchet when Sam Moscatel came between a brave exchange and streaked unguarded for a hoop that put MI up 16 -9 in the opening moments of the second.

"I have to admit that I was concerned," said Segadelli. "I didn't want to get too far down."

The Islanders stretched the lead out to 20-14 before Wickstrand and company woke up and responded with a quick three buckets and took the lead on a Murray free-throw.

The two teams traded buckets to intermission with Blanchet leaving the court up 28-26.

With both Lammers and Schwabe in foul trouble, Blanchet was able to work the Islanders inside and escape the third stanza on a 39-34 cushion.

Schwabe hit two big buckets in the opening of the fourth and Light glided through the key to pick up a pretty three-point play giving Mercer Island the lead at 41-39.

Light hit again three minutes later breaking a 45 -45 deadlock, and the Islanders went into a stall.

Wickstrand forced the turnover and was fouled by Schwabe enroute to what would have been an easy layup. The foul sent Schwabe out of the game and Wickstrand to the stripe for two attempts with 1:19 remaining.

Wickstrand bricked the pair, Zenier collected the rebound and was fouled by Snyder.

Zenier, who finished with seven points, hit one of the two. Dammkoehler did the same at the other end and Wickstrom got the last two hoops.

In getting to the final district playoff game with Blanchet, the Islanders disposed of upstart Inglemoor the previous night, 67-51.

Schwabe, Lammers and Rob Mitchell held Inglemoor's 6-7 Kevin Love to six points. The East Coast transfer had terrorized Juanita in earlier action, scoring 30.

Lammers once again intimidated the middle, blocking seven shots in the back-to-back games.

"We would've been playing better when we got into the state tournament," lamented Pepple the morning after. "That's the kind of kids these are." Instead, Pepple's cagers hang up the sweat socks for another year. "But" warns the coach: "We'll be back.

The summer of 1983 would prove to be eventful for basketball fans on Mercer Island. On June 23, Paul Dammkoehler appeared in the state all-star game, hosted by Mercer Island High School, where he scored 12 points suiting up for the "City" team against the "State" team in his final game in the Mercer Island gym before enrolling at the University of California at Santa Barbara.

A capacity crowd of 1,600 fans packed the gym, including Pepple, who witnessed the State team outscore the City team 121-105. "City seemed to rely much more on one-on-one basketball, and consequently found themselves taking hurried and bad shots, whereas the State team played together much better, and seemed more concerned with team victory than individual statistics," Pepple told the Seattle Times.

The weeks of June 20 and 27th, Pepple held training clinics, as he did each and every summer for boys in grades 3-12 at the Community Center at Mercer View.

Meanwhile, incoming juniors Quin Snyder and Brian Schwabe spent their summers preparing for what would be their breakout season, one that would bring national prominence to Mercer Island basketball and produce two highly-touted Division 1 recruits.

PART FOUR
1983-1984

"I don't think the people of this state have seen the last of Mercer Island.
We will be back."

- Ed Pepple

November 29, 1983

Island cagers making a safari through the KingCo jungle

By John Shanahan

Few people who follow prep basketball in Washington would argue the fact that the KingCo league is a jungle, and Ed Pepple is king.

In 16 years on the KingCo prowl, Pepple and his Islanders have dismembered opponents in and out of the league, compiling a 314-87 record. Along the way Mercer Island has picked up nine league titles in the last ten years, while ranking in the state's top ten teams six times.

With the 1983 KingCo "hunting season" about to open, Pepple says the jungle has become a lot trickier, but still not too tricky for Mercer Island. "KingCo will be tougher than ever," he says. "And our Sea-King division will undoubtedly be the toughest in the state, but I think Mercer Island will have the versatility and talent to play anybody."

At the center of Pepple's versatility is a motion offense that revolves around starting low post Brian Schwabe (6-9 junior). Schwabe is a returning forward from last year's squad. As a sophomore, he was third in Islander scoring behind departing seniors Paul Dammkoehler and Jorgan Light. Schwabe also shot an impressive 54.9 percent from the floor and averaged 8.5 points a game. When Schwabe wasn't shooting he also managed to grab 198 rebounds on the season.

"I'll LOOK FOR Brian to carry the bulk on offense," Pepple says.

"He's our Jack Sikma. I'm sure he will be one of the best big men in the state for the next two years, and we'll be going to him a lot when the pressure is on.

"But we have enough balance so that no team will be able to key in on just one or two players."

Along those lines, the starting combination of co-captain Sam Moscatel (5-9 senior), and Quin Snyder (6-1 senior) at point and shooting guard positions ought to open a can of offensive worms suitable to jinx any defense.

In Pepple's motion offense, the point guard does most of the ball handling. "It takes an intelligent player who knows how to guide the other players under pressure." Pepple added. "That's just the kind of player that Sam (Moscatel) is."

Last year Moscatel, playing at point, had 63 assists and 39 steals, while averaging 3.6 points on 57 percent shooting from the field.

Snyder will be looked upon to do the scoring from the other guard slot. Last year he was fourth in overall team scoring, averaging 7.6 points a game on 45 percent shooting. Snyder also got 123 assists and 53 steals on the year.

"I expect Snyder will be one of the best, if not the best guard in the state," Pepple adds. "The thing about him that is so special, is that he can shoot out or drive in. He can also play point guard if we need him there, and that will leave another option open to us, but we really don't need him at point with Sammy there."

At backup shooting guard the Islanders can call on either co-captain Rick Hodge (6-0 senior), or Scott Norwood (6-2 senior).

"The thing about Hodge and Norwood," Pepple says, "is that Hodge is left-handed, and Norwood is right-handed. That should give defenses something to think about on coverage. I also expect Hodge to be a very aggressive player this year, because he missed nearly the entire season last year due to knee injuries."

A PLAYER THAT Pepple will be taking off the injured shelf from last year, to start this year, is small forward Mike Williams (6-4 senior). "Mike is probably the most versatile player we have on the team," Pepple says. "He can play short forward, or guard, and can shoot from the outside or drive."

Williams should have graduated last year, but a severe back injury forced him to stay out of school most of the year. In 1981 Williams averaged 6-4 points per game on 46 percent shooting, while pulling down 9-1 rebounds, 40 assists and 27 steals.

Rounding out the starting five for MI is Scott Weller (6-3 junior). "Weller is the glue to our team," Pepple says. "He is not a great scorer, but he's intelligent, unselfish and he can play the good defense."

Pepple looks for Shawn Lightning (6-0 senior) to be making a sizeable contribution from the bench, along with Gregg Dean (6-1 senior), Chris Strickland (6-2 senior), and Geoff Swanson (6-6 junior).

Mercer Island opens its 1983 season with a jamboree starting at 7:30 p.m. on Dec. 1 at home against Lake Washington, Eastside Catholic and Kennedy. On Dec. 3, the Islanders will travel to Blanchet at 7:30 p.m.

"The Blanchet game should be a good match." Pepple says. "Last year they beat us by one point in the consolation final at Sea-King, to stop us from going to state.

Mercer Island beat Blanchet in their season opener. On December 6, Quin Snyder had 24 points and Mike Williams 23 to lead the Islanders in a 75-44 win over KingCo rival Bothell.

Three nights later, the Islanders, playing without center Brian Schwabe (out for the second straight game with a sprained ankle) had no trouble taking care of Bellevue, beating the Wolverines 79-52 behind Quin Snyder's 20 points, with Sam Moscatel adding 12 and Mike Williams, 10.

The next day, Mike Williams' 19 points led the Islanders to a 78-31 victory over visiting Davis of Yakima, improving their record to 4-0.

December 12, 1983

All in the family

From grid to hoop, Schwabe brothers a talented trio

By John Shanahan

Most families consider themselves lucky to be blessed with a single athletic child, and rare are the parents who count two athletic prodigies among their offspring. But when MIHS Principal Larry Smith married Carolyn Schwabe and adopted her sons, he found that athletes, and good luck, come in threes.

"When I met their mother, and married her," Smith said, "I knew that was good, but I had no idea the boys would turn out to be such a bonus."

The first signs that these were unusual kids came in 1973 when the family lived in Vancouver, Wash., where Smith was principal of Columbia River High School. In the fall of that year, the eldest Schwabe boy, Paul, then 11, took an interest in kicking footballs. By the time Smith accepted the principal's job at MIHS and the family moved here in 1974, Paul was booting the pigskin up to two hours a day, while brothers Brian and Eric assisted him.

AS A PRINCIPAL, Smith was no newcomer to youthful endeavors in sports. His own son, Mark, even grew up to play college football for the Missoula, Montana Grizzlies, but Paul's kicking was different than that.

"I've never seen a kid so dedicated to something at such an early age," Smith said. "He (Paul) would be out there rain or shine, day in and day out."

Apparently, Paul's dedication started to pay off by the time he hit high school age. Punting and playing split end for Dick Nicholl, Paul started what became a Schwabe tradition of winning varsity letters in all three high school years.

After being intensely recruited by the University of Washington, the Air Force Academy and Montana State, Schwabe graduated from Mercer Island High in 1980, and decided to attend the University of Oregon as a walk-on.

Beating out a highly touted scholarship kicker to win the starting nod in his freshman year, Schwabe went on to letter all four years at the UO. As a senior this past season, the (6-1, 185 pound) 21-year-old tied an Oregon record for most successful field goals (12 of 18) in a single season. In two games Schwabe hit three field goals, including one for 51 yards in the 16 to 17 Oregon victory over Stanford.

A 30-yard Schwabe boot was also the only thing that stood between the Huskies and a shut-out when they beat Oregon 32 to 3 earlier this year.

Schwabe will graduate with First Team, All-Academic Pac 10 honors this spring. At that time, he'll hope to put his French-speaking ability, and international relations degree to work in a business capacity. That is, if some football scouts don't come knocking on his door first.

"If someone gives me the opportunity, I would love to give pro ball a try," he said.

While Paul is proud of his football, the thing he is most proud of, he said, "is being able to compete and keep up my academics as well."

COMBINING ATHLETIC and intellectual pursuits is apparently a Schwabe tradition. Middle brother, 19-year-old Eric (6-5, 195 pounds), graduated from MIHS in 1982 with academic honors, as well as three varsity letters from Ed Pepple's basketball program.

In his freshman year at the UW, Eric walked on the junior varsity basketball squad. This year he is sitting on the varsity bench, "putting in his time," he said, until the day when he might hold down a starting position.

Also much like his elder brother, Eric takes both school and sports seriously. "I study pretty hard, because I'm trying to get into the school of business next year," he said. "It can be tough mixing classes and a varsity sport in college. That doesn't leave you with much time for either."

Since the family moved to Mercer Island, Eric has focused on his basketball as his principal outlet, but in Vancouver he was a competitive tennis player. And in the sixth grade, he became the second runner-up in the state of Oregon Chess Championships for that age group.

With Eric's secondary school athletic career already behind him, and his collegiate career just getting started, he said he doesn't know where all this will lead him but he's content just the same. And being born between two brothers who also happen to be sports stars hasn't caused any sibling discord yet.

"Paul, Brian and I are at a good balance of friendship and competitiveness," he said, "It is a good kind of competitiveness, and I like being in the middle. That way I can both give and get advice, especially where Brian is concerned."

As a (6-9, 200 pound) 16-year-old junior and starting center for MI basketball this year, Brian is the "baby" of the family. He traces his competitive basketball days back to when his sixth grade Little Dribblers basketball team won a national championship. "That experience really showed me what it's like to have a future in basketball," he said.

Since that time, Brian's goal has been to play Division I basketball. It is a goal he moves closer to every year. This summer, Brian was selected by University of Washington coach Marv Harshman as one of the best high school players in the state and sent to a special Athletes For Better Education Seminar at Princeton University.

"There were scouts there from all the best basketball schools in the country." Brian said. "Being the youngest brother out of three to play for MI, people put a lot of pressure on me to perform well in the basketball program here, but after this summer, I can see the pressure is going to get a lot tougher as time goes on. But I know in my own mind, that I have got to keep my priorities straight. For me, right now, academics are number one."

FOR LARRY SMITH, raising three bona fide jocks has not been difficult at all. "I really credit the programs up at the high school a lot for helping these kids," he said. "But the most surprising thing has been how much they support one another. They call each other on the phone all the time to see how things are going."

Sometimes, Smith said, he wishes the boys wouldn't be quite so supportive of one another. "The long-distance calls alone this year back and forth from Seattle and Mercer Island to Eugene have cost a fortune."

December 20, 1983

BOYS' BASKETBALL

Mercer Island boys' basketball tightened their grip on KingCo's Crest division first place, with an 80-48 victory over Interlake on Dec.13, and a 67-56 decision over Redmond on Dec. 16.

Mercer Island jumped out to a 19-10 lead over Interlake at the end of the quarter, and in the third period, MI outscored the Saints 28-2.

Leading the Islanders offensively were Quin Snyder, and Sam Moscatel, each with 18 points. Brian Schwabe had 15, followed by Mike Williams with nine, Shawn Lightning with eight, Rick Hodge with six and Geoff Swanson with four. Chris Strickland and Eric Brandy each had one point.

In the game against the Redmond Mustangs, MI's Schwabe had 21 points, Snyder had 17, Moscatel 12, Weller six, Williams six, Lightning four and Hodge one.

MI will travel to O'Dea on Dec. 21 for a non-league game.

December 27, 1983

Hoopsters pull off win despite icy conditions

For years Ed Pepple's squads have done a good job of leaving tennis-shoe tracks all over their basketball opponents, but on Dec. 31, the MI hoopsters squad might have been better off to wear ice skates.

Despite freezing conditions better suited to a hockey match than a basketball game, the MI boys' basketball team avoided both O'Dea and frostbite long enough to pull off a 71 to 56 victory in the unheated O'Dea Gymnasium last Wednesday night.

The non-league win upped the Islanders' season record to 7-0 and proved that it takes more than a very aggressive division AA team and a mild ice storm to bring down this year's Islander squad.

"O'Dea is one of the better AA teams in the state," Pepple said after the match. "Their center, Eric Nelson, has an excellent chance of being all-state in Division AA this year.

"Playing them at O'Dea in an unheated gym right before the holidays was a very good challenge for us, and I think the boys did a good job. O'Dea is a very physical, aggressive team."

Besides containing Nelson's offensive threat and coping with Old Man Winter's wrath, the Islanders went into the contest short-handed. Senior guard Rick Hodge, who was back in the lineup for a Dec. 26 Hawaiian departure, missed the entire O'Dea game with a knee injury, while point guard Sam Moscatel played with stomach cramps.

But if Moscatel was hurting, he hid his agony well, scoring 8 points and getting three steals. "Sam did an outstanding job of running the offense," Pepple said, "He had a perfect game in terms of having no turnovers of his own." Moscatel also tied Quin Snyder for a game high 7 assists.

Junior center Brian Schwabe contributed significantly to the overpowering Islander offense, adding a game-high 24 points to the MI total. Schwabe's point total equaled a season high set by Quin Snyder against Bothell on Dec. 6.

On defense, Schwabe was faced with the task of containing Nelson, whom he held to 23 points, 11 on free throws.

"Brian played well against Nelson," Pepple said, "Nelson was smaller and faster than Brian, so it was tough for Brian to cover him, but he still did a good job." Schwabe had a team-high 8 rebounds, followed by senior forward Mike William's 6.

"All the boys played well," said Pepple, who stuck to a conservative game plan that had only six Islanders see action until the final moments. "The game didn't warrant a lot of substitutions," Pepple added. "I just stuck with what I call my 'Iron Men,' my starters."

And all of Pepple's "Iron Men" produced. Both Snyder and senior forward Mike Williams scored 11 points. Junior forward Scott Weller tallied 9, and senior forward Shawn Lightning 6. In the final moments of the game Omar Parker nailed his first-ever varsity points on two free throws.

In the fourth quarter, MI as a team made 14 to 16 free-throw attempts, as a desperate O'Dea tried foul their way back into the ball game. Throughout the game, MI made 17 of 21 free throws, while O'Dea sank 16 of 17.

Islanders Island-bound

The Mercer Island boys' varsity and junior varsity basketball teams will depart Mercer Island for slightly more exotic Hawaiian environs this week. The teams will see action at Waipahu on Dec. 29, then travel to a second match at Iolani on Dec. 30.

For the Islander squads, however, their Hawaiian breather will be short and sweet. The teams will hit the boards with Newport on Jan. 4 on Mercer Island.

January 3, 1984

Hoop squads show OTHER Island Islander talent

Mercer Island High School cagers highlighted their holiday trip to Hawaii with basketball wins at Iolani and Waipahu.

The MI basketball team humbled last year's Hawaiian prep state champion Iolani squad by a score of 79-45.

MI's Brian Schwabe ripped through the Iolani defense like a monsoon through a straw hut for 23 Islander points. But the Islander game plan was definitely not a one-man show as Chris Williams added 15 points, Gregg Dean 10, Rick Hodge 7, Quin Snyder 6, Mike Weller 5, Omar Parker 4, Geoff Swanson 3, Paul Roberts 2, Shawn Lightning 2, and Sam Moscatel 2 to round out the Islander effort.

ON DEFENSE the Islanders also had a good night, holding Iolani to just four points in the third quarter.

The cagers warmed up for Iolani with a 64-44 luau a-la-Pepple at Waipahu High School on Dec. 29.

Snyder scored 16 points in the game for an MI game high.

The Islanders had strong offensive showings from many players, including Williams with 10 points. Hodge, Strickland and Schwabe each had 8.

The Islanders outscored Waipahu 20-11 in the first quarter, and 38-16 in the first half.

The hoop squad will meet Newport at home on Jan. 4, then travel to Inglemoor on Jan. 10.

Fresh off the heels of their Hawaii excursion, Mercer Island returned to their gym where they dismantled Newport, 101-51. Quin Snyder contributed 30 points on 14-16 shooting, while Brian Schwabe added 20 points and 12 rebounds. At the time Mercer Island was ranked the 12th best high school boys basketball team in the nation by USA Today, with their KingCo rival Juanita coming in at #10.

January 17, 1984

Roundballers win two more

MI boys' basketball jumped out to a 13-2 lead over Inglemoor, before squandering their lead, and narrowly defeating the Vikings 59-54 on Jan. 10.

Mike Williams missed the game with the flu, and Scott Weller was less than 100 percent, said coach Ed Pepple.

"The only good thing about this game was that we hit some free throws in the stretch, and did not choke in the pressure situations," Pepple said.

On Jan. 13, the Islanders won a 54-49 decision over Sammamish.

Pepple credits guard Sam Moscatel with excellent defense on Jim Toole of Sammamish, who had been averaging 13 points a game this season. "Weller also had a good defensive game," Pepple said. "It was our defense that won this one for us since we were both outrebounded and outshot."

MI, now 13-0 and ranked 1st in the state this year, will meet 2nd-ranked Juanita tonight, Jan. 17, and Issaquah on Jan. 20.

January 17, 1984

Tonight's the night

Fans gets some good basketball tonight

Tonight, when the No. 1-ranked Islanders' invite No. 2-ranked Juanita into the Mercer Island gym for some hot basketball action, the outcome won't decide the state championship.

It won't even clinch this year's KingCo title race.

In fact, Mercer Island head coach Ed Pepple says, "At this point in the season, our most important games record-wise are within our Crest division of KingCo." (Juanita is in the Crown division.)

Nevertheless, when the maroon-and-white Islanders meet the Rebels tonight at 7:30 p.m. in the MIHS gym, it will be about the biggest game any Islander team has ever played.

Both Mercer Island and Juanita head into "The Game" with 13-0 records. AP has ranked the Islanders 1st and the Reb's 2nd in the state, while nationally, Juanita is 10th, the Islanders 12th among prep squads ranked by USA Today.

In most contests, such rankings would overshadow everything else, but tonight the rankings will take a back seat to something much more important – pride.

IT STARTED in 1971, when an upstart school named Juanita entered the KingCo league. Today, 12 seasons later, it has developed into the hardest-fought rivalry in the history of the league. In the past dozen seasons, MI has run up a 13-7 edge in games with the Rebels.

In that same period, MI has captured nine league titles, while Juanita has bagged three.

Last year the Islanders and the Rebs each won a game as the series continued. Mercer Island handed Juanita its first loss on Rebel turf since 1978, ending a 46-game Juanita home hot streak. But Juanita redeemed itself by clipping MI in the KingCo title game.

"Tuesday's game is just like round one of the wars we are going to be having with Mercer Island this year," said Juanita guard Todd Webster last week. Webster averages 11 points a game, and along with Juanita forwards J.D. Taylor and Steve Evenson, carries the brunt of the Juanita scoring load. "This is a big game, a very big game and a big rivalry for us," he added.

"This game is going to be for the state and national rankings, but it's also going to be for the pride of both schools," said MI's 6-9 center junior Brian Schwabe. "Just look at the traditions these schools have going."

Coach Pepple enters the game with a career record of 326 wins. Juanita's coach Robert Anderson, meanwhile, has built up a 415-159 record. Anderson has already announced that this will be his last year of Rebel coaching, and his leaving adds yet another dimension to "The Game," since his squad will surely want their coach's memories of the Islander gym to be pleasant ones when he hangs up his whistle a few months hence.

BOTH coaches downplayed the importance of the state and national rankings, and said that despite the ranking, they will try to keep the game in perspective.

"Games are not won on television, or in radio station and newspaper ratings," Anderson said.

"I think being number one is what it's all about," said MI coach Ed Pepple, "but I want to be number one when it counts, at the end of the state tournament next March."

Pepple said he doesn't expect any big surprises in tonight's game. "When you have two teams who are 13-0, you won't see anybody changing things very much."

That means the Islanders must settle down and play good defense on Taylor and Evenson, 2nd and 5th in KingCo scoring, averaging 21.8 and 16.4 points apiece. At the same time the Islanders must run their "motion" offense, which revolves around league top scorer Quin Snyder, who averages 22.2 points a game, and Schwabe, who averages 18.2.

"The guys from Juanita are all good guys," Schwabe said. "We've all known each other a longtime, but we are going to have to put that friendship aside for one night and play with the better friends on our own team."

January 24, 1984

REBELROUSERS

They showed no mercy to the gang from Juanita

By John Shanahan

Brian Schwabe and Quin Snyder were thick as thieves, but it was the Islander team defense that ripped the Rebels when Washington's No. 1-ranked Mercer Island met No. 2-ranked Juanita in "The Game" on Jan. 17.

And the MI animal band couldn't have been happier.

The lanky Snyder, the Islanders' 6-1 junior point guard, blistered Juanita for 22 points with his patented outside jump shot mixed with drives to the hoop, while the 6-foot-9 Schwabe dissected Juanita's defense underneath for 22 points and 14 rebounds.

Sam Moscatel contributed 6 points from the number 2 guard spot, and Scott Weller added 9 Islander points from his forward slot.

"Of course I was pleased with the way Schwabe, Snyder, Moscatel and Weller played," said MI coach Ed Pepple, "but those boys can go out there and do that every night. The two kids I'm especially happy with are Geoff Swanson (6-6 senior center) and Paul Roberts (6-6 junior center)."

Swanson and Roberts were just two of five players Pepple used to fill in for Mike Williams (6-4 junior forward), MI's third leading scorer who injured a foot against Sammamish.

SWANSON AND ROBERTS did not play that much (about 10 minutes each) nor did they score a lot of points (6 combined), but the two played a crucial role in the game plan that Pepple used to torpedo Juanita's one-two offensive punch of J.D. Taylor and Scott Evenson.

Coming into "The Game," the 6-7 Evenson and the 6-5 Taylor, both of whom have already signed letters of intent to play Husky hoop ball for Marv Harshman next year, had a combined average of 37.4 points a game. But Mercer Island denied the two hotshot Juanita stars with a 2-1-2 zone defense that held the duo to just 26 points. A key part of that zone was the intimidating presence of Swanson and Roberts on the MI baseline.

The zone defense, unusual for the Islanders who normally play man to man, was the idea of Ed Pepple and his brain trust of assistant coaches.

"Juanita had scouted us every single game this year, and so we thought we would do something to surprise them," Pepple added. "It was our game plan to come out in a zone. We felt like we had to stop them on the baseline and force them to beat us outside."

To say the least, Pepple's ploy was a success.

In the first quarter, Juanita's Evenson was held to no points at all, and even though Taylor scored 8 in that period, MI held a 16-10 edge going into the second quarter.

On offense, the Islanders repeatedly passed the ball to Schwabe, forcing a direct matchup between MI's and Juanita's big men. "We wanted to get pressure on Taylor and Evenson," Pepple said. "We did not want to let them just stand there."

IN THE SECOND PERIOD, Evenson was temporarily retired to Juanita's bench with 3 fouls and 2 points. He returned to score 10 points in the second half, but the Schwabe-Taylor mismatch worked to the Islanders' advantage.

Mercer Island opened its largest lead of the game at 23-14 in the middle of the second period. Juanita closed that gap to 27-24 with a minute to go in the half, but MI entered the locker room with a 31-26 lead.

In the third period, the Snyder-Schwabe connection boosted MI to another 9-point spread of the night as the Islanders led 42-33 mid-way through the period.

But in the words of Islander guard Moscatel, "Those guys just wouldn't quit." And from the middle of the third to the middle of the fourth period, Juanita outscored the Islanders 12-4.

Evenson capped the Juanita surge when he stole an Islander inbounds pass, bringing the Rebels to trail, 46-45 with 6:51 to go in the fourth quarter.

With just 1:08 on the clock, MI breathed easier as Moscatel sank both ends of a 1-1 to put the Islanders up 59-55.

The last seconds ticked off the clock as Roberts fittingly pulled down the game's final rebound – after J.D. Taylor's last second prayer missed.

INSTANT MAYHEM broke out among the 2,000 mostly-Mercer Island fans packed standing room-only the gym.

The crowd swarmed onto the court to the raunchy strains of the Animal Band's rendition of "Another One Bites the Dust."

MI'S 65-57 victory over Juanita extended the Islanders' season record to 14-0, established MI as the undisputed frontrunner heading into the postseason tournaments, and set up a rematch with Juanita – who else? – in the Feb. 13 KingCo title game.

"I don't think we had any trouble running our offense," Pepple said after the game. "We came down and shot selectively. We just didn't crank up the first decent thing that came along.

"Another factor was we didn't have many fouls," he said. Juanita had 25 team fouls compared to Mercer Island's 18.

Mercer Island made use of the team foul situation with one of its hottest displays of free throw shooting this year. Led by Quin Snyder, who went 12-13 from the line, MI sank 27 of 33 free throws for 82 percent.

"We were a poor free throw shooting team early in the year," Pepple said, "but if we keep going at this rate, we might break the team free throw record."

When asked if he thought "The Game" lived up to all the pregame hype, Pepple responded, "I don't think it was anything less than it was supposed to be. Everybody thought this would be a big game and it was. The teams thought so and the fans thought so. I'll bet the 300 people who didn't get into the gym thought so."

After posting a 27-33 free throw shooting performance against Juanita, Seattle Times staff writer Craig Smith asked Coach Pepple how his team did it. Pepple credited a drill he'd picked up from Morgan Wooten, the nationally famous coach at Maryland's DeMatha High, and brought back to Mercer Island.

The drill is to shoot sets of 10 free throws. A player hitting 9 or 10 gets a "permission", 7 or 8 is "break even" and below 7 is "suicide". Any player with a suicide must run sprints. A permission can be used to cancel a suicide or it can be traded or sold to another player. A "privilege", more valuable than a permission, is earned for good play in a scrimmage, hitting 20 free throws in a row, or offered at Pepple's discretion.

Some ticket-holding fans were left out in the cold

Reports that "several hundred" ticket-holding fans were turned away from last Tuesday's Mercer Island-Juanita game are "totally untrue," said Gary Snyder, Mercer Island High School's associate principal in charge of athletics.

Snyder said that 142 ticketed fans were not admitted to the contest. Of the surplus ticket holders, 140 purchased presale tickets at Juanita High school.

"It is a standard KingCo policy that schools sell advance tickets to away games (Juanita sold 400), but such tickets are subject to availability of space," Snyder said. "Just holding a ticket is no guarantee that you are going to get into the game, you also have to be in line."

Snyder added that ticket holders are not the only people entitled to get into regular season games. KingCo season pass holders, parents of team members, the press, college scouts and any students with an Associated Student Body (ASB) card need not purchase tickets to attend games.

For the Mercer Island-Juanita game, the large turnout of students, press and parents, as well as hundreds of people buying tickets at the doors, overflowed into space which would have been used by presale ticket holders.

Snyder said the crush of fans was so great that an estimated crowd of over 2,000 filled the gym in less than 40 minutes. After filling the bleachers which seat 1,800, the crowd filled another 140 seats which had been set up at the normally open east end of the court, and onlookers stood or sat in virtually every remaining space left in the gym.

All 142 fans who had tickets and did not get in received refunds.

January 24, 1984

Hoopsters trample Issaquah

With Quin Snyder shooting 10-16 for 23 points, MI boys basketball trampled Issaquah 57-44 Jan. 20.

Islander guard Sam Moscatel added 8 assists and 6 points. MI will play away at Bellevue tonight, and at Interlake on Friday.

Coach Ed Pepple says Shawn Lightning, Moscatel, Eric Brady and Mike Williams are doubtful to play in this week's games due to injuries.

January 31, 1984

Upset time

Nobody was as surprised as Ed Pepple last Friday night when Interlake tripped up the then-undefeated Islanders 69-60 in a contest at Interlake.

The Islanders had been coming off a 38-35 escape of Bellevue's delay game tactics on Jan. 24.

Interlake played the Islanders in a man-to-man defense, which held them to within 4 points of the Islanders, ranked 10th in the nation by USA Today, until late in the fourth period.

The Interlake loss was the first of the season for the now 17-1 Islanders.

February 7, 1984

Juanita showdown coming Feb. 13

Mercer Island guard Sam Moscatel's first quarter steals helped the Islanders build a commanding 20-4 lead by the end of the quarter, on the way to clobbering Bothell 82-48 on Jan. 31.

Moscatel ended up with five steals for the game, as coach Pepple emptied his bench, allowing 13 Islanders to see action.

Quin Snyder scored a game high 18 points for the Islanders. Brian Schwabe hit for 13, while Moscatel had 11.

Snyder's 10 third quarter points were what the Islanders needed to break open a 27-20 half-time score on the way to beating Woodinville 66-41 on Feb. 13.

Brian Schwabe hit for 13 points and grabbed nine rebounds in the game. Rick Hodge tallied 10 points on 5-5 shooting from the field.

Mercer Island missed the services of the starting trio of Mike Williams, Scott Weller and Sam Moscatel against Woodinville. Coach Ed Pepple said it is possible one or more of the sidelined players will be healthy to play against Redmond at Mercer Island on Feb. 7 in the Islanders' final regular season contest.

Mercer Island will then meet Juanita in the KingCo championship game on Feb. 13 in the Seattle Arena at 8:30 p.m. Depending how they do in that game, they will play in a district play-off game on either Feb. 17, 21 or 24.

February 14, 1984

Lightning helps zap Mustang streak

Riding high atop a nine-game win streak, the Redmond Mustangs built up an 11-5 lead over Mercer Island, before being zapped by none other than Shawn Lightning and falling 63-52 to the 19-1 Islanders in Mercer Island's final regular season game last Tuesday night.

Mercer Island then advanced to the KingCo Championship game against Juanita on Monday night. If they win, they will meet either Redmond or Sammamish on Friday at Interlake at 7 p.m. If the Islanders lose the Juanita game, they'll play Ingraham at Woodinville at 7 p.m. on Friday.

COMING OFF the bench in last Tuesday's game, Lightning creased the Mustang defense with passes to Brian Schwabe, who exploded for a team high 25 points on 10-16 shooting underneath. Quin Snyder was MI's second leading scorer with 17.

"One of the keys to this game was Shawn Lightning," said MI coach Ed Pepple. "He was the catalyst that got the ball in to

Schwabe." Pepple also credited Lightning with shutting down Redmond's offensive threat, Joe Meinecke. "Stopping their top scorer is as good as scoring yourself," Pepple noted.

MI's Paul Roberts went 3-4 for 9 points, as the 19-1 Islanders hit for 49 percent from the field to Redmond's 45 percent.

On February 14, the Seattle Times reported on Mercer Island's KingCo Conference championship game against Juanita, played before a sellout crowd of 5000 fans at Seattle Center Arena, where the Islanders beat the Rebels, 54-49.

The nets came down just before the Islanders were presented the school's sixth KingCo conference trophy since 1974, the year the league went to a title game format.

The Islanders built a 36-18 halftime lead, with Quin Snyder scoring 10 of the Islanders first 12 points. The Islanders were outscored 13-7 in the third as Juanita gained composure. "We weren't executing," said Coach Pepple, "we were reaching for the ball standing around..."

In the fourth quarter, the Rebels cut the lead to 45-37 and Juanita's Sam Spiller drove for a lay-in with 4:10 left to make it 45-39.

Sam Moscatel, who Pepple said "isn't our best three throw shooter except in the clutch," hit a pair to make it 47-39 and another pair at 2:13.

Snyder scored 14 points in the first half and finished with 16.

Mercer Island plays Sammamish Friday night at Interlake High in the first round of the Sea-King district playoffs. Third ranked Juanita opens the same night with Ingraham at Woodinville.

Also on February 14, the Times ran a feature on Islander point guard Sam Moscatel under the headline, "Sammy is what makes MI Run". Coach Pepple was interviewed for the story and referred to

Moscatel as "the engine in the chassis, the real catalyst to our basketball team, the guy who makes us go."

Sam, the younger brother of former Mercer Island star Al, got his first ever varsity start in the 1983 KingCo championship game, after regular starter Quin Snyder sat out with a bruised thigh.

Although Mercer Island lost the game on a tip-in at the buzzer by Juanita, Moscatel scored 10 points and played "near flawless ball," said Pepple.

"The job that he did was just incredible."

Moscatel never figured he'd factor in much on the varsity team. "I was hoping I'd be able to play. I wasn't able to shoot the ball that well and I was short. They list me at 5-9. I guess defense plays off in the end," he told the Times.

"We have a formula which we call team value based on different things - turnovers, points scored," Pepple said. "In terms of team value, the leader on our team is not even close. Sam has the highest team rating by probably 25% over any other player."

Pepple said the only real similarities in the way Sam and his older brother Al play is their intensity and their competitive nature. "Sammy leads our team in all the things that don't show up in statistics," said the coach. "He's our captain as voted by the players. He's also the key to our defense."

In the previous season, Moscatel started on the varsity but was demoted to the JVs, where he got the team back on track. After four games, Pepple brought him back up to varsity and he's been there ever since.

"He's shooting 62% from the floor for the season," said Pepple. "People don't think of him as being a great shooter. But the thing that makes him so valuable is that he doesn't take any bad shots. He is handling the ball for us most of the time and his turnover ratio is incredible.

"I'm never surprised at anything Sam does because his heart is as big as a gymnasium."

On February 17, Mercer Island (21-1) beat the Sammamish Totems (12-11) 82-47 to open the District tournament, with Quin Snyder putting up 17 points and adding 5 steals. Brian Schwabe also contributed 17 points. "That's my kind of start," Ed Pepple told the Seattle Times.

February 28, 1984
Islanders take on Curtis, push for shot at a state title
By John Shanahan

A 79-55 rout is nothing to be happy about, but Islander coach Ed Pepple didn't need to look far to find a silver lining after last Saturday's loss to Juanita.

After beating the Rebels once in the regular season, and again for the KingCo title, losing the class AAA boys Sea-King District title to them was bad, but not that bad.

"If there is ever a good time to lose to a team, this was it," Pepple said. "We knew coming into the game that we already had a berth at the regional tournament, and so this game didn't have the impact that a loss to Juanita would have had earlier this season."

MI (22-2) will continue in the Region II tournament Friday against (22-1) Curtis at Renton High. The game is tentatively scheduled for 9 p.m. If the Islanders win that game, they'll automatically qualify for the state tournament March 8, 9 and 10. If MI loses, they'll play a must-win game on Saturday to continue in the tournament.

AGAINST JUANITA, trouble came soon for MI, when 6-9 center Brian Schwabe picked up his fourth foul at only 5:03 in the first quarter. With Schwabe on the bench, Juanita's J.D. Taylor and

Steve Evenson led the revenge-starved Rebels to an early 16-8 edge. On the night, Evenson and Taylor would combine for 39 points, while Schwabe was destined to play a total of only 4:23 before fouling out for good in the third quarter with no points.

And center wasn't the only position where MI was short-handed. Sam Moscatel, MI's star point guard, saw only 12 minutes of action due to injury, while Paul Roberts and Rick Hodge sat out the entire game due to sickness and injury.

"It's just one of those things," Pepple said.

Another one of "those things" was Scott Weller's inspired performance in the losing MI effort. Weller shot 7-10 from the floor and 8-8 from the line to lead MI with 22 points. MI guard Quin Snyder hit for 19 points on 9-20 shooting, but the show was all Weller's. "Scott played the best game I have ever seen him play," Pepple said.

MERCER ISLAND REACHED the Juanita game by winning a 57-53 decision over the Garfield Bulldogs last Tuesday.

MI forward Mike Williams scored 18 points, including a pair of clutch free throws with 23 seconds left to put MI on top to stay 54-51. At the end of the first half MI led 29-18, and the Islanders pulled out by as many as 13 in the third quarter, before Garfield outscored MI 16-5 in the start of the fourth quarter to go on top 47-46 with just 3:14 to go. Garfield led by as much as three before Williams hit a jumper and Weller nailed two free throws to go ahead 50-49.

"These kids had a lot of courage to battle back like that," Pepple added.

March 6, 1984

Islanders 'steal the show' in final-seconds drama with Curtis

By John Shanahan

When Sam Moscatel graduates this spring, Islander hoop coach Ed Pepple might just hang a sign in the Mercer Island gym saying: "THIEF WANTED, EXPERIENCE UNNECESSARY." Because when it comes to basketball steals, "Sammy" is King; he will be missed.

Though Moscatel leads Mercer Island with 72 steals this season, those other robberies pale in comparison to last Friday's supreme rip-off when – with 23 seconds to go – Moscatel stripped the ball from Curtis guard James Redburg, drove the length of the floor and scored the winning basket in a 54-52 comeback win in a Region II state playoff game at Hec Edmundson Pavilion.

IT WAS A PIECE of first-class hoop thievery. Call it Sammy's Whammy, because it was nothing less than grand theft basketball. But unfortunately for the Curtis Vikings, that's not a felony in Washington.

Not only did the steal give 23-2 MI the game, the victory catapulted the Islanders directly into the final eight-team showdown in the Boys AAA State Basketball championships this Thursday, Friday and Saturday at the Center Coliseum.

Adding insult to injury, the MI win snapped a 19-game Curtis win streak, while sending the Vikings into a must-win qualification game with Auburn last Saturday night.

IN THE FIRST round of Coliseum action, MI is slated to meet the 22-1 Richland Bombers at 10 p.m. in the quarterfinals Thursday night. If the Islanders win that game, they'll play at 8:30 p.m. on Friday against either Garfield or Foss in the semi-finals. If Mercer Island wins the game, they'll advance to the championship game at 9 p.m. on Saturday.

If Mercer Island loses in the first round against Richland, they will advance in the losers' bracket action at 10 p.m. Friday.

Presale tickets for the Thursday and Friday games will be on sale at Mercer Island High School this week.

"Richland is a big rivalry for us," said MI coach Pepple. "We have a big following, and so do they."

There is also no love lost between the two teams, since Mercer Island defeated Richland by two points in their last meeting at the 1981 state quarter finals. "It should be a hyper night," Pepple added. And the coach, facing his seventh "final eight" appearance in 14 years, isn't looking for his squad to advance into the losers' bracket on Friday either.

"If we play our best, our chances are as good as anybody's to go all the way. We are going to have to get a lot of performances out of a lot of kids, but if we are playing our best, we can beat any other team that is playing their best."

WHILE NO MERCER Island team has ever captured a state title, if a team ever played like a champion, this one did last Friday night.

"It was a gut win," Pepple said after the game. "There wasn't any coaching, no finesse. It was just the kids out there. This was their win."

MI fell to a 12-2 first quarter deficit, and trailed 32-43 late in the third quarter, before battling back to take a 50-49 lead on a Brian Schwabe free throw with 3:01 left. Schwabe scored 13 of 16 MI fourth quarter points, and a team high 25. A Schwabe bucket with 1:02 remaining tied the game at 52, and Curtis was playing for a last shot, when Moscatel looted the Viking hopes for a win.

Thursday night, March 8, the Islanders stormed past Richland in a 69-53 first-round victory to open up play at the state tournament. The next day, the Seattle Times ran a photo of Quin Snyder on the front page of the sports section going for a layup over two Richland players, with an accompanying headline, "Mercer Island shooters bomb Richland in the am."

After hitting only one of his first six shots, Snyder sank his next six jumpers, finishing with 22 points on 10-18 shooting from the field. Schwabe contributed 16 points and 9 rebounds.

"I don't think anybody could have beaten us tonight," Ed Pepple told the Times.

The Islanders were supported by "a couple thousand MI residents and the wacko Islander animal band that showed up wearing a variety of nuclear related clothing – construction helmets, protester garb and lab coats, plus WPPS signs in the tubas" (a nod to the now-decommissioned Hanover Nuclear Reactor site near Richland). The crowd was the biggest of the eight-game day, with a total of 10,876 fans inside the Coliseum to watch.

On March 9, Mercer Island punched its ticket to the state championship game by beating Foss of Tacoma, 59-43.

Brian Schwabe scored 19 points - 17 in the first half - and grabbed a game-high 18 rebounds over the Falcons. Of his performance, Foss Coach Wayne Dalesky told the Times, "We haven't played anybody that big who is that good. He's everything everybody said about him."

"The fourth time's the charm, I hope," said Pepple when asked about his chances of finally winning a state title.

The biggest story of the tournament, however, would be the showdown between the top two teams in the state in the championship game, both ranked nationally by USA Today throughout the season.

Juanita coach Bob Anderson, preparing for retirement after this final game, said about Mercer Island: "They're who we wanted to play, absolutely. We wanted to play them for two reasons: first we want to wipe out the minds of everyone that the KingCo's conference can't win a state championship. And then from the rivalry standpoint, they pounded us twice and we wanted to play them again.

On March 10, 1984, Brian Schwabe and Quin Snyder were the only juniors named to the Seattle Times' Star-Times list of the top basketball players from Seattle-area schools for the '83-84 season.

March 13, 1984

Lost opportunities lead to a heartbreaker at the hoop

By John Shanahan

Ed Pepple stood outside a quiet Islander dressing room at the Seattle Center Coliseum after Mercer Island lost a 59-56 heartbreaker to the Juanita Rebels in the class AAA state basketball championship Saturday night.

Pepple's voice – normally loud and brimming with the confidence of a coach who has amassed 411 prep varsity wins – was reduced to soft tones as he discussed the game with reporters.

"When you have two outstanding teams on the floor, one of the team's got to win," he said. "They just played three points better than we did tonight.

"Mercer Island and Juanita are both definitely great teams. You could have them meet each other ten times, and they'd probably each win five times."

In fact, Mercer Island and the Rebels did meet four times this year, with each squad winning twice. Mercer Island beat Juanita in the regular season, and again for the KingCo championship. Juanita took home victories in the Sea-King title game and last Saturday's state title match, which was Juanita coach Bob Anderson's last game before retiring as head Rebel.

"My leaving won't change this rivalry," Anderson insisted.

"Every time these two teams meet it'll be a great rivalry."

In character, Mercer Island and Juanita played like great rivals last Saturday.

THE TWO CLUBS battled to early ties at four, six and eight points, before Juanita opened up a nine-point lead at 27-18 late in the first half. Despite shooting a lukewarm 10-28 from the field, MI came back to close the margin to 3; the score was 31-28 in favor of the Rebels at halftime.

In the third quarter, Quin Snyder got eight of his game-high 24 Islanders points to spark the Islanders to a 14-4 scoring spree, giving MI a 42-35 lead with 2:48 to go in the third quarter.

But the game's momentum swung to the Rebels, as MI starters Scott Weller and Brian Schwabe fouled out of the game within 90 seconds of each other in the fourth quarter. When fouls sent Schwabe to the bench, MI still led 52-48 at 5:15. Juanita's J.D. Taylor, the game's MVP, tied the game and put the Rebels on top by sinking two free throws a minute later. But it could have been anybody's ballgame down to the closing seconds.

MI's Rick Hodge sank two free throws to bring MI to within one with 2:19 on the clock. With the score unchanged and just 25 seconds left, Snyder missed the front end of a 1-1. Juanita grabbed the rebound and Bobby Taylor sank a lay in off the Rebel fast break. With just 15 seconds to go MI trailed by three. With just five seconds on the clock, Juanita's Ernie Shreve sank two free throws to put the game out of reach. MI's Sam Moscatel scored the game's final bucket with one second to go.

"WE HAD OPPORTUNITIES to win this game," Pepple said. "When you don't capitalize on those opportunities you lose.

"Missed free throws and missed opportunities made the difference. You can't have missed free throws at crunch time."

But, Mercer Island's head Islander added, "we have nothing to be ashamed of. We have been to the championship game in three of the last four years. Not many people can say that."

Mercer Island was state runner up to Roosevelt in 1982, and Shadle Park in 1981.

"I want to congratulate Bob Anderson on a great win," Pepple said, "but I don't think the people of this state have seen the last of Mercer Island. We will be back."

And Pepple has every reason to be optimistic in looking to next year. Though the Islanders are losing a bevy of talent to the college ranks – including Sam Moscatel, Mike Williams, Geoff Swanson, Shawn Lightning, Chris Strickland, Gregg Dean and Rick Hodge – junior standouts Brian Schwabe and Quin Snyder will be back in the maroon and white jerseys next year.

"The future always looks bright for this team," Pepple said.

In the summer of 1984, Quin Snyder and Brian Schwabe teamed up as part of the Northwest Nike team to compete in the Great Western Shootout in Huntington Beach, California. There, they lost to Mid Valley of California, 62-59. On July 24, the team competed at the Basketball Congress invitational tournament in Tempe, Arizona, where they beat San Fernando, 83-49. In that game, Schwabe contributed 12 points, with Snyder adding 10 points and 10 assists.

Meanwhile, the basketball community on Mercer Island was rocked by a scandal of sorts, involving a player who had been kicked off the team during the 83-84 season for apparently violating the athletic code of conduct.

July 17, 1984

Family takes dispute with MIHS athletic officials to school board

by Doug Cooley

A simmering dispute involving a Mercer Island High School student whose parents contend he was "forced off" the varsity basketball team last December has landed in the lap of school board members.

"We consider (the incident) to be the greatest travesty of justice either my wife Nancy or I have ever witnessed," V. Lee Norwood told board members at a special hearing July 12. "The story is ugly."

Norwood is the father of Scott Norwood, 18, who graduated from MIHS in June. Until December 12, 1983, Scott was a member of the basketball team and had played in varsity games.

On that date, prior to a practice, team members reported to head coach Ed Pepple that they smelled alcohol on Scott's breath. Pepple escorted the ballplayer to associate principal Gary Snyder's office for disciplinary action.

What transpired at that meeting has been at the crux of the complaint waged by his parents. Though Scott allegedly had a history of drinking, he denied drinking that day. But Snyder said the youth confessed to drinking earlier in the basketball season and, in step with district policy and the athletic code, suspended him from the team for five days.

Scott's version is that he told Snyder he had been with friends who were drinking, but that he himself never drank during basketball season. His parents believed him.

Snyder met with Scott and his parents the next day. Nancy Norwood, a nurse, explained that the alcohol on his breath the previous day was from cough syrup she had given him earlier that day. But Snyder decided the suspension would stick based on the admission of drinking earlier in the season.

The Norwoods said their concerns were somewhat relieved because Snyder - father of standout player Quin Snyder - assured them that Scott could rejoin the team without recrimination after sitting out a week.

At a meeting Dec. 19 that followed the suspension, Lee Norwood and Scott discussed the next step with Snyder and Pepple. Pepple told Scott he did not want him back on the team. When Scott asked about the team's feelings, Pepple agreed he could attend a team meeting that afternoon and discuss it with them. After the discussion, Scott left the room and the team voted on reinstating him. Pepple afterward told him the vote was split, and he still didn't want him. Scott said he was "surprised".

"I was told I was not wanted and that if I did return, I'd have to start all over again," Scott told the school board. "I was told I should turn in my practice uniform to Mr. Snyder".

But Snyder insists the young hoopster was not forced to quit. "Pepple said he didn't want you, but you chose to leave," Snyder, also at the meeting, said. "You were never told you couldn't play basketball."

Pepple, contacted at home last week, confirmed he wanted Scott off the team, but that he "legally had a right to stay".

Norwood dismissed the argument. "If the coach doesn't want you on the team, a kid is not about to say, 'it's my legal right'."

Both Pepple and Snyder say they wanted to help Scott with his "drinking problem."

"I was concerned about him as a person," said Snyder.

Pepple said he had spent hours counseling Scott, and that the team also wanted to help him. But he said Scott's drinking had become a "morale problem" for the players.

"There was no doubt in my mind that he had been drinking during the season," he said. "I did what I had to do for the good of the team and would do it over again."

Norwood admits his son "discovered" alcohol in his sophomore year. But he said several incidents prejudiced school staff opinion of him as a "problem alcoholic." First was his arrest at age 16 for driving while intoxicated, he said. The local newspaper reported the charge, he said, but failed to report that he was found not guilty.

The father also recounted that his son injured himself during the basketball team's trip to New Zealand last summer after he and his teenage host broke into the family liquor cabinet.

"Coach Pepple was called in the middle of the night and took Scott to a hospital emergency room," said Norwood. "It appears he has been unable to forgive Scott for this incident which, had proper supervision been imposed, would never have happened."

Norwood said he and his wife, who have two other children attending Mercer Island public schools, are not ignorant about alcohol and drugs. He said both of them work with the Salvation Army's Harbor Light Center, a program designed to help recovering alcoholics.

But last year Scott had begun to change and become more concerned about the effects of drinking on his academic record, said his father. "He was also excited about his final year of basketball."

SNYDER TESTIFIED that he told Scott the suspension could be appeared to Principal Larry Smith. The Norwoods said they rejected that option because they were assured by Snyder that Scott could rejoin the team. Snyder, however, claims to have made no promises.

In February, Scott's father sent Smith a three-page letter protesting "the grossly unfair suspension" and requesting Scott have the suspension rescinded and letters of apology from Pepple and

Snyder. Norwood said he delayed because he "didn't know how to approach it. It also took me that long to be certain in my own mind that Scott had been completely candid."

That letter has triggered a stream of correspondence this spring between the Norwoods and school officials. Failure to produce an admission of wrongdoing on the part of school staff prompted the Norwoods to request a public hearing before the school board.

Norwood, a semi-retired businessman, told board members they must decide who's "lying." He would also like to see Snyder and Pepple disciplined for violating district policies. Snyder, he contends, violated Scott's stated right of freedom from incrimination. Pepple, he said, made "a mockery" of district policy that states interscholastic athletics are "to promote physical, mental, moral, social and emotional well-being of the individual participants."

"The mental anguish created by this incident is extreme and substantial for all three of us," said Norwood.

The father asked the board to consider letters of apology to his son, revoking the suspension and financial award for loss of possible basketball scholarship money. Scott will attend the University of Southern California in the fall and plans to try out for basketball.

Board president Gretchen Ilgenfritz said the Norwoods will receive a reply to their complaint this week.

"Make no mistake in assessing our determination to pursue the matter to its ultimate conclusion," Norwood told the board members. "Although our three children are all now in college, we feel a civic duty to do all within our power to expose abuses within the school system."

Norwood said his attorney will take over the complaint if no settlement can be reached.

Pepple thinks it's a little too late to make amends. "All they're doing is bringing attention to their problem," he said.

PART FIVE

1984-1985

"1985 was truly a championship year – a long time coming but well worth the wait."

- Ed Pepple

By November of 1984, national recruiting interest in senior guard Quin Snyder and senior forward Brian Schwabe had reached an all-time high.

"They're singing the blues elsewhere, but in Durham, N.C., today the Blue Devils are happy," wrote Seattle Times staff reporter Ranny Green in the Monday, November 5 edition of the paper. "That's because one of the nation's most highly recruited prep-basketball players, Quin Snyder, a 6-foot-2 guard from Mercer Island High School, announced he will attend Duke University."

As it turns out, Snyder had turned more than a few heads the previous summer at the Athletes for Better Education (AFBE) camp and the Basketball Congress International tournament in Tempe, Arizona, becoming the object of interest for 100 schools nationwide.

Snyder eventually trimmed his list down to Washington, Virginia, Stanford, Arizona, and Kansas before selecting Duke. "This was one of the toughest decisions I've ever had to make," Snyder told the Times. "I chose Duke because I felt most comfortable there. Coach K and his staff made me feel like a part of the family. I felt that I fit right in with the players, too."

Snyder's father, Gary, the athletic director at Mercer Island High School, was interviewed for the piece on Coach Ed Pepple's involvement in his son's recruiting process. "I can't say enough about Ed's assistance," he told the Times. "Earlier this year, Tonette (Quin's mom), Ed and I had dinner together to map out some recruiting guidelines. From that point on, he has been available whenever Quin or the family needed him."

The younger Snyder talked about how all the notoriety was impacting him. "Things became so hectic in late August early

September before school started that I moved out for a while, staying overnight with friends for about a week or 10 days," Snyder said.

"I got pretty uptight at times," he continued. "I tried my darndest to keep cool, but I couldn't get the college selection matter off my mind."

The Times also covered the ongoing recruiting of Snyder's teammate, Brian Schwabe. "Seldom does one high school have two highly coveted basketball players at the same time but the Islanders do this year," Ranny Green wrote. "Although the long-time teammates - they've played together since the fourth grade - compare notes, Snyder said his decision was made totally independent of what Schwabe may decide."

The story went on to quote legendary Duke basketball coach, Mike Krzyzewski, who was instrumental in recruiting Snyder to his school.

"It made my weekend," he told the Times. "Quin's a great student and an outstanding young man. When he visited Duke last month, he left a lasting impression on the players. To a man, they felt he was as well-rounded a player as has visited here in three years. Almost everyone on the team has asked me right along if Quin is committed anywhere. Quin struck up a rapport with our players right away."

In the story, Snyder made clear his long-term ambition to pursue a career in the National Basketball Association, something he has since achieved as the head coach of the Utah Jazz.

Pepple acknowledged the media focus on Snyder and Schwabe specifically. "Having all the attention lavished on two kids can be upsetting to others," he said. "But they have all accepted it in stride. From another standpoint, it can be inspiring to the young player seeing something like this firsthand."

The article highlighted Snyder's teammate and friend, guard Jeff Thompson, who had volunteered as Snyder's unofficial librarian, helping to organize all the college literature he'd received which had been piled up in his room. "I think he enjoyed it, however," Snyder said. "It gave him a chance to scan material from a lot of the schools."

Lastly, the story quoted Snyder's mother, Tonette. "It's nice to get it over so things can get back to normal." she said. "More important, I have my son back again."

On Monday, November 12, an item appeared in the sports section of the Seattle Times under the headline, "Islander's first work out a yawner".

In the story, Times staff reporter Eldridge McCready described the scene outside the Mercer Island High School gym that morning: "Dressed in a tail tuxedo at 12:08 this morning, Bob Burmeister glanced at a nearby door where a dozen teenage girls and short skirts waited patiently. The girls cheer when the doors open. No rock stars appeared, but 32 high school basketball players did.

"Turnouts had begun at Mercer Island High School."

Burmeister, the girls track coach at MI and basketball game announcer, was there along with 12 cheerleaders, parents and friends to watch Coach Pepple and Assistant Coach Bill Woolley put the players through a strenuous workout.

"I can't remember," Pepple said when asked how the early morning turnout tradition started. "I imagine I stole the idea from somebody."

After the two-hour workout, the team, ranked #2 in the nation by Street and Smith's magazine, went to breakfast together.

November 13, 1984

Hoop duo sets sights on new heights

By John Shanahan

Quin Snyder and Brian Schwabe, who officially started basketball practice for the 1984-85 season at a 12:01 a.m. practice session early Monday morning, actually started making news a week before the balls started pounding on the gym floor.

Not many prep athletes hit the headlines before they hit a jump shot or two, but the Islander duo, representing two of the country's most sought-after high school players, is a slight exception.

A proven expert at turning KingCo and various other opponents on their ears, Snyder, Mercer Island's unassuming point guard extraordinaire, was up to his old tricks again, this time pulling a preseason alley-oop by announcing Nov. 5 that he's taking his state-of-the-art basketball skills to Duke University next fall.

Snyder's announcement inspired an instant print and electronic media blitz. The story ran for two days in the state's largest daily paper. Snyder was interviewed live on local television, and wire services carried the story nationally.

Snyder intends to sign a Duke letter of intent on Nov. 14, the first day of a week-long autumn signing period allowed by the NCAA.

TEAMMATE SCHWABE, a highly recruited candidate himself, has narrowed his field to six colleges - Stanford, Santa Barbara, Arizona, Northwestern, Kansas and Washington - but says he may not make up his mind during the autumn signing period. Schwabe visited the University of Arizona over the weekend, in his sixth and final college visit allowed by NCAA rules.

"I have two options," Schwabe said. First, he could make his choice during the autumn signing period. Second, he could narrow his field from six to just three schools, one of which he has already decided would be Washington and inform the other schools he's not interested. Then, Schwabe said, he could just "see how it pans out" as the season develops.

Snyder, the 6-foot-3 Islander senior, one of the nation's top six high school guard prospects, has been swarmed for months by college recruiters hoping to sway his attentions.

After making his announcement, Snyder said the welcome but relentless pressure from the colleges had "toned down," leaving him to concentrate, along with the rest of the Islanders, on winning the state AAA championship they lost in the finals last year to Juanita.

November 27, 1984

Islander prospects: Rare coach psychs up national-ranked squad

By John Shanahan

He's at it again.

Ed Pepple, Mercer Island's head basketball coach, is once again doing what he does best - turning Mercer Island high school's gymnasium into Motivation Central. Islander Airlines Flight 1985 is about to take off.

Possible destinations include KingCo and District titles, a state AAA championship, and maybe even a national championship. At least one preseason national forecast has pegged Mercer Island as the nation's number two ranked high school team.

Spectators should keep seatbelts fastened, because before it lands, this flight is sure to hit pockets of violent emotional uplifts and pass through huge clouds of media hype. Oxygen masks are advised.

And Pepple, although he's not only driver but also chief engineer of a program that, for lack of a better description, is utterly remarkable in its success, gives the lions' share of the credit to his players.

Pepple has led the Islanders to 411 wins in 17 years. Although the state championship has eluded his group, he's been a step or two away over and over again. He's the first mortal ever to build a national prep hoop title contender from this state. Whether or not he wins a title, People ranks among the shrewdest high school basketball coaches this state, or maybe any state, has ever seen.

Even as the Islanders taxi towards this season's liftoff at a jamboree against Kennedy, Lake Washington and Eastside Catholic at home this Thursday (Nov. 29), People wants the attention to focus on his players, not himself.

That's a little like Albert Einstein dodging credit for the Theory of Relativity.

BUT PEPPLE likes to talk about himself about as much as he enjoys giving up three-point plays to Juanita. His standard retort to a reporter, trying to shine a little light his way, begins something like:

"Don't do (a story about) me. I've been done to death. It's these kids…"

It's hard to argue with the coach's logic. During his time here, some amazing talent has suited up for the Islanders. In 1968, there was Steve Hawes. 1977 saw Peter Gudmundsson. This year, of course it's Brian Schwabe and Quin Snyder, the Islander's answer to Batman and Robin.

And they are backed up by a wealth of talent, including Scott Weller, Paul Roberts, Omar Parker, Mike Mathers, Eric Brady, Russell Easter, Jeff Wood, John Gilliland, Doug Marriott and Jeff Thompson.

BUT THE PLAYERS come and go, and Pepple stays on to build another team.

He understands the meaning of words like "tradition" and "motivation" and he knows how to impart those concepts to players. There is a mental aspect to making teams tick, and Pepple, whether he'll admit it or not, is a master at it.

"The tradition is the biggest thing," Pepple says. "I think all of the kids know that if you don't play with the team, you don't play. That's been our strength over the years."

One of Pepple's strengths has been a personal flair as distinctive as the maroon warm-up suit he wears to each practice. His coaching regimen includes a midnight practice session to open the season. It's not an idea for which he takes credit, but it's "a good motivator," Pepple says.

Besides the midnight practice, People takes the team on a preseason weekend retreat to promote closeness and define team goals for the year. He also beefs up the Islander's schedule with trips to tournaments like the Holiday Prep Classic, which Mercer Island will be attending in Las Vegas this Christmas. "We are interested in seeing how good we are, not just winning games," Pepple says.

"They (the players) have got to learn about each other," Pepple says, adding that two things which can be fatal to developing a proper team spirit are jealousy and players striving for personal accomplishments. If all of the individual goals fit into the team goals, you've got a chance.

"You'd think that just because these kids all go to the same school they'd be close, but that's not always the case."

Pepple says that may be especially true of this year's team, which is comprised of seven seniors, one junior and four sophomores. With such a difference in ages, players don't spend much time together off the court.

Pepple adds that he's never had two players who have been recruited to the extent of Schwabe and Snyder - a situation of lavished media and collegiate attention that could form rifts in the squad. Pepple says the only option is to look at the situation positively. "The way we approach it is that if Quin and Brian didn't get all the attention, then no one would ever come and see the other players. They all benefit from the hype."

"THERE'S NO QUESTION this team has a lot of talent, but we've got to blend it all together. We are not smooth right now. There is no consistency out there. There are times we look awesome; at other times we look phlegmatic. Our depth still has to be proven."

Besides Schwabe and Snyder, the team returns starter Scott Waller, a 6-foot-4 senior forward from last year. He'll start at small forward this year, Pepple says. Paul Roberts, a 6-foot-6 senior, also from last year's team, will be at power forward. The 6-foot-9 Schwabe will be back at center. With the 6-foot-3 Snyder starting at one guard position, Pepple says the 6-foot senior Mike Mathers will be starting opposite.

Other guards include junior Omar Parker, and 5-foot-9 senior Jeff Thompson. The guard ranks are filled with sophomores 5-foot-11 Jeff Wood and 6-foot-4 John Gilliland. Gilliland could also play at forward, as will sophomores 6-foot-3 ½ Doug Marriott and 6-foot-7 Eric Brady. Russell Easter, a 6-foot-5 senior forward, will also see action at forward.

December 11, 1984

After wins over Bellevue and Bothell, hoopsters to take on unbeaten Redmond

Mercer Island's boys basketball squad, 2-0 in KingCo after wins over Bellevue and Bothell last week, will meet the Crest Division's only other unbeaten squad, Redmond, tonight (Dec 11) at Mercer Island.

"They (Redmond) will be very competitive," predicted Mercer Island coach Ed Pepple. And with the Islander juggernaut starting to roll, Redmond will have to be.

Mercer Island zapped opponents from Lake Washington, Eastside Catholic and Kennedy Nov. 29 at a Mercer Island Jamboree, where the Islanders outscored the competition 61-18.

It was a showing Pepple describing as "dominating".

It was also a showing that did nothing to prepare the Islanders for the Bellevue Wolverines, who nipped at Mercer Island's heels throughout the Islanders' season-opening contest Dec 4.

Midway through the third quarter, Bellevue trailed Mercer Island 32-31, a state of affairs that, needless to say, did not have Ed Pepple feeling very good. "We were playing below average," he said, "quite a way below average. It looked like our first game of the season."

Mercer Island overcame an off night (13 for 24) from the free throw line and 17 of 35 from the floor, to finally down the Wolverines 59-49.

But at least against Bellevue, the Islanders showed a hint of their depth. After Brian Schwabe (16 points, 12 rebounds) went to the bench with foul trouble and Mercer Island leading by one point in the third quarter, his absence was filled quickly by the efforts of Eric Brady (9 points), Paul Roberts (3 points) and Scott Weller (11 points, 8 rebounds).

Quin Snyder finished the contest with 14 points, while Omar Parker, Mike Mathers and John Gilliland each had two points.

AGAINST BOTHELL, Mercer Island's depth became glaringly apparent. Playing all 12 players from his bench - Schwabe and Snyder for just 16 minutes - Pepple's squad still ran away 80-31 from some very discouraged Cougars.

December 18, 1984

'Tis the hoop season to be merry

If you are a Mercer Island boys' basketball fan, 'tis the season to be jolly.

Last week, Mercer Island left an 83 to 39 whipping in Redmond's Christmas stocking, before gift wrapping Woodinville 59-29.

The next guests invited to the 4-0 Islander Christmas party will be Interlake today and Sammamish on Friday.

The Islanders will leave December 25 for Las Vegas, where they will play in the Holiday Prep Classic Tournament. The first game on the Islander schedule will be against Bishop Gorman High School, defending Nevada AAA state champions, in a match-up at 7:30 PM December 26.

Quin Snyder's 17 points topped the Islanders scoring against Woodinville. Brian Schwabe had 12 points and seven blocked shots, while Mike Mathers and Eric Brady combined for 11 points.

Schwabe led the rebounders with 12, while Mathers and Brady each had 6.

From the floor, Mercer Island shot 21-45 for 46.7%. Woodinville shot 11-37 for 29.7%.

"We played well defensively," said Mercer Island coach Ed Pepple. "We intimidated inside."

Besides Schwabe's seven blocked shots, Brady contributed several. Snyder added four interceptions. Mathers and Snyder each had four assists.

Russell Easter exploded for 12 points against Redmond.

Schwabe topped all scores, netting 18 points in 12 minutes before being taken out of the game. Snyder had 15 points, while Omar Parker and Brady each had 8.

On Tuesday, December 17, Quin Snyder's 17 points helped Mercer Island squeak past the Interlake Saints, 56-49. Brian Schwabe contributed 17 and Eric Brady, 12.

The headline of the Prep Page in the Saturday, December 22 issue of the Seattle Times read, "Islanders crush Sammamish 87-39" with a photo of Eric Brady driving against a Totems' defender. Quin Snyder scored seven field goals and two free throws in the first ten minutes of play to lead the Islanders (6-0 in conference play) over their league rival. Brian Schwabe finished with 25 points. Pepple seemed satisfied with the results. "A lot of players had their best games," he told the Times.

January 2, 1985

Hoopsters enjoy prep spotlight, take 3rd in Las Vegas classic

By John Shanahan

Ranked briefly as the nation's top prep basketball team, Mercer Island found itself playing Goliath to a host of potentially murderous Davids at last week's Brooks Holiday prep Classic Basketball Tournament in Las Vegas.

After Initial wins over Bishop Gorman and Rancho high schools, both of Las Vegas Dec. 26 and 27, Goliath looked unstoppable.

He wasn't.

Before clobbering Chaparral of Las Vegas 76-69 to take third place in the Prep Classic Dec. 29, the Islanders ended their eight-game win streak and hopes of a prestigious tournament title in a losing battle with Flint Hill of Oakmont, Va. 60-56 in the Dec. 28 tourney semifinals.

In the topsy-turvy world of fast-lane high school basketball, Mercer Island's reign on the prep hoopdom throne was frustratingly brief – just a few days.

If Julius Caesar had his Ides of March, Dec. 28 was, for Mercer Island, the Ides of December (apologies to the ancient Roman calendar.)

BUT MERCER Island Coach Ed People didn't have any harsh words for Brutus – Flint Hill Coach Stuart Vetter. "It was a great team. We just came up a little short."

"A little short" translated into a Flint Hill 32-27 lead at the half. Mercer Island could shave the lead to no less than two points throughout the second half.

"We just couldn't make the big plays. They hit the key free throw," Pepple said.

In the tournament's opening rounds Mercer Island was anything but short. The only plays they bothered to make were big ones.

In a town full of shows, Mercer Island's was one of the class acts.

Brian Schwabe scored 29 points and grabbed 23 rebounds to lead the Islanders to a 65-48 trouncing of Nevada state champion Bishop Gorman Dec. 26. Schwabe shot 12-21 on field goals and went 5-6 from the free throw line. Schwabe scored 10 in the first quarter to lead MI to an 18-8 lead. In the first half, which ended with the Islanders holding a 31-18 lead, MI led by as many as 18.

"He was the difference," Pepple said of the 6-foot-9 Mercer Island center.

The key to Schwabe's statistics was that he managed to stay out of foul trouble, Pepple said.

While Mercer Island's 6-foot-3 guard Quin Snyder went 3-15 from the floor, and Mercer Island's top 3 guards shot only 5-24,

Mercer Island's Schwabe, Jeff Thompson and Eric Brady filled the scoring void. Brady scored 13 points and Thompson hit for 6.

While still impressive, the Mercer Island first round win left coach Pepple nonplussed.

"We can compete with any team here, but we've got to play better than we did tonight," he told reporters after the Bishop Gorman game.

Against Mercer Island's second round opponent Rancho High, Pepple need not have worried.

Snyder exploded for a season high 25 points - 10 in the third period alone, and Schwabe added 24 of his own as the Islanders dressed-down Rancho 83-71.

Scott Weller also added 6 points in the third period - on the way to his first double-figure scoring effort of the season (16) - to help Mercer Island widen a narrow 39-37 halftime lead. Mike Mathers also scored 10 points.

But it was Snyder who ignited the Islander offense. The senior guard added three steals and nine assists. According to Pepple, Snyder "really broke it open. He controlled the ballgame down the stretch."

Rancho, whose tallest player was only 6-foot-4, retaliated with brute strength.

"This was a war," Pepple said. "You wouldn't believe the pace and intensity of the game. It was a real hard fought... well, war is the best word I can use. It was very physical."

Mercer Island won the war with blistering 58 percent shooting from the field.

Brady added 6 points and Omar Parker had 2.

Greg Anthony, Rancho's 6-foot-1 junior guard, led his team with 29 points.

Saving perhaps the best for last, Schwabe, who was named to the tournament's all-star team, scored 47 points on 19-25 shooting from the floor. He was 9-9 from the foul line.

Mercer Island was red hot from the free throw line in the late going.

Leading 66-65 the Islanders sank 10 free throws, all in the last 53 seconds to ice Chaparral.

Weller had six of the free throws, while Snyder, who sat out injured much of the game, had two and Schwabe added a pair

Mercer Island, who as a team has been sporadic from the line this year tallied 18 points on foul shots, while Chaparral had only 7.

Chaparral outscored Mercer Island 62-58 on the floor.

The Islanders outrebounded Chaparral 35-27.

Mercer Island, 9-1 overall and 6-0 in league, will resume league action on Jan. 4 at Newport.

Back home, the Islanders dismantled Newport, 101-51, in front of the Knights' home crowd. Highlights of the game included Quin Snyder hitting 14 of 16 shots from the floor for a game-high 30 points, and Brian Schwabe's 20 points and 12 rebounds for the Islanders.

January 15, 1985

Issy tried, but they couldn't do it

By John Shanahan

Issaquah came to Mercer Island hoping to find the state's number one prep basketball team napping.

They weren't. The Islanders, who meet Juanita away tonight (Jan. 15) and Lake Washington at home Friday, were wide awake.

Indian coach Rich Brines said entering the contest he hoped his team could "sneak up on" the Islanders, who he hoped were tired after a tough holiday tournament in Las Vegas.

But Mercer Island was wired, not tired. They were soaring, not snoring.

The final score was 60-48, although the Islanders led by as much as 21 (50-29) late in the third quarter, before Coach Ed Pepple drained his bench with the game iced late in the fourth period.

Issaquah's only lead of the night was 2-0. Mercer Island then scored 12 straight points, and never really looked back.

WELL, MAYBE ONCE, for just a minute.

The game looked briefly as if it might be in some sort of jeopardy when 6-3 Quin Snyder, who scored 13 points, collided with 6-foot-9 teammate Brian Schwabe, then crashed headlong into a bench. With 2:50 left in the third quarter, a bloodied Snyder retired to the locker room for an appointment with a butterfly bandage.

Though Mercer Island led 46-27, Schwabe picked up a quick two fouls and momentum was suddenly runnin' with the Indians.

But in the closing moments of the quarter, Islander 6-0 senior guard Mike Mathers sank two key buckets to keep the Indians under control.

While Schwabe, who fouled out with 1:49 to go in the game, scored a game-high 23 points (including 15 rebounds), the Mercer Island trio of Eric Brady, Scott Weller and reserve Mathers combined for 18 points. Weller and Brady took advantage of Issaquah's triple-teaming of Schwabe in the first quarter to score eight of those points.

"Early on in the game their strategy seemed to be to allow Weller to shoot," Pepple said.

"That is a mistake."

But while Mercer Island ran their offense freely, the Islanders slowed the Indians to a crawl at the other end of the floor.

"Defense has been the name of our game for a long time," Pepple said.

Snyder exemplified the Islander defense by holding 5-11 Issaquah senior Kevin Landdeck, who had been averaging over 18 points per game to just 5 points.

Schwabe meanwhile played air traffic control in the lane, and Weller shadowed 6-4 forward Mark Ainsworth.

Mercer Island, now 9-0, 12-1, went on to trample the Bothell Cougars 68-33 on Friday.

High scorers for the Islanders were Schwabe and Snyder with 24 and 15 points respectively.

On January 15, Mercer Island escaped with a 48-46 win over Juanita, thanks to Jeff Thompson's two free throws, which gave the Islanders a 48-44 lead in the final 30 seconds. Brian Schwabe scored 20 points.

On January 18, the Islanders had quite a scare, almost giving up a league game to Lake Washington if not for a heroic 30-foot shot from Quin Snyder with no time left on the clock.

Scott Rolfness, the Kangs' leading scorer, scored a lay-in with six seconds left to tie the game 54-all. The Islanders called time out, then inbounded the ball to Snyder, who put up the winning shot.

"I looked up at the clock and saw a '1'," Snyder told the Seattle Times. I shot a little quicker going to my left. They had everybody up court covered, so I just put my head down. I figured I'd get as close as I could."

Snyder finished the game with 14 points; Schwabe had 10 and Scott Weller 11 in the 56-54 Islander victory.

January 22, 1985

The Other Guys: Even without Schwabe and Snyder, it's a quality basketball squad

By John Shanahan

Mercer Island's boys' basketball team is actually a combination of two teams.

Everybody has heard of the first: it's made up of Quin Snyder and Brain Schwabe. The second team is slightly less famous, and possibly undeservedly so.

It's made up of "The Other Guys" — a group of excellent basketball players whose accomplishments usually remain in the shadow of their more recognized teammates.

To opponents, however, "The Other Guys" are anything but invisible.

"Mercer Island is a phenomenal basketball team," said Issaquah Indian Coach Rich Brines after Mercer Island handed Issaquah its only loss (60-48, Jan. 8) "I'm of the opinion you could take (Quin) Snyder and (Brain) Schwabe out of there and still have a quality class AAA basketball team."

Last week, the number one ranked Snyder, Schwabe, and Co. proved they are at least that.

Mercer Island, now 15-1, eeked out a pair of wins over Juanita 48-46 on Tuesday and Lake Washington 56-54 on Friday. Mercer Island will play Bellevue at 7:30 p.m. today (Jan. 22) and Woodinville at 8:15 p.m. Friday. Both games are at home.

FOR MERCER Island Coach Ed Pepple and his team, coping with the lopsided publicity generated by his outstanding duo has been a season-long challenge the squad has so far been up to.

"I don't think it's helped us," said Pepple of the massive media hype that began with the pre-season signing of Quin Snyder and Brain Schwabe with Duke and Northwestern Universities respectively, "but I don't think it's hurt us either. We've only lost one game, and we've generally played pretty well.

"I would prefer not to have so much individual attention, but I think one of the great things about our players is they know what it takes (for the team to win). They realize Quin and Brian are special talents and they don't begrudge them the attention. I think they realize that by being in the reflection of those two they have received some added attention themselves, so I think they have handled that pretty well."

Pepple likes to talk about the talented "other team," which seems to score everywhere but in the headlines.

Ranked by minutes played overall (after 15 games) that team includes Scott Weller, Eric Brady Mike Mathers, Omar Parker. Jeff Thompson, Russell Easter, Paul Roberts, John Gilliland, Doug Marriott and Jeff Wood. Weller, Mathers, Thompson, Easter and Roberts are all seniors.

Weller, who is third in total minutes played only to Schwabe and Snyder, has averaged 5.9 points per game, while leading the team in free throw percentage (83.9) but Pepple said Weller's real strength is on defense.

"Scott Weller for the last two years has been, really, I think, one of the best defensive forwards in the state," Pepple said. "He's guarded every top forward, and we've played some very good ones. He's done some incredible jobs."

BUT PEPPLE added that Weller is "a much better offensive player than people give him credit for." Something not as evident as it might be, because the 6-4 Weller "subverts his talents for the rest of the team. He plays off of Brian and Quin and does not assert himself as much as he should offensively. He is another person that gives us steadiness and stability."

Mathers, 6-0 guard, Pepple described as "a very explosive type of player. He is an outstanding shooter and very quick defensively (23 steals). What he has to work on is his passing. If he ever becomes a good passer, his game will go right to the sky, because he does everything else."

Of forward Jeff Thompson, Pepple said, "Thompson may be the most intelligent player we have in terms of knowing what we want to get done. He probably comes the closest to getting the most out of his abilities as anyone on the team. He works hard all the time. He is an excellent shooter, though he doesn't take a lot of shots." For the season, Thompson has shot 13-26, including two key hoops late in the fourth quarter of Mercer Island's 48-46 win over Juanita.

Against Juanita, Roberts, a 6-6½ forward, scored a season-high 9 points.

"Paul is experienced. He was instrumental to our success last year, especially at the end of the season."

Overall, Roberts has only played basketball for slightly over two years, Pepple said.

"He gives us a very steady inside player with an excellent shooting touch for a big guy."

Easter, who sprained his ankle in the contest against Juanita, "has a lot of ability," Pepple said.

"He's strong, very aggressive and tough inside. He is improving on his defense and he only needs to get a little more experience."

On January 22, Mercer Island improved their record to 15-1 and clinched the Crest Division title with a 59-39 defeat over the Bellevue Wolverines. High scorers for the Islanders were Quin Snyder (20) and Brian Schwabe (17). Schwabe also pulled down 19 rebounds.

On January 25 in the Mercer Island Gym, Schwabe scored 22 and Quin Snyder, 17, in an easy win over Woodinville, 75-38. Both Schwabe and Snyder only played half of the game.

The next night, the Islanders played host to Melbourne, Australia's Bulleen-Templestowe club team on the last stop of their two-week tour of Washington.

February 5, 1985

Islanders finish league play tonight, look ahead to KingCo action Feb. 12

Mercer Island left Interlake high and dry in the Islanders' lone league game last week with a 76-44 decision Tuesday.

The hoopsters second game of the week, scheduled against (2-12) Bothell on Friday, was rescheduled to last night (Monday, Feb. 4) due to snow.

Mercer Island will finish regular-season action tonight (Feb. 5) at Redmond, looking ahead to Feb. 12 KingCo championship play.

FOR SENIORS Quin Snyder Brian Schwabe, Paul Roberts, Russell Easter, Scott Weller, Mike Mathers and Jeff Thompson, last Tuesday night's game marked their last home court appearance.

Islander fans will be sad to see them go, but Interlake probably won't. Mercer Island blitzed the Saints at both ends of the court.

"I thought we played some of our best basketball of the year," said Mercer Island Coach Ed Pepple. "We had excellent defense and our fast break was great."

Snyder and Schwabe combined for 36 first-half points, as the Islanders opened a 42-23 halftime advantage.

Schwabe finished the game with 29 points and 16 rebounds, while Snyder ended the effort with 19 points, two steals, and six assists. Neither Schwabe nor Snyder played the final quarter.

Defensively, Schwabe and Eric Brady each blocked two shots.

Mercer Island as a team shot 33-62, while the Saints hit 19-49.

Islander team scoring went as follows: Doug Marriott had eight points, Omar Parker had four points and four assists, Mathers had four points, Jeff Wood and Easter each had three points. Brady, John Gilliland and Roberts each had two points.

The likely matchup in the Feb. 12 KingCo final at the Seattle Center Arena will be Mercer Island against Issaquah.

"They are in the top 10 in the state with a 15-3 record, so I would expect a tough ballclub," Pepple said.

On February 4th, the Islanders held the Bothell Cougars to 10 points in the second half and came up with a 67-30 win behind Brian Schwabe's 19 points and Quin Snyder's 17, improving their overall record to 19-1.

February 12, 1985

Hoop showdown tonight, Islanders meet Issaquah

The Mercer Island boys' varsity basketball squad meets Issaquah at 8 p.m. tonight, Feb. 12, in the KingCo title game at the Seattle Center Arena.

Mercer Island (20-1), ranked number one in the state, defeated the Indians (17-3) by a score of 60-48 in their prior meeting on Jan. 8.

Mercer Island tuned up for the big game with an 87-52 clobbering of Redmond in the regular season's final game last Wednesday.

Any question that Mercer Island is ready for postseason action? Not really.

"We probably played as well as we did all season," said Mercer Island coach Ed Pepple of the Redmond contest.

Brian Schwabe led the Islanders with 25 points and 10 rebounds. Quin Snyder had 17 points of his own. Scott Weller had eight points, while Mike Mathers, Gerald Piper, Omar Parker, John Gilliland and Paul Roberts each had six points.

Mercer Island jumped to a 38-20 halftime lead and then coasted throughout the second half, outscoring the Mustangs 49-32. The Mustangs shot 43.8 percent from the field compared with Mercer Island's 70 percent.

"Mercer Island is so big, so quick, so good," said Redmond coach Al Williams. "There's no question they are peaking at the right time this year."

Tickets to the KingCo Conference Championship will be available at the door.

February 19, 1985

Hoop hopes heighten

Islanders grab KingCo title, forge ahead on road to state

By John Shanahan

Coach Ed Pepple said it last year. He said they would be back, after losing in the 1984 state AAA Championship game.

He wasn't kidding.

Last week Mercer Island took two giant steps toward the 1985 state tournament. They won the KingCo Championship 72-38 over Issaquah on Tuesday, then beat Lake Washington 68-58 in the first round of the Sea-King District tournament on Friday.

Not only were KingCo's undefeated Islanders back, they were back with a vengeance.

"We were really ready tonight," Mercer Island guard Quin Snyder said after the Islanders' dismantling of Issaquah.

"You fans are the best in the state," said Mercer Island senior Scott Weller, holding high the KingCo trophy for a cheering Seattle

Center Arena crowd after last Tuesday's game. "And that's what we're going to be. This is our first step."

THE ISLANDERS will likely take some more steps this week.

A win over Blanchet last night would have clinched a berth in the preliminary rounds of the state tournament and put the Islanders into the District title match at 8 p.m., on Thursday in the Arena.

A loss would have put the team into the District's consolation semi-finals at 8 p.m., Wednesday, in the Arena.

The way Mercer Island has been playing, though, they should wind up in Thursday night's championship against the winner (probably Garfield) of last night's Garfield—Issaquah contest.

Garfield, Metro's champion, toppled Bellevue, KingCo's fourth place 86-68 in Sea-King's first round Friday. The Bulldogs are led by 6-foot junior guard Craig Murray, 6-2 junior forward Chris Fogerson, 6-8 sophomore center Craig Jorgen and 6-4 senior forward Phil Ross.

Issaquah qualified to play them by beating Eastside Catholic, KingCo's sixth place, 59-54 Friday.

HERE'S HOW it went last week.

The Islanders routed Issaquah enroute to their 11th league title since 1968, jumping out 21-4 in the first quarter. To describe it as a "decisive" quarter would be an understatement. It was devastating. It was instant crunch time for Issaquah, who never got back into it.

It was also not the first time Mercer Island has blasted off at tipoff time.

"We've had starts as good as that before," said Pepple.

Mercer Island's Quin Snyder and Brian Schwabe, who finished the game with 13 and 10 points respectively, got 17 of them in the first quarter.

Snyder, hampered with three second-quarter fouls, eventually fouled out.

"Quin and Brian didn't have one of their better games tonight, neither one of them," Pepple said last Tuesday, but added that the rest of the team more than made up for it.

"Brian and Quin were really the neutralizers and everybody else came through productively tonight," Pepple said.

Eric Brady, a 6-7 sophomore, scored just two points in the first half, but exploded for 13 second half points for a team high 15. Brady scored 11 of those in one five-minute stretch of the third quarter, to put Mercer Island up 32-27 after a 34-17 halftime lead.

"Eric Brady really came of age tonight," Pepple said. "I think he proved that he's really one of the better players in the league.

"Brady was sensational. The easiest shot he had of the night he missed, but I think that was the only one he missed," Pepple joked.

EQUALLY DEADLY as Brady was the duo of reserve guards, 6-foot senior Mike Mathers and 5-10 ½ junior Omar Parker, who peppered Issaquah with long range shots for a total of 16 points.

"I thought Parker and Mathers both did a great job coming in for the guard spots," Pepple said.

The two guards hit 5-for-5 from the field in the first half.

Pepple lauded the team's efforts at both ends of the floor as the best of the season.

"I think no question about it, this was our best game of the season overall," he said. "We had more people productive offensively and defensively. I think without question though you can look at the 72 points or whatever it was, but it was (also) really the defense," Pepple said.

Scott Weller, a 6-foot-4 senior, did "a masterful job of defense and also hitting the open shot" in holding Issaquah's leading scorer Mark Ainsworth, averaging over 15 points per game, to just four points. Weller scored six points.

Pepple criticized rough play on the part of the Indians, who have picked up the reputation of KingCo's Bad Boys. "I don't feel good about the game, because it was far too physical," Pepple said, "At times it was not basketball. I can understand being physical, but not that, especially in the end when the game is over. Double fouls (there were two of those) and things like that. That's not basketball."

Issaquah's center David Lavine led the team with 16 points. Kevin Landdeck had five points.

A 35-FOOT JUMP SHOT at the buzzer by Snyder tripped the Lake Washington Kangaroos 56-54 on Jan. 18 and left them hopping mad — and looking for revenge.

For a while Friday, it looked like they might get it.

The Islanders rolled to a 22-14 lead at the end of the first quarter, but Lake Washington battled to ties at 32 and 34 in the third quarter.

But revenge in Mercer Island's gymnasium comes about as often as short sleeve weather in Antarctica.

The cold snap which froze the now 16-7 Kangaroos' hopes of an upset came in the form, once again, of Quin Snyder. For the Kangs, it was Jan. 18 revisited.

Snyder started the Kangaroos' woes in the first quarter when he stole the ball then got an assist on a pass, setting up Schwabe for the first bucket of the game.

Snyder finished with a team high 25 points, also a season high for the Duke-bound senior.

"Snyder is just a great athlete," Lake Washington coach Mike Cashman said, "He's sensational when he's on and he was on tonight.

"When he's hitting, the only way you can stop him is to deny him the ball, and we didn't do a good job of that."

Schwabe added 17 points to the Islander total. Jeff Thompson and Weller each had 8 points. Eric Brady had 6.

In the February 19 edition of the Seattle Times, staff Reporter Eldredge McCready reported on the Islander's game against Blanchet in the second round of the Sea-King AAA District Tournament.

The Islanders beat Blanchet 67-53 due in no small part to Quin Snyder and Brian Schwabe's combined 51 points and set themselves up for a championship match against KingCo rival Issaquah (19-4), who had upset Garfield 71-61 the night prior.

"Mercer Island," as reported by McCready, "has been favored to go all the way this season by sportswriters and broadcasters who repeatedly have voted the Islanders the No. 1-rated boys' show in the state."

The Blanchet game opened with a Snyder-tossed back-door, alley-oop pass to Schwabe, setting the stage for things to come ``They worked well together," Coach Ed Pepple told the Times. ``Quin did a good job of getting the ball inside to Brian, and Brian kicked it back out to Quin.

"That was the Snyder and Schwabe show tonight."

A few nights later, Quin Snyder scored 25 points to lead the Islanders past Issaquah 50-41 in the Sea-King District AAA championship game at the Seattle Center Arena.

Despite only scoring five fourth-quarter points against Issaquah, Mercer Island came out on top. ``I thought our effort and execution were below our standards," Ed Pepple told the Seattle Times.

Snyder connected on 11 of 16 field-goal attempts, had six assists and scored 11 straight Islander points prior to fouling out with 1:25 remaining. Brian Schwabe added 12 points, 15 rebounds and two blocked shots to the score sheet.

In order to get to the state tournament March 7-9 at the Coliseum, the Islanders would need to beat Auburn, ranked just behind Mercer Island as the No. 2 team in the state.

Coming into the game, Auburn, at 22-1, was the North Puget Sound League champion, and had a big-time player in 6-foot-6 ½ center Doug Blair, who averaged 17.1 points per game.

On Friday, March 1, in front of a capacity crowd of 5000 at Seattle Center Arena, Mercer Island beat Auburn 60-41 to earn their way into the state tournament.

Led by Quin Snyder (17 points) and Brian Schwabe (16 points, 10 rebounds), the Islanders outscored the Trojans 20-6 to take a 47-29 lead into the final period.

``Now we get a No. 1 seed,'' Pepple told the Seattle Times.

On March 5, in anticipation of the upcoming tournament, staff reporter Craig Smith contributed 1811 words for the Seattle Times about Pepple's 35-year quest under the headline, "Will this be Pepple's year?"

In the story, Smith highlights Pepple's time as a player at Lincoln High School in Seattle, where his team lost the championship game in overtime to South Kitsap high school in 1950.

He introduces Pepple's father, Raymond, who returned wounded from combat in Korea and spent the final 27 years of his life as a paraplegic, but still managed to teach school.

Pepple played basketball and met his future wife Shirley at Everett Community College, before transferring to the University of Utah, where, in his senior year, the team was ranked No. 6 in the nation and lost in the 1955 NCAA playoffs to the eventual champion, the University of San Francisco.

The story traces Pepple's time in the Marines, his coaching and teaching assignment at Fife High, his time as an assistant at Meadowdale High in Lynwood, one year as head coach at Mark Morris in Longview, to his landing on Mercer Island in 1967.

There, Smith wrote, Pepple "organized a youth basketball program that later adopted the name Little Dribblers. It's been called "Pepple's pipeline" because it continually restocks the Islander program with fundamentally sound players who have had a taste of national age-group competition. High-school players are expected to referee Little Dribbler games and help to pay back the help they received as youngsters. The Little Dribblers program has been envied and much copied."

Smith then goes into detail about the infamous 1981 Shadle Park game and the fallout with the WIAA. He describes the Islanders' three subsequent seasons, setting the stage for their big opportunity as the #1 seed heading into the 1985 state championship tournament.

March 5, 1985

Islanders to state: Starting Thursday morning, it's crunchball for Mercer Island's Region I champions

By John Shanahan

Wipe the slate clean.

For 25-1 Mercer Island, the basketball season that has been under way for three months starts all over again at 9 a.m. Thursday morning. That's when Mercer Island meets Puyallup in the first round of the State Class AAA basketball finals, to be held March 7 through 9 at Seattle Center Coliseum.

Sure, Mercer Island is the KingCo League and Sea-King District champion. It's strutting into the state Class AAA finals ranked No.1.

It doesn't matter.

For Mercer Island, just like the other teams left in the Final Eight of the state tournament, every game from here on out – there are three for each team – is do-or-die to win the state championship.

Mercer Island has played basketball all season. Starting Thursday, they'll play crunchball.

Of course, crunchball is what Mercer Island coach Ed Pepple has been getting the Islanders ready for all season.

"That's what it's all about," he said after his team beat Auburn last Friday night to make it to state.

That's why his team played in the Brooks Holiday Prep Classic in Las Vegas over the Holidays. In the Brooks format, teams play four games in as many days – much like Washington's AAA format which has the Final Eight playing three games in three days. Whoever makes it through the state tourney undefeated wins the title.

The Islanders qualified for the Final Eight with a win over No. 2 ranked Auburn 60-41 in Region I action at the Arena last Friday night, March 1. Other Final Eight teams also qualified in games last weekend. The field includes Garfield, University, Issaquah, Curtis, Richland, Snohomish, and Puyallup.

Mercer Island was matched against Puyallup in a Sunday afternoon tournament drawing. At that time the 9 a.m. playing time also was set.

The winner of the Mercer-Puyallup clash will play either Snohomish or Richland at 2:30 p.m. on Friday. The winner of that game advances to the championship game scheduled for 7 p.m. Saturday. Losers in the double-elimination tournament's first two rounds drop into a separate bracket, playing for at best third in the state.

Tickets for single games or passes for the entire tournament will be on sale from 10:40 a.m. to 12:30 p.m., today and tomorrow (March 5 and 6), at the Mercer Island High School Mushroom,

Mercer Island High School Athletic Director Gary Snyder said. Prices vary for students and non-students. Tickets will also be available at the door of the Coliseum before the games Snyder said.

Thursday, March 7

FIRST ROUND: MI vs. Puyallup

The "Egg McMuffin game," so-called because of its 9 a.m. tipoff, nearly turned into "Burned Toast" for the heavily favored islanders.

The Vikings were led by senior guard Jay Vogt's 14 points and senior forward Lance See's 13 points.

Puyallup never led in the contest, though the Vikings played the Islanders close throughout the first half and closed to within one point twice in the fourth quarter.

Three Snyder (20 points) jump shots boosted the Islanders into a 13-5 lead midway through the first period. The Vikings managed to close the gap to 13-17 on two Vogt lay-ins and four foul shots before the end of the quarter.

Puyallup's Jeff Rescue hit the front end of a 1-1 to bring the Vikings within 1 point at 21-20 with 3:12 left in the half.

Mercer Island then scored five points in the period on a field goal by Brady (11 points) and free throws by Schwabe (19 points) and Mathers (1 point), to run to a 16-10 halftime lead.

Puyallup closed to within three points at the end of the third quarter (36-38) and to within one (40-41) at 6:46 in the fourth.

Omar Parker (4 points) hit a critical foul-line jumper to put Mercer Island up 43-40 at 6:29.

"Coach Pepple just says to keep popping and they'll fall," Parker said. "Today they started to."

A Vogt jumper again closed the gap to one point (42-43) at 6:10 in the fourth quarter.

Mercer Island then outscored Puyallup 14-6 to put the contest out of reach.

Friday, March 8, 1985

SEMI-FINALS: MI vs. Snohomish

AGAINST SNOHOMISH Mercer Island looked unstoppable.

Snohomish opened with a 1-0 lead on a Nate Duchesne free throw, before Schwabe answered with three Islander baskets in a low-scoring first quarter that finished with Mercer Island leading 6-3.

"The good news in the first quarter was that we doubled their score, the bad news was that we only had six points ourselves," Pepple said.

Mercer Island, paced by three Snyder (17 points) jump shots, took a 21-15 halftime lead.

In the third quarter, Mercer Island again held Snohomish to three points – but this time exploded for 16 of their own.

Schwabe (16 points) opened the scoring with two foul shots at 6:52 and then a tip-in at 4:44. Brady (6 points) then hit a pair of lay ins of assists from Snyder and Schwabe, which touched off an eight-point Snyder scoring spree in the period's final 2:23.

"He was the catalyst," Pepple said.

In the fourth quarter, the Islanders outscored Snohomish 16-8. Mercer Island got two points apiece from Mathers, Weller, and Gilliland in that quarter.

Omar Parker finished with eight points.

"When the Parkers, Wellers, and Bradys start hitting some shots, we break things open," Pepple said.

The win over Snohomish set up the heavily favored Islanders for a showdown against Curtis in the 1985 AAA state championship game.

March 12, 1985

STATE AAA TITLE: MIGHTY Mercer Machine ramrods AAA field to finally take the big one

By John Shanahan

Last week Mercer Island basketball lost Ed Pepple's voice, some of Quin Snyder's words and the reputation as a perpetual also-ran in state AAA basketball competition.

The team won everything else.

It thundered to the state championship — a first-ever for the school and for coach Ed Pepple — with wins over Puyallup (57-46), Snohomish (53-26), and Curtis (47-28) in the state class AAA basketball tournament at the Coliseum.

Along with the title came all the tangible rewards of winning the state AAA basketball tournament: the trophies and recognition.

The intangibles may be even more important, though, because Mercer Island finally shrugged off its reputed inability to "win the big one" – an inability that has haunted Islander coach

Pepple since he played in Lincoln High School's losing effort in the tournament final 34 years ago.

Last week Mercer Island, second at state in three of the last five years, won the big one in a big way.

"COACH PEPPLE has coached a lot of great victories, but this has to be the greatest one of all," stand-out guard Snyder said after Mercer Island's 47-28 quashing of Curtis in the final.

But when asked how he felt about the win himself, Snyder suddenly found himself speechless.

"I'm at a loss," stammered the Duke-bound guard. "It feels great."

Pepple was having difficulties speaking as well, though for a different reason.

"Our strategy was to play defense and shut them down," he told reporters in a hoarse, strained voice after the Curtis win. "I have never in my life seen a high school team play such excellent defense in the three toughest games they've had to play all season."

"Defense was the key to the whole thing," out-going Mercer Island assistant coach Pat Strong said. "We shut top scorers down and when you do that, and play good offense, you win." Strong is leaving his part-time coaching position of four years to pursue a business career.

He won't be the only one leaving the program this year.

Seven seniors will graduate in June, including Brian Schwabe, Snyder, Scott Weller, Jeff Thompson, Paul Roberts, Mike Mathers, and Russell Easter.

Schwabe and Snyder averaged 18.5 and 18 points respectively in the tournament.

DESPITE Mercer Island's strong team defense in the final, the presence of Snyder and Schwabe dominated the final game.

That domination started with the first tipoff, which Schwabe (21 points, 13 rebounds) swatted to Eric Brady (two points). He passed to a streaking Snyder (16 points, seven assists, five rebounds) who halted and fired a jumper from the top of the key for Mercer's first score.

Elapsed time: 3 seconds.

Snyder and Schwabe connected for 35 of the team's first 37 points. (John Gilliland added a second quarter jumper.)

Curtis held early leads at 4-3 and 6-5, but a Snyder top-of-the key jumper put the Islanders on top 7-6 to stay in the first quarter.

By halftime the Islanders had opened a 25-18 lead.

In the first half Mercer Island shot 12-24 (50 present) while Curtis hit an icy 5-20 (20 percent).

Mike Matz, the Curtis center (season avg, 14.2) finished the half with three points, the game with six (12-24 shooting). Curtis as a team hit 9-44.

Curtis' other top scorers, Jeff Larson and Spencer Bonter (combined season avg. 27), finished with 13 total.

SCHWABE ATTRIBUTED the Islander defensive showing to scouting and a sound game plan.

"The scouting really helped a lot. What the coaches wanted me to do was to play baseline," Schwabe said.

That forced Matz, who prefers the baseline drive, into the key, where he met Brady and Scott Weller. Much of the credit should also go to the unheralded Weller, who put the defensive clamps on. "Weller is a superb team player," Pepple said.

Snyder cut off Larson at the top of the key while Thompson harassed the Curtis ball handlers in the open court.

The third quarter began with the same Schwabe-Brady-Snyder tipoff combination that yielded 2 more points in five seconds.

Curtis trailed 33-23 at the end of the quarter.

The Islander defense held Curtis to just five points in the fourth quarter and scoreless in the game's final 2:28.

Down the stretch, Mercer Island shot eight for eight on free throws by Weller, Brady, Thompson and Schwabe.

With 17 to go, Snyder passed from the top of the key to hit Easter underneath for a game-ending layup.

Easter, Weller, and Thompson each finished with 2 points.

"I was very impressed with their defense," Curtis coach Don Huston said. "People don't talk about their defense very much but they are an excellent defensive ballclub."

Islanders savior their state hoop title

Ed Pepple's powerhouses pour on the right stuff

by John Shanahan

Past Islander trips to the AAA state finals have typically ended with Islander Coach Ed Pepple congratulating the opponents and rallying his own stunned players' hopes for a better showing next year.

That "next year" – which has eluded Pepple since he played in the high school tournaments final himself 34 years ago – finally came last Saturday night in the Seattle Center Coliseum, where the Islanders flattened Curtis High School of Tacoma 47-28 in the championship final.

For Pepple and Mercer Island, who had lost in three of the previous four championship finals, it was a long, emotional odyssey to the top.

The team hit a dead end in 1981, when Shadle Park beat Mercer on a buzzer shot that Pepple still disputes. The Islanders fell to Roosevelt in 1982, and last year Juanita came from behind in the fourth quarter to sink MI in the final.

BUT THE CLIMB for the Mercer Machine finally peaked as Pepple climbed a step ladder placed under one of the Coliseum's goals Saturday night. With one swipe of a scissors, Pepple simultaneously cut loose the net and the estimated crowd of 9,000.

The gesture brought pandemonium to the 5,000 Islander fans on one side of the arena. Curtis rooters cheered courteously from across the floor.

Pepple, his voice nearly spent from consecutive days of sideline yelling, was later given a microphone.

The coach, who has four times congratulated winning teams in the state final, did that again – only this time talking about his own team, not someone else's.

The team, Pepple said, had not buckled, even though under "more pressure than any team in the history of the state of Washington."

But Pepple also had some words for the fans.

"We'll see you back at the gym," Pepple's hoarse voice, amplified by the Coliseum's sound system, assured the crows.

PEPPLE'S CROAKED invitation drew about 800 fans to the Mercer Island High School Gymnasium for a post-game rally. They arrived carrying enough plastic leis and wearing enough gaudy-colored shirts to qualify Mercer Island as an honorary member of the Hawaiian Islands.

Outside the gym, leis sprouted everywhere, like multi-colored plastic fungi which thrive on victory. They hung from car antennas, bumpers, windshield wipers and trees.

Inside they hung from necks, wrists and foreheads. One even adorned the recently won state trophy, which stood amidst the crowd on a table in the middle of the gym floor. Another was wrapped around the microphone with which Pepple addressed the crowd.

But perhaps leis were the appropriate garb of the night, because the ceremony permanently "laid" to rest the "jinx" that Mercer Island basketball couldn't win it all.

"As you know, the pressure on this team was unbelievable," Pepple told the crowd.

"Outrageous!" someone yelled from the student section of the crowd.

"They were outrageous," Pepple answered, smiling, getting a laugh from the fans.

But the team rose to the occasion, Pepple said. "At Mercer Island we made defense a trademark, but I have never seen a team that played defense like this team before."

Pepple said he has been trying to win the tournament for 34 years, "but I probably don't look that old."

TRI-CAPTAINS Scott Weller, Quin Snyder and Brian Schwabe also spoke to the crowd and thanked fans for their support.

"I'll take you out to lunch sometime," Weller joked to show his appreciation to two especially gung-ho rooters wearing Indian war paint on their faces.

Later, between hugs and handshakes with the jubilant, something he called "the fringe benefit of coaching," Pepple would issue no rallying cries for next year's season to an interviewer – not yet anyway.

"We're just going to savor this one for a while, and that's it," he said.

Undoubtedly, that's another of coaching's fringe benefits.

March 12, 1985

Team managers: Lots of work, little glory

Mercer Island Australian transfer student Stuart Page says he is a little surprised at how preoccupied American high schools are with athletics.

He ought to know. For the past three seasons, he's been manager of the Mercer Island High School's boys basketball team, perhaps the most successful and attention-ridden prep sports program in the state.

At times, all that activity can be a little overwhelming – times like last Saturday night, when the Islanders snatched the Class AAA state title.

"I never dreamed it would be this wild or this big a deal," Page said.

What was he planning to do when it was all over?

"I'm just going to go out, sit back and relax somewhere," he said.

While managers grab few headlines, they work nearly as hard as the players on the team.

Page says he keeps busy at practices and games taping players' ankles and keeping tabs on team equipment, such as towels and ice.

It adds up to hard work that page says he could not handle were it not for the help he gets from co-manager John Meek.

Page has attended special athletic training courses at Pacific Lutheran University and at the University of Idaho. A senior, Page has been with the team since his sophomore year.

Mercer Island Coach Ed Pepple offered him the job after the coach taught Page in a physical education class.

"That started a really good relationship," Page says. "Here I've really found a home. People are really nice."

Page, along with the rest of his family, expects to return to his permanent home in Canberra, Australia in August, when his father, who has a commission in the Australian Navy, finishes his tour of duty in Seattle.

On April 1, the Seattle Times reported on Quin Snyder's performance in the 12th Annual McDonald's Capital Classic, played before 10,000 fans at the Capital Centre in Washington, DC.

In the game, Snyder scored 8 points and contributed 5 assists, helping lead the U.S. All-Stars to victory over the Capital All-Stars, 142-120. The game also featured Snyder's future teammate at Duke, Danny Ferry, a 6-10 center out of DeMatha High School in Hyattsville, MD.

April 12, 1985

State hoop champs still being fetted

Mercer Island High School's 1985 State AAA basketball champions took home the hardware in an impressive awards program last week.

Before a large crowd of fans and parents in the high school auditorium, the Islanders were awarded trophies as KingCo Champions, Sea-King Champions, District Champions and State Champions. Principal Larry Smith presented a large state champion banner to be placed on the gymnasium wall. Also on display was a third-place trophy from the prestigious Holiday Prep Classic in Las Vegas.

Frosh Coach Pat Strong, who is leaving the Mercer Island program to accept a business opportunity in California, opened the program by honoring the first-year players, who ended the season 12-8. King County Councilmember Bruce Laing presented plaques of honor to all of the varsity players, coaches and one to the student body. Cheerleader advisor Jill Leslie presented "Gimme a Shock – Let's Rock" t-shirts to all the varsity players.

Sophomore awards were presented by Coach Dan Absher. The sophs won the KingCo Conference title with an 18-1 record. An emotional KING TV special, "Thanks for Being a Friend", produced by Bill Rockey, was played for the audience and presented to the high school.

An outstanding junior varsity team, which finished the season 18-1, was presented certificates by Coach Bill Woolley.

The highlight of the program was a black-out sequence which reviewed the championship season and spotlighted each varsity player. Mercer Island finished the season with an 18-1 record, ranked No. 1 in Washington and No. 13 in the nation. In the state finals, the Islanders held opponents Puyallup, Snohomish and Curtis to an average of 33 points a game and combined shooting percentage of 26%. The 1985 Islanders broke the all-time field-goal percentage by shooting 54.2%. A perfect 9-9 free-throw percentage in the Redmond game set a single game record

Brian Schwabe broke Peter Gudmundsson's career blocked shot record with 112. He set records for field goals in a season, and for a career. Scott Weller set a new career free-throw mark with 79.5%, breaking David Milloy's 1975 record.

All team members were presented with plaques embossed with the team victory picture provided by the parents, and maroon state championship sweaters donated by Larry Mounger. Coach Ed Pepple received a maroon and white chair engraved with the players' names and 1984-85 game results.

Individual top awards included: Top rebounder – Brian Schwabe. Top free-throw shooter – Jeff Thompson (81.3%, season). Captain awards - Schwabe, Quin Snyder, Scott Weller. Most improved – Eric Brady. Coaches award – Weller. Most inspirational – Thompson. Fans of the year – Wynn and Barb Kampe, Warren and Doris Williams.

Schwabe was presented with a plaque for being named all KingCo, All-State and honorable mention All-American. Snyder was also honored all KingCo, All-State and first team McDonald's All-American.

On Saturday, April 13, millions of Americans got their first look at Quin Snyder when ESPN broadcast the 1985 McDonald's All-American Boys Game from the Moody Coliseum in University Park, Texas.

Snyder played in the game as a member of the West team, matching up against the East team, which featured future Duke teammate Danny Ferry, and Pervis Ellison, another highly recruited center.

In the game, Ferry scored 17 points, leading the East team over the West, 128-98. Of the 25 players in the game, 15 went on to play at least 1 game in the NBA.

July 2, 1985

Hoop shot pyrotechnics: Schwabe, Snyder dominate all stars

There's no place like home for Quin Snyder and Brian Schwabe, Mercer Island basketball's Wizards of Awesome.

At least that was the case at last Wednesday night's state Class AAA – AA basketball All-Star game.

The two Islanders scored a combined total of 62 points to lead the state All-Star team to a 128 to 104 victory over a city All-Star squad in the Mercer Island High School gymnasium. It was the second time the game has been hosted by the island. Also featured in the contest were Mercer Island Coach Ed Pepple, and Islander team manager Stuart Page.

But Snyder and Schwabe, playing their final game in an arena they have dominated for the past three years, stole the show.

"They had some very good games in this gymnasium, but they finished with their best," Pepple said.

Snyder's career high 34 points, many scored on his trademark jumper, earned him game Most Valuable Player honors. His final bucket, scored with 2:01 remaining, broke the game all-time scoring record set by Al Moscatel, also of Mercer Island.

"We really wanted to show people what we could do," Schwabe told reporters. "I'm really happy that Quin played great, and I played good. It was really fun to go out this way."

Schwabe was hot right from the start of the contest, which evened the score from a 108-106 State loss to the City squad the previous night in Yakima. The state All-Star series included one game played on each side of the Cascades.

Schwabe scored six of the eight points as State jumped to a lead it never lost. By the end of the first quarter, the squad was up 37-27, 16 of the state points coming from the Islander twosome.

The 128 points scored was also a record for the series.

"When you score 128 points it's hard for somebody to beat you," Pepple said.

In June of '85, Ed Pepple contributed an end-of-the season wrap up for the Mercer Island Reporter:

It was a great year for Mercer Island basketball. The Islanders were the preseason choice as Washington state's number one team and were barraged by media attention all season long.

Through the intense pressure the team maintained its poise and dedication of purpose. Solid senior leadership by co-captains Brian Schwabe, Quin Snyder and Scott Weller was a key factor in compiling a 28-1 record.

Mercer Island clinched the 1985 State AAA title with convincing wins over Puyallup, Snohomish in Curtis. In an awesome defense of display, the Islanders allowed their three final opponents an average of only 33 points per game on 28% field goal shooting.

The record of accomplishments included the KingCo Championship, Sea-King District Championship, Regional Championship and State Championship. The Islanders finished third in the prestigious Las Vegas Holiday Prep Classic in December. USA Today ranked the Islanders as the number one high school basketball team in the nation on December 26, 1984.

Individual honors also were abundant. Snyder, Schwabe and Weller were named to All-Conference teams. Quin Snyder and Brian Schwabe were selected All-Region and All-State. Both played in the All-Star game at Mercer Island on June 26, 1985. Schwabe broke school records for field goals and shot blocks and was named Honorable Mention All-American. Snyder was named to the McDonald's All-American team and played in the Capital Classic in Washington DC and in the All-American game in Dallas.

The team success was a total effort - seniors Mike Mathers, Jeff Thompson, Paul Roberts and Russell Easter were major contributors. Omar Parker, a junior and four sophomores, Eric Brady, John Gilliland, Jeff Wood and Doug Marriott complemented the veterans and gave promise for the future.

1985 was truly a championship year – a long time coming but well worth the wait.

EPILOGUE

While 1985 was no doubt a zenith year for Ed Pepple and Mercer Island High School basketball, it was hardly the end of the program's successful run – if anything, the '85 championship served as a catalyst for what would ultimately become a high school basketball dynasty in the state of Washington.

In 1993, the underdog Islanders entered the state tournament with six losses on the season. Miraculously, the team everyone discredited knocked out highly-touted Federal Way (led by future NBA player Michael Dickerson) in the semi-finals, behind sharp-shooting junior Jason Cooper's game-high 20 points.

Appearing in the championship game again for the first time since 1985, Mercer Island rose to the challenge, defeating Ferris High School of Spokane 59-54 behind another big night from Jason Cooper. Cooper, who stayed up practicing at a local elementary school playground until 2 a.m. the night before the semi-final game, lit up the Seattle Center Coliseum, shooting 61% (11-16) from the field for 23 points.

The Seattle Times interviewed Pepple the day after the game, asking him how he felt about his second state championship. "Tired," he said. "I didn't get to bed until five in the morning, and I got up at seven. I always get up to play tennis on Sunday.

"You don't think I'm going to stop playing just because we won the state title?"

1997 produced perhaps the most dominant Islander basketball team Pepple had delivered since the '85 team, as Mercer Island won their third state championship in a 61-57 victory over top-ranked Mount Vernon.

The team was led that year by 6-2 Bryan Brown, the youngest of former Seattle Supersonics star guard "Downtown" Freddy Brown's three sons. At the state tournament, Brown scored 31 points in a semifinal victory over Prairie, 80 points in four games, and was named tournament MVP.

Despite Brown's heroics, the '97 championship game belonged to sophomores Josh Fisher and Elliott Prasse-Freeman. Coming off the bench, Fisher scored 16 points and Prasse-Freeman contributed 14 points and nine rebounds. The Islanders finished that season 28-2.

Two years later, Mercer Island again appeared in the state championship game. The 1999 Islanders had four seniors committed to play Division 1 basketball: forward Tyler Besecker (Stanford), Josh Fisher (Pepperdine), Prasse-Freeman (Harvard) and Pepple's grandson, Matt Logie (Lehigh). The state championship appearance was especially meaningful for Logie, who'd grown up in the shadow of the '85 and '93 championship teams. "I've been looking forward to this my entire life," he told the Seattle Times.

In one of the last sporting events ever played at the now-demolished Seattle Kingdome, Besecker and Fisher combined for 36 points, 20 rebounds and 5 assists to lead Mercer Island over Metro competitor O'Dea, 60-44 for Pepple's fourth state championship in 14 years. That year's team finished the season with an impressive 27-3 record.

Pepple continued coaching at Mercer Island High School until March of 2009 when he retired after 42 seasons with a whopping 952 victories, still the most of any high school basketball coach in

Washington state history. Former player Gavin Cree, a 2000 graduate, inherited the program and still coaches to this day.

Pepple enjoyed his retirement, spending time with friends and family on Mercer Island where he remained an active member of the community. He could often be found enjoying breakfast at his favorite local haunt, Chace's Pancake Corral, in Bellevue, where they even named a dish after him – the "Coach's Pick" (crepe style pancakes filled with apple glaze).

In 2012, having already been inducted into several halls of fame including the National High School Coaches Association and Washington Interscholastic Basketball Coaches Association, Pepple was inducted into the Washington Sports Hall of Fame in a ceremony at Century Link (now Lumen) Field.

But for all the wins and championships that became his signature, Pepple is remembered most by the people who knew him for the impact he had on his players.

Omar Parker, a 1986 MIHS graduate, member of the '85 championship team and now, head basketball coach at Liberty High School in Renton, describes Pepple's legacy as: "People. Excellence. A model for how to build not just a high school basketball program but how to build any organization. (He produced) 100's of successful businesspeople. Nordstrom as an example. Pete and Eric both played for Ed."

Parker goes on to share his sentiments about the Little Dribble program, another hallmark of Pepple's extraordinary career. "MI basketball was something kids could touch. The Little Dribbler program invited an entire community to play basketball and be close to something that in the MI community was great. As a third, fourth, fifth, sixth or seventh grader, Mercer Island Basketball was the greatest."

Quin Snyder, who went on to play at Duke, coach at Division 1 Missouri and who now serves as the head coach of the NBA's Utah Jazz, agrees with Parker. In an interview with the Reporter in 1993, Snyder called out the Little Dribbler program specifically when asked about his childhood basketball memories.

"The (1985) state title certainly was one of the highlights of my formative years," he told Therrien. "But sixth grade is still the best year of my life."

In terms of Pepple's coaching style and approach to basketball, Brian Schwabe believes legendary UCLA coach John Wooden played a vital role in helping shape Pepple's idea of what a basketball team could be. "John Wooden obviously was an inspiration to a lot of coaches, but I think Coach Pepple used him as a symbol of success."

Schwabe, like Parker and Snyder, says that Pepple "had a profound impact on me as a person."

On Monday, November 14, 2020, after a life well-lived, the years finally caught up with Ed, and he died in his sleep of causes related to cancer. He was 88.

The community and basketball world at large mourned the loss of a legend. When word of Pepple's decline spread, the Pepple family received more than 100 notes, cards and letters from former players, opponents, managers and stat-crew members, as reported by the Seattle Times.

Today, one need only walk into the Mercer Island High School gymnasium to recognize the impact Pepple continues to have on the school. A framed maroon blazer, previously worn by Pepple, hangs on the wall below an ever-growing list of KingCo championship banners. Next to the blazer, a sign dedicating the gym to Shirley and Ed hangs in full view. Next to that, a framed jersey of Chris Kampe, #23, captain of the 1981 team, whose life ended prematurely in 1993 after a battle with cancer, a player Pepple always spoke highly of.

Quin Snyder, interviewed by the Seattle Times the day of Pepple's passing, probably said it best about his former coach:

"You play for him your whole life."

ACKNOWLEDGEMENTS

First and foremost, this book could not have been possible without the generous support of Josh O'Connor at Sound Publishing, owner of the Mercer Island Reporter, who believed in the project and allowed me to use the words and images of the newspaper to construct the narrative.

In researching the book, I had the opportunity to speak with past Mercer Island High School basketball players who shared their experiences with me. Special thanks to Brian Schwabe, Omar Parker, and especially Matt Logie, who took time out of their busy schedules to talk with me about their memories of Coach Pepple.

Special thanks to Priscilla Ledbetter, who wrote her own book about Mercer Island for Arcadia Publishing, for her support and feedback on the subject matter and format of this book.

I would be remiss if I didn't thank the sportswriters and photographers from the Mercer Island Reporter, who did most of the heavy lifting for this book with the many articles and images they contributed over the years to the Reporter.

Lastly, I'd like to thank Ed Pepple, who made a lasting impact on me as a student at Mercer Island High School and helped shaped me as a coach and supporter of youth sports.

CPSIA information can be obtained
at www.ICGtesting.com
Printed in the USA
LVHW032352180222
711410LV00001B/108

9 780578 337005